REUNION IN MOSCOW

Books by Markoosha Fischer

REUNION IN MOSCOW

THE RIGHT TO LOVE

THE NAZAROVS

MY LIVES IN RUSSIA

Reunion in Moscow

A RUSSIAN REVISITS HER COUNTRY

by

Bertha Mark

(MARKOOSHA FISCHER)

HARPER & ROW, PUBLISHERS

NEW YORK AND EVANSTON

To my grandchildren

Library of Congress catalog card number: 62–9888

Contents

v

vi / Contents

Prologue

This is the story of my recent visit to Russia after an absence of twenty-one years. I had left Russia in 1939, leaving behind shattered hopes, friends in prison or in graves with bullets in their hearts or backs, others alive whom I never expected to see or hear from again. After I had written and spoken openly about my experiences in Russia I could never, not even in my wildest dreams, see myself walking again the streets of Moscow and talking with her people.

And this is a sequel to my book *My Lives in Russia*, a book in which I told of my childhood and youth in Russia and other European countries, of my years in the United States between 1916 and 1921, and the return to Europe and Russia. But mainly it was the story of the years in Russia from 1927 to 1939, of the life of our family there, of keeping house and bringing up two boys, of my earlier expectations and later heartbreaks. And it was about our return to the United States in 1939 with a dream smashed into never-to-be-mended pieces.

How and why did I go to Moscow in 1960? I wish I could answer that with an impressive statement. But I cannot. For years I had been hearing and reading the reports of people who made trips to Russia, even members of my own family. But they were all born

Americans. Never once had it occurred to me that I, a former Soviet citizen, who had written uncomplimentary things about the Soviet Union, could be one of them. Would the Soviet government ever let me in? And if they did would they respect my American citizenship and let me out? I was far from certain that the answers would be yes. So I kept reading and listening to reports.

And then one wintry Sunday morning, in the *New York Times Travel Section*, I came upon a most extraordinary notice. The Soviet authorities had eased all entrance restrictions. They would welcome the visits of former Soviet citizens including even those who had fled Russia during and immediately after World War II. They also promised to give a combined entrance and exit visa, thus eliminating the fear of being detained there. The price of hotel room and board was about half the previous high cost if no guides and limousines were required, and travelers would be free, within the limits of general restrictions for foreigners, to go wherever they wished.

It sounded unbelievable but good, and no sooner had I finished reading the notice than my decision was made. Next morning I made some telephone calls, and within a few weeks everything was taken care of. I had a contract for a book, a visa to enter and leave the Soviet Union, and a plane reservation for the end of May. I wanted to arrive in Moscow after spring had definitely taken over.

Then came a time of waiting and reflection. What did I want to achieve on this trip? What did I want to do and see in Moscow? One thing was clear beyond any doubt. It was going to be Moscow only and no side trips whatever. Nowhere else would I have a chance to see so many people I had known before, and nowhere else in Russia, except in Leningrad perhaps, can one get lost in a crowd and soak in what goes on around. But what should I do in Moscow? Shouldn't I work out a definite plan and follow it so as not to waste any time? I started to prepare a list of questions to which I wanted to get answers. When I reached question

No. 125 doubts began to cast a long shadow over my list. Would I have time to get answers to all those questions? And for me might it not be better simply to whiff the atmosphere than to make a lot of ponderous inquiries. The decision was taken: never mind the 125 questions. What did I have eyes and ears for? I would let them, and my curiosity, guide me, talk to as many people as happened within earshot, soak up every impression I possibly could. I did not tear up that list, however; I still have it, and though I did not take it along and hardly ever thought of it, almost every one of the 125 questions received an answer.

During the period of waiting I told myself to try to forget the heartbreaks of the past, to go with an open mind, to think of the past only in order better to understand the present. This was not an easy task. It is one thing to read about today's favorable changes in Russia and another to forget the past murdering, jailing and exiling of millions as well as the brutal destruction of souls and minds. It was not easy to force myself to clear my mind of old memories, bitter disappointments and resentments. I kept reminding myself that attitudes, emphases, tempers keep changing everywhere, that the United States of today is different from the country it was in the thirties, in the forties, even in the fifties, and that we take it as it is today without constantly thinking of dark pages in the past.

The feelings I was now trying so hard to overcome had not developed overnight. They had grown slowly and painfully through at least a decade. Very slowly at first, then more and more rapidly when the question: Was anything on this earth worth so many heartaches, so much human misery? began to demand a definite answer. Especially when the "anything" no longer encompassed the lofty ideals of the early Revolution? The deepest attraction that the Soviet revolution had had for me was its internationalism. To me that had meant in the fullest and most literal sense the brotherhood of man, the equality of people everywhere, each attached to and loving his own little world but feeling a kinship with every human being on earth. The Marxist "Proletarians of all countries unite, you have nothing to lose but your chains" I translated into no more sweatshops anywhere, no more exploitation by the mighty of the weary and helpless, especially of children, equality for women. It meant making the advantages of progress and science available to all, not only to the privileged; it meant that no one, especially no children, should go hungry anywhere in the world. It meant a great many things which, I realize, might sound naïve and sentimental today to sophisticated minds. But I am talking about things and using words that meant a great deal to me in my youth. And if today these goals sound unrealistic, even childish, they did not then to a great number of people besides me.

All this it was important for me to remember now, because it was what had made me so enthusiastically and wholeheartedly accept the Bolshevik revolution. After the many social injustices I had seen in a number of highly advanced countries, and after the nightmare of the First World War, I was ready to accept the violence of the revolution for the sake of making this a better world. Hadn't we more than once accepted the horror and sacrifices of war for this very aim?

I know better now. But in 1917 and for about two decades after that I did not know. In 1917 the Bolshevik revolution to me was the inevitable result of conditions that had become too hard for people to bear. There is not the slightest doubt in my mind now that had the democratic Russian revolution that overthrew the czar succeeded, with its moderation and respect for human rights, our world would have been a better place to live in today. But recognition of this, too, came to me much later than 1917.

Before I continue chronologically I will make one jump ahead. During the forties I did a great deal of lecturing in the United States. In order to explain to my audiences my acceptance of the Soviet revolution I would describe the deplorable state of Russia under the czar. During a lecture tour in Vermont I shared the platform with Alexander Kerensky, the head of the Russian Provisional government which was overthrown by the Bolsheviks in October, 1917. He spoke on 1917-1918, I on 1927-1939. He spoke on the political events of the period, I on everyday life during the years I lived there. He found the picture I gave of Czarist Russia much too dark and said so in his talk. What he said sounded almost like an apology for czarism. He brought one argument after another to compare favorably the czarist with the Communist regime. When the chairman gave me time for rebuttal I asked: "Mr. Kerensky, if czarism was so attractive, why did you overthrow it? You did, I didn't." This went over very well with the audience but when I later thought it over I was not proud of my flippant remark. I had to agree with a great deal of what he said and when I met him some time later I told him so.

It had taken me quite a number of years to realize that czarist Russia with all its cruelties and ignominities had much less terror than Stalin's Russia. In the czar's days the execution of a political adversary was not a daily occurrence but an event that people in Russia as well as the outside world talked about for a long time. Families of political prisoners, even of those accused of genuine plots against the government, were not held responsible for their kinfolk's views; neither were their friends and coworkers, as they were under Stalin. When I was in high school my older sister, a Socialist, was arrested along with the other members of her group. I was as proud as could be and came next day to school all radiant and was the hero of my schoolmates and, I am certain, of many of our teachers. Our family was never molested during her prison term. My parents regularly visited her, sent her clothing and food packages. This could never have happened under Stalin.

I could go on endlessly with comparisons of life in Czarist and Soviet Russia. Years ago I would not have believed that I would ever go to such length to exonerate the Czarist regime, whose abuses had made it so easy for me to accept the Bolshevik revolution.

The seeds for this acceptance were sown early in my childhood. My father and mother were both involved in a number of philanthropic organizations; my father was also politically active and from an early age I heard a great deal about poverty and social injustice. I was deeply troubled by what I heard and saw and couldn't understand. Most of the ills and injustices I saw seemed to me to lie at the czar's door. I did not know the outside world then. When I did at the age of fifteen come to know other countries I found plenty of injustices outside the czar's domain. None of those countries—Switzerland, Germany, France, Scandinavia— seemed to have as their main purpose the creation of a good life for everyone. Everywhere there were people much more privileged than others.

Even in the United States, which since my early childhood had seemed to me a beacon of light, I found much injustice. When I first came here in 1916, sweatshops, child labor, the lack of safety devices in factories, the lack of aid for the disabled and the old, and endless work hours were the concern of a few "crackpots" only, agitators, Socialists, anarchists, generally considered undesirable people. It was against this background of disenchantment with the Western world that I saw in the slogans of the Russian revolution a promise to humanity that I did not find anywhere else, and so came easily to believe that Russia was on its way to true brotherhood, that in Russia I would find no social injustice, no exploitation of man by man, that it would truly follow the precept so important to me: that "all men are created equal."

Of course, I well realize now that my eyes should have been opened much earlier. But at the time I accepted the premise that such a fundamental upheaval, not only in the political system but also in human nature, could not happen overnight and certainly could not be brought about, to quote a term of that period, while wearing "silk gloves." Tragic as the sacrifices were from the very beginning, I sincerely believed that after a period of sacrifices the millennium would come.

For years my hopes helped me not only to disregard personal discomforts—they seemed such a small price to pay for the goals ahead—but to close my mind and my eyes to the injustices and cruelty around me. These were years of hope, exaltation, fierce inspiring discussions, inner searchings, when no sacrifices seemed too hard to bear if they would help to bring about the radiant vision of the future. They were the years when Russians still argued freely about politics, economics, art, literature and education. There was enthusiasm, exhilaration, excitement. And then by and by, as the years went on, there was less and less of it. Slogans and lies, absolute censorship, a dry, uninspiring bureaucratic terminology took over, the intellectual excitement faded away. Personal initiative and originality of word, thought and behavior disappeared; there was no deviation from the narrow path laid out by official dictate. Gone was the daring, the urge to change the old, to bring fresh ideas into art, human relations, everyday living. There was still a great deal of official prating about a new life, especially about a new Soviet man, a creation of the revolution; but it was all talk. The forward surge had stopped. A gray conformity settled down over everyone and everything.

When doubts began to stir in me and voices inside began to question, I tried for a long time to banish them. Giving up ideals is very hard, one feels so unprotected and naked without them. But in the years of Stalin's purges my questioning voices were hard to ignore. The thousands and thousands of pages describing the purges have never come near to telling the whole ghastly story. One after another the petals of that cherished flower—hope—fell and the naked stem stood exposed. But it still stood. And then one day the stem itself broke and I took the decision to return to the world from which I had come in search of my ideal. I suppose that really the stem had been ready to break for some time and that it needed only a little thing to make me aware of it. But to me then the little thing that made the final break loomed very large. I had for several years accepted a great deal against my better judgment, always hoping that when the end finally came it would justify the means. But there was something I could definitely not accept. That was the revival of Russian chauvinism presented under the more palatable name of nationalism. Whatever motives Stalin had in reviving it—it was certainly not for Russian nationalism that I had come to live in Russia.

As I have said, the deepest attraction that the Soviet revolution had held for me was its internationalism. Stalin's turn to pure unadulterated nationalism gave the last blow to my indecision about leaving Russia, though it was already obvious that nothing remained to make living there worthwhile for me any longer. But it was not an easy decision to take and when my husband, Louis Fischer, came on a visit from Spain in the fall of 1938 we discussed it for days and days without my being able to say the final word. And then—I quote from *My Lives in Russia:*

> One day the boys came home from school all flushed with excitement. In both schools, in identical high-flown words, they had been told about the wonderful heroes Russia had in the past —Alexander Nevsky, Minin, Pozharsky, Kutuzov, Suvorov, etc.— and what freedom-loving patriots they were. Old czarist generals were presented to Soviet children as nineteenth-century anti-fascist fighters. . . . I did not mind the children being made aware of the heritage of Russian culture . . . But I strenuously objected to the dragging out of the historic corpses of czarist princes and generals to arouse Russian patriotism. I felt very strongly on this point. There was enough confusion and insincerity already in what the boys were being taught. I did not want them to absorb more of it and to ruin their minds forever for clear honest thinking.

At that moment my mind was made up. We applied for an exit visa for the boys and myself and, after many nerve-racking months of questioning and refusals, with the help of Washington we happily landed in the United States in April, 1939.

Now, twenty-one years later, I was going back. And of course there would be changes.

I don't remember ever in my life having had so many conversations with myself as I had during the weeks I was preparing to face Russia again. I think that in the end these self-monologues proved to be of great help. But I knew that, even though I should not judge what I saw by constantly harping on the sins of the past, I must, in order to be able to understand and judge the present, compare it with what I had known before. This I have tried to do.

This is not a book on Soviet intellectuals, not a book on a chosen few, on those who may, not openly of course, think and search and doubt. I saw several of these but mostly I saw ordinary people busy with everyday living. The book is about them.

CHAPTER ONE

Passport Fiasco

The plane trip was uneventful if one accepted as a normal event ten-and-a-half flying hours from Idlewild, New York's airport, to Vnukovo, the Moscow airport. There were two distractions during the flight. First, the arguments between several passengers going to visit relatives in Russia over who had not seen them for the longest time. The winner was a 75-year-old cabinetmaker from California who had left his native Ukraine sixty years before.

The other distraction took place during our short stop on the Brussels' airdrome. While we were being ushered into one of the waiting rooms I heard a Russian-accented English-speaking voice ask something like "Do you have your music with you?" and there was a smiling Van Cliburn following Hurok into another waiting room. This created a pleasant flutter, especially among our younger female pasesngers.

It seemed not long afterward that the pilot called our attention to the first view of Moscow. I had never before approached the city by air but could well imagine how different this approach must have been years ago. What remained unchanged, of course, were the Kremlin walls and the glittering towers of the cathedrals and churches. But the new tall buildings, the many broad boulevards with rows upon rows of new houses, the many cars and

1

trucks gave me even in the air the feeling that the Moscow I was going to see was definitely not the one I had left in 1939.

Then the plane was on the ground. No one from Intourist met us, the tourists, either when we came down the ramp or when we entered the huge waiting hall, but a crowd of several hundred enthusiasts, among them many young women with flowers in their hands, met Van Cliburn with shouts, embraces, even tears. He was showered with flowers which soon covered the ground. I couldn't bear seeing flowers trampled on and for several days my hotel room was graced by the booty of my first minutes in Moscow: white lilac and lilies-of-the-valley.

Some domestic planes arrived at the same time ours did, and the Russians, knowing their way around, were taken care of long before we found out what we were expected to do. Since most of my fellow travelers knew little or no Russian, I helped make out the necessary declarations, discovered where our luggage was and where our passports had to be handed in. And all the time my mood was of joyful expectation, close to exhilaration, despite the noisy confusion around us. What amazed me was that after several years of intensive international travel a smoother way of meeting a foreign plane had not been worked out. Finally we had finished with all the formalities, an Intourist guide appeared, and we lined up for our passports before boarding the Intourist bus. One by one my plane companions received their passports and were escorted to the bus until there were no more passports left to hand out. But I did not get mine.

The man who had returned them to the travelers said that he had nothing to do with the passports but to hand them to those to whom they belonged and that I was to wait; someone would come out and talk to me. After a few quite dismal moments a handsome man in a dashing uniform came through a door marked by a large sign "Strictly Forbidden to Enter." He held my passport in his hand but it was obvious that he had no intention of letting me have it. I suppose that at that moment there were few sacrifices I would not have been ready to make to hold that passport in my own hands again. With a pleasant smile and most politely he asked me whether I knew that I had arrived in the Soviet Union on an expired visa. "This couldn't be," I assured him. But it could, and still keeping the passport he showed me that it was! My visa had expired exactly five days before my arrival in Moscow. Later I realized the reason for it. I had postponed the trip for a week, since I had wanted to know Khrushchev's mood after he returned to Moscow following the failure of the Paris summit meeting. His mood was all right as far as American tourism was concerned. But meanwhile my visa had expired and, though the postponement had been cleared with Intourist, the expiration of the visa had not occurred to anyone.

The next few hours I spent first sitting on the luggage counter behind which stood two lonely suitcases—my own. After a while I was invited to sit in a comfortable armchair in an adjoining small lounge. From time to time the same or another man in uniform would open the forbidden door behind which my fate was being decided and tell me not to worry, that everything would be all right, that they were trying to get an answer by telephone. Those who didn't know that I spoke Russian kept telling me "Don't worry, wait just a leetle beet," a phrase obviously learned to calm impatient foreigners. It definitely needed more than these few friendly words to make me stop worrying.

There was at least one advantage in the thoroughly unpleasant—to say the least—mess I found myself in. I had more first impressions than I normally would have had at the airport, and since there was nothing on earth within my power to do to change whatever verdict was awaiting me, I tried to get in as many impressions as I could. For I was certain that these would be the only ones I would be permitted to take back to the United States—on the first plane leaving Moscow on that very day, which, of course, would have been the happier of two imaginable endings. I tried not to think of the other. I had no doubt that if the authorities were out to detain me they would not hesitate to charge me with whatever sinister anti-Soviet activities their fertile minds might come up with. I worked hard at trying to forget whatever I remembered of descriptions of Soviet prisons. And whenever I succeeded I looked around with wide-open eyes.

What impressed me first were the young girls rushing around with papers in their hands, as Russian secretaries have always done. They looked quite smart with their wide bright skirts, frilly blouses, painted fingernails, modern hairdos and fancy shoes, some with spiked heels. There were, of course, the others too, slightly disheveled, in dresses of indifferent color and cut, lips unrouged, nails uncared for, girls I well remembered from the past. But now they were the exception; the smart ones dominated the scene. In their looks and their clothes they were poles apart from the charwomen in clumsy mannish clothes and boots, with kerchief-covered heads and red rough hands, who kept moving around picking up things, mopping floors, dusting counters, emptying wastebaskets, exchanging an occasional word with the porters.

Without exception, everyone was most attentive and friendly. Some Russian travelers, the clerks and the porters, all informed of my predicament, came to talk to me, and they all, having heard the officials say it, kept repeating that I shouldn't worry, that everything would be all right. Later, when my brain began to function normally again, it occurred to me that no one was afraid to be seen talking to me. How did they know that it was going to end all right? They all knew that my passport had been held up. Suppose in me they had caught a spy? It was only a couple of weeks after the U-2 incident, and the press was still full of it. This was a tremendous change from the past, when fear would definitely have prevented anyone from being seen talking in a friendly way to someone whose passport was detained by the authorities.

Finally, after three hours—hours that seemed longer than I ever thought three hours could possibly be—one of the men came out with an even bigger smile than before and with my passport in his hand, kept holding it out toward me from afar. This was a most considerate gesture showing that he did not want to waste any time in relieving me of my anxiety. "We finally," he said, "were able to get in touch with Intourist" (I would have loved to know with whom else) "and they confirmed your reservation for today. So everything is all right and your car is waiting for you." As simple as that! In no time my luggage was in the car and so was I. The clerks and the porters saw me off and kept waving till we were out of sight.

With my passport securely in my bag I relaxed. I had the Intourist car and the driver to myself. I sat in front with the driver, as I did subsequently in all my daily cab rides in Moscow, and listened avidly to his explanations. The wide new road we were on had only a few short years ago been nothing but dense woods, he said. This was easy to believe. The dense woods were still there, right behind the road. And they were right behind the hundreds of new houses which lined the road as we came closer to Moscow, as they not long ago had covered the ground on which these houses now stood. With great pride the driver pointed all this out to me and as a contrast he called my attention to some old shanties which, he said with contempt, were the kind of houses people used to live in. His voice sounded proudest as we approached Moscow University. He slowed almost to a stop to let me have a good look. He was quite astonished when I told him that I had seen many pictures of it in the American press. "Do they permit you to print such pictures there?" he asked in disbelief. I was glad I could leave no doubt in his mind that "they" really do permit it, since I was able to describe the building before we approached it. This question was a foretaste of hundreds of similar questions throughout my stay.

After a while it was his turn to ask me questions and I had another taste of what was ahead of me. There was not a thing about the United States he was not interested in, he said, and all his questions and reactions were most friendly. It must not be forgotten that Intourist drivers are not ordinary cab drivers. They are chosen and trained for contact with foreigners. If not for a casual remark of his on the U-2 incident and a short not too violent comment on Eisenhower's speech defending the flight, which had interrupted the soft music on the car radio, one could easily have forgotten that such a thing had ever happened. I felt the comparatively moderate radio comment, as well as the driver's reaction, was a good omen.

All along the road to Moscow I watched the people who were strolling at the edge of the woods. My first fleeting impressions were the same as at the airport. Children looked healthy and full of bounce, the dresses of the women were gayer than I remembered them, the men's sport shirts looked more mid-twentieth century than their old garb used to be; shoes were more up to date too. The people looked like working people anywhere out for a walk after work. Few were without young green branches or bunches of field flowers. It was a homely sight and it was good, after the past disagreeable hours, to have a glimpse of Moscow in these friendly family groups and young lovers.

I was finally deposited at the Ukraina, Moscow's newest and largest hotel and one of Moscow's "tall buildings," as the Russians call them, refusing to adopt the too American-sounding word "skyscraper." I found bedlam there and my airplane companions all over the lobby. A convention which was supposed to have ended in the morning had had its last session in the afternoon. The convention delegates were still in their rooms, which had been assigned to the new arrivals, among them our American group. Several members of this group had been met by their relatives at the airport. Now more had come to greet them in the hotel. They were quite well dressed, seemed relaxed and not as awed by the splendor of the hotel and the many foreigners around them as in my recollection they were in the past. I heard them talk freely over the hotel telephones, informing others loudly and excitedly about the arrival of the American relatives. They helped them send off cables to the United States. They clamored at the receptionists' desks for rooms for them. That was another good first impression. People did not seem to be afraid of being seen with Americans, even of announcing their close ties with them, and they were not afraid of a hotel housing foreigners. Here I hasten to say that I later found this to be not a general attitude, particularly where nonrelatives were concerned.

All the clamoring at the receptionists' desk did not, however, produce rooms for us. Quite exhausted by this time, I went through the first stages of a tourist's arrival in a foreign country—sending off the cable home and changing American money. Then I had to go through the purely Soviet travel procedure of getting Intourist coupons for the three daily meals which had been paid for in New York. The Intourist and hotel employees were extremely friendly and helpful despite the turmoil created by the mass of roomless people and their friends, augmented now by the mass of the finally departing convention delegates who filled the lobby with their luggage and their friends.

In my exchanges with the Intourist officials and the hotel clerks I had not expected the light badinage that is associated more with American than Russian ways. This lightness was something new to me. And on that first day, unnerved by my airport experience, I began, during the long wait for a room, to be worried over this extreme friendliness toward me, wondering whether there wasn't something suspicious in it. Suppose they all had been instructed to give me special attention so as the better to watch me. I was still wondering about it while getting my meal coupons from a young Intourist girl, who kept chatting and joking with me, when I heard my name called. And there was one of the hotel receptionists, a well-groomed dark-haired young woman who had left her busy desk and was looking for me to tell me that she had a room for me. "I let you have the first available room," she informed me with a flashing smile. At her desk I found my plane companions still waiting to have rooms assigned to them.

Considering that I arrived at the hotel several hours later than they, I no longer had any doubt that my suspicions were justified. I was now convinced that I was being singled out for special attention, and that this attention, added to the unusual procedure of letting a person with an expired visa enter the country without asking her even one question, was the final proof that the Soviet authorities had sinister designs concerning me. However, since, as at the airport, there was nothing in the world I could do about it, I continued to go through all the motions expected of me. Finally I was in my room, with a beautiful view of the Moscow River. A room with an excellent bed, comfortable chairs, a large round table for meals and—what I never stopped appreciating throughout my stay—an enormous desk with numerous drawers. The porter who brought up my luggage and a few minutes later the chambermaid who brought me a vase for Van Cliburn's flowers, which had miraculously survived the ordeals at the airport and in the hotel, explained the reason for this kind of desk, which usually is not found in hotels. Since this was not exclusively a tourist hotel, many of the rooms were used, especially during the off-season, by convention and conference delegates, by representatives of industrial plants and farms, and in general by people with bulging briefcases for whom desk space is essential. The bathroom was large, clean and modern, and had every convenience in it, including hot pipes for towels and a huge man-size bathtub with two showers, one to take standing, another sitting.

On the desk were two lists, one in English and the other in Russian, with telephone numbers for room service, theater tickets, Intourist, general information. I dialed the number of the small snack bar of which there was one on each of the thirty floors. A few moments later, after twenty-one years, I again came face to face with that motherly warm human being, the ordinary Russian woman. After the waitress had spread out the food (caviar, an omelet, black Russian bread, and tea), delighted over my ability to speak Russian, she began to fuss over me. She was concerned about my being tired after the long journey, urged me to leave the unpacking for the morning, to go straight to bed and to sleep as late as I felt like. She made me feel that I was not alone, and that I had a friend. I ate, I did unpack, and I slept very well.

The next morning I was served breakfast by another pleasant and motherly waitress who also advised me to take it easy and to rest after such a long tiring trip. I am afraid I did not follow her advice. After writing a note to my family I left the room—to return to it fifteen hours later. My suspicions and anxieties of the day before almost entirely evaporated in the bright sunshine and with the help of a rested head and satisfactory breakfast. Again everybody in the lobby and in the Intourist office was exceedingly cordial and helpful and smiling, but now I didn't see anything suspicious in it. My conscience was clear, my intentions were friendly, and after a quick glance over the theater programs for the coming week I was out to rediscover Moscow.

Before many days had passed I found it hard to imagine the censorship and espionage of the old days. One knew then without any doubt that every single foreign letter, every single private phone call from abroad (and most domestic letters and calls as far as foreigners were concerned), every single visit paid or received was noted by the proper authorities. In those days one well knew and almost greeted as old friends the men assigned to watch one. The great majority of people I talked with about it now assured me that the strict censorship and spying of bygone years no longer existed, but few were certain that there was not some kind of control still.

Whatever form it took now, it was clear that the clumsy methods of Stalin's day were a thing of the past. Then the spies followed one step by step, left unmistakable signs of having opened letters, made no attempt to disguise the telltale telephone clicks. The Russians have learned so much in the intervening years that I am sure they have learned new and more discreet ways of following whomever they want to follow and of keeping an eye on whatever foreign mail and telephone calls they want to keep an eye on. For several days there would not be a single letter from abroad on the floorlady's desk where we picked up our mail. Then one day the desk would be covered with them. There must be a reason for that and it is not a lack of planes to carry mail. Numerous planes arrive in Moscow daily from the West. It is also hard to explain why some letters from New York took five days to reach me and others fifteen, though all were mailed on the same day. No one I asked about it could explain this phenomenon and I had no access to those who could. But whatever ways of keeping tabs on foreigners are used now they are very different from the old ones.

I never for one moment was conscious of anyone's watching or following me. Never once did I feel that anyone was interested in my goings and comings. Never once did I notice any suspicious character around. Never once did I have the feeling that anyone talking with me was trying to provoke me into some indiscretion. The only moments when the old fears and suspicions returned came when I was taking pictures. People were taking them everywhere, adults and children, foreign visitors, Moscovites, and out-of-towners. And still I was uneasy. I tried never to take pictures that bystanders might object to. I knew how touchy Russians were in this respect. They suspected that foreigners were out to catch on film whatever negative aspects of Soviet life they could find. Suppose somebody became suspicious of me? This idea never ceased to be disturbing.

Before I plunge into this rediscovery, a few words about my hotel, the Ukraina. I heard from several American travelers that the moment they entered the noisy lobby and faced the crowds of every color under the sun speaking a babble of incomprehensible languages, they rushed to the Intourist office asking to change their hotel. Though the thought that I was being followed soon disappeared completely, during the first day or two I felt safety in numbers and preferred to be lost in a crowd. Besides, I preferred large crowds where one could politely eavesdrop or join in a conversation, where one could without any effort gather and share impressions. I never regretted staying in the Ukraina. My room was quiet and comfortable, the lobby crowded—both exactly as I wanted them.

CHAPTER TWO

Old Friends

When I stepped out of the elevator into the hotel lobby my first morning the place was swarming with a colorfully clad delegation. This, I was to find, was usual. There were delegations and tourist groups galore in Moscow, of all shades of color and dress, of all ages and professions and backgrounds. They came from every corner of the earth, were treated like long-lost brothers and sisters, were well housed and fed, and were received by the proper authorities and their Soviet opposite numbers. I doubt whether any of them, except the students, ever have any contact with ordinary Russians not chosen by the authorities. And judging by the fact that the government found it desirable to create Friendship University, exclusively for students from underdeveloped countries, I would guess that the authorities do not look upon these student contacts with confidence. The adult delegations and organized tourist groups are certainly carefully shielded from any unofficial contacts. I usually saw them within their own groups, as a rule shepherded by a guide.

The impression of color and movement created by the scene in the hotel lobby was reinforced when I went into the street to find a cab to take me to my first reunion. Flowers were being sold everywhere. At street corners old peasant women were selling bunches of lilies-of-the-valley, forget-me-nots, violets, lilacs. As the weeks of my stay rolled on, cornflowers, daisies, poppies, peonies, and whatever else was coming into bloom were seen at these corners. And, as school doors closed, I saw children helping the old women. Men and women overloaded with briefcases and groceries would stop to buy and somehow manage to tuck in a bunch of flowers among their packages. All over town the more expensive, cultivated flowers were on sale at state-controlled kiosks. The collective farmers sell these same field and woods flowers on the open market along with their poultry, vegetables and dairy products. And another thing struck my eye—the enormous amount of greenery everywhere. There had always been the two rings of tree-lined boulevards circling Moscow as well as trees in the gardens of the old private mansions. But this cannot be compared with what has been planted in Moscow during the past years. Wherever the eye turned there were trees, shrubs, grass and flowers. But whenever I mentioned this to Moscovites with praise they demurred. This was far from enough, they said; other cities, like Kiev, for instance, were so much greener; there were still streets in Moscow without trees and back yards without any greenery. And besides, and this complaint came up whenever the word "tree" was mentioned, "there would have been more of them if not for someone's blunder." When a few years earlier the Garden Ring was being modernized for the demands of present-day traffic the huge trees in the middle of the boulevard were removed. There are persistent rumors that the Ring may get the trees back even if it involves great expense and great labor. But considering how many had to be cut down to make way for new roads and how many were destroyed during the war, hundreds of thousands of new trees must have been planted since I left in 1939. The linden tree, always a favorite on Moscow's boulevards, is now growing all over the city. The old poplars are still around, and while I was there their blooms, to the delight of the children and the exasperation of their mothers, floated everywhere, covering the ground as well as rugs and furniture with a snowlike soft blanket.

On that first morning ride in Moscow I sat, as I had the day before, next to the cab driver. And on that first ride I learned a lesson. I started the conversation with "Moscow has certainly changed since I saw it last." The driver showed little interest as he politely asked, "Where do you live now?" assuming that I had moved from Moscow to another Russian city. My Russian obviously sounded genuine enough. My answer "In the United States" electrified him as it did every cab driver and noncab driver after him and inevitably led to a shower of questions and an exchange of information about our families and life in our respective countries.

My first visit was to be to old friends, the Volgins. My son George had been in Moscow only a few weeks earlier and had told them I was coming. They had even wanted me to stay with them, which to me was the greatest proof that things had changed quite fundamentally in Russia. In the past the idea of a foreigner's sharing the room of an ordinary Russian family would have been totally unthinkable. And here I was, ringing the same doorbell I first rang thirty-three years earlier and last rang twenty-one years ago. I had meanwhile forgotten the proper number of rings—six families live in this particular apartment and each has a certain number of long and short rings. I rang the wrong combination. A tall gaunt woman who seemed vaguely familiar in the dark entrance hall opened the door and when I mentioned my friends' name first informed me, for the future, of the proper number of rings for them. Then she called out in the direction of the kitchen: "Sonya, someone for you." Unhurried familiar steps not expecting anything important, then a cry. It was 10 A.M. when we embraced in that dark hall and it was after midnight when a car deposited me again at my hotel. Through George we both knew the general outlines of each other's lives, but for women to fill in the general outlines with details is an endlessly satisfactory process.

Later in the day when her husband Mikhail, a high school mathematics teacher, and the two daughters came home, the deluge of emotions and words again threatened to engulf us. The last time I had seen the girls they were two and four years old. Now the

older, Kseniya, a lawyer, had two babies of her own, while Masha
was teaching in a kindergarten. Their mother, my friend Sonya,
fifty-seven years old, had retired two years earlier after a successful career as a pediatrician in order to help Kseniya with the babies.
Soon Miron, Kseniya's husband, brought the children home. They
had spent the day with his mother. There was no suitable neighborhood nursery and the two grandmothers in turn took care of
the children.

I had forgotten how families lived in Moscow and this visit
brought it back vividly. Sonya, her husband and Masha shared
the larger room, which also served as study, dining and living room.
The young couple and their two children had the smaller room.
Kseniya bubbled over with excitement; they were almost certain
soon to get two rooms of their own in a new building. Sonya's
eyes filled with tears at the thought of their moving away. They
had never been separated before, not for even one day, and even
the thought that she and her husband would have a room to themselves did not console her. We ate a huge dinner which, they all
assured me, was exactly the kind of dinner they would have eaten
had I not come. I believed them. Sonya had spent every minute of
the day with me and did not do any shopping. The daughters,
who brought home bags of food, did not know I had arrived. We
ate and we drank and we talked and we laughed and we were sad.
So many had died since I left. After dinner neighbors began to
drop in. No one had moved out of the apartment in the twenty-one
years and I had known all of them, including the gaunt woman
who had opened the door for me. Young people came in whom I
had known as children. They remembered me only as the mother
of two boys, of course. I have not the slightest idea what we
talked about that first evening. There was too much for one day.
When I was again alone in my room I was totally drained and not
able to make any notes.

Often during the next weeks I returned to my room completely
spent. The demands on my brain and my emotions seemed at
times too much to bear. But I tried never again to miss my note-

taking before going to bed. Anything left for the next day would have been pushed out by the impressions of that next day.

My second day in Moscow brought another warm reunion with friends equally close and dear, the Rozovs, and again it lasted through the day and long evening. Again young people I had known as children now had their own children. And again there were neighbors I knew dropping in, since the Rozovs too lived in the same apartment they had had since 1927. And again there was a table covered with food, this time embellished with a rich assortment of excellent jams and jellies, in which the newly acquired daughter-in-law, Sofochka, a budding actress, excelled.

Russian hospitality, it was clear, had not changed; in other words, it was still overwhelming. The idea that I might have regular hours for meals or had had a large meal an hour or two before was preposterous. Wherever I went I was almost forcibly fed as if I had just returned from an arctic ice floe after days without food. Even when I went to spend an hour or two with friends after a dinner engagement they knew perfectly well about, the table was set for me and I was expected to eat and drink and eat and drink some more.

There was one big difference between the Rozovs and the Volgins. In the Volgin family and among their neighbors there were both Communists and non-Communists. The Rozovs were all Communists, old and young, and so were their friends and the friends of their neighbors. The head of the family, a professional Communist, had been killed at the front. Anna, his wife, a retired school superintendent and my dear friend, had remained a faithful Communist, though the purges had left a not completely healed scar on her. Their only son, Nikolai, a surgeon, and his actress wife were members of the Komsomol. They all lived in two rooms. Anna felt that she was a most fortunate woman to have a room all to herself though the price of it, the death of her husband, was a heavy one. Her son definitely felt that one room for a family of three was exactly what was needed and, though Sofochka expected another baby within four months, the idea of applying for an extra room did not seem proper to them. As good Communists they felt that only when living conditions were satisfactory for everyone would they have the moral right to seek better accommodations for themselves. I did not realize then, as I did very soon afterward, that the Rozovs' idealism was far from typical. With only a few exceptions, the people I met, even orthodox Communists, were more concerned with bettering their own lot than that of other people.

As on the night before, I returned to the hotel after midnight with a blurred head, physically and emotionally exhausted, and thoroughly happy. It was an endless joy to see people who occupied such a large spot in my heart and who only a very short time before I had never expected to see again.

One of the reunions I had eagerly looked forward to was with another cherished friend, Maya, a woman doctor. She had been a beautiful blonde in her thirties when I first met her, with an old-fashioned Russian yearning for sentimentality and romanticism, and a universal feminine longing for beautiful clothes. She used sometimes to come to our apartment at the end of an exhausting day in her office in a large factory on the outskirts of Moscow, after she had helped the maid feed the family, after she had put the children to bed, after her husband, an engineer and active party member, had left for a meeting. We would lower the lights, curl up on the couch, and listen to sentimental old Russian songs on records prohibited in Soviet Russia, which our family used to bring from Paris. She used to say that if not for these occasional evenings she would be unable to take the eternal noisy propaganda, the tensions and duties of her days and evenings.

Now we sat again on a couch, a different one this time, without lowering the lights, without listening to sentimental songs, and talked about our families. Maya was a widow now, retired, had an adequate pension, was completely indifferent to clothes, though she dyed her hair. She visited her children regularly and was one of the very few people I met who lived in a room by herself. She was not interested, she said, in anything besides her family and her daily household chores. But whenever I permitted myself even a hint of criticism of anything Soviet, Maya would deliver a speech of the kind I heard constantly from others too about the sacrifices of the Russian people during the war and about the Allies' refusal to come in until they were sure that the Germans had already been beaten by the Russians. From Maya I heard what many later repeated—that the canned food which the United States sent to Russia during the war was sarcastically called by the Russians "The Second Front." I had never in the past heard Maya make a political speech and had always considered her to be far from a great admirer of the Soviet system.

Though I tried not to argue, at times it was thoroughly impossible for me to listen patiently to misinformation without being provoked into a denial. As a rule I had a great deal of patience when we talked about the war. It was hard to disagree or to dispute while listening to tales of personal suffering. But even then my patience would sometimes give out, particularly when the Russians showed their deep resentment over the late opening of the second front and, as they all insisted, on a much smaller scale than their own effort. They would reproach the West for the millions of dead they had lost before the Americans lost the first soldier.

Invariably they responded with little warmth and interest when I spoke of the sacrifices that England made during the period of the Stalin-Hitler pact; indeed they showed little interest in any sacrifices but their own. The fact that England held off Hitler's forces while Russia was supplying him with oil and wheat did not penetrate minds that were totally absorbed with themselves. In none of these conversations was there much warmth and interest for anything but Russia. Without exception every one of the many conversations about the war was exclusively centered on their own sacrifices which, they were sure, could have been so easily lightened by the West. The Stalin-Hitler pact, England, Poland, Holland—nothing has a place in their thinking when the talk is about the war.

To get back to the story of my reunions, throughout the years I had more than once wondered about my friend Yelena, a young chemistry student when I first knew her. She had joined the Communist party at the age of seventeen, was a disciplined, unswerving party member, tough and efficient in her exacting work but in her personal life a most gentle soul. When purely nonpolitical sentimental films were still being shown around Moscow we never missed one and when I at times felt tears smarting my eyes I was not embarrassed by her presence. She had made several trips abroad in connection with her work, knew foreign languages, recited Heine and Yeats, loved Tchaikovsky and was heartbroken during the years when his music was prohibited. When I first met her in the twenties she had just gone through the breakup of her marriage, and her second marriage a few years later did not work out either. She was an ardent internationalist and though she loved her native land there had never been a trace of narrow nationalism in her feelings and thinking. And now? Was she still an internationalist or only a good Russian?

I found Yelena in the same old apartment, with the same old neighbors and the same overcrowded kitchen. Her son and his wife joined us after putting their baby to bed. They were both bright young people and their knowledge of internal affairs was excellent even if one-sided. Of the outside world they were totally ignorant but they did not know that they were ignorant. They had not the slightest understanding of any other point of view but their own, which was the official one, of course. Yelena, who reads a great deal, including foreign literature in translation or in the original when she can get it, showed slightly more understanding, but in her quiet way disagreed with me on everything. This was quite contrary to her attitude in the past, when she had made no secret to me of her critical attitude toward Stalin and the purges and about being cut off from the outside world. In short, I had the answer to my primary question: Yelena had remained a devout Communist, which meant that by 1960 her internationalism had been transformed into ardent Russian nationalism.

When I commented on their crowded rooms they, like the Rozovs, insisted that their life of three adults and a child in two rooms, plus prolonged visits of Yelena's brother, was completely satisfactory. They were obviously well adjusted to it. They told me the story of some neighbors of theirs, a couple who got divorced and had to remain in the same room. They divided it with a large closet and a curtain. The divorced wife lived on one side of the curtain with their child, the husband with his new wife and her child from a previous marriage in the other half. Two years after the divorce, when their own baby was half a year old, the ex-husband and his new family miraculously succeeded in getting a room of their own. A divorce in itself is no reason for being assigned a new room. "How dreadful!" was my comment on the story. "Nothing dreadful about it," was Yelena's answer. "They have adjusted very well. After all, they are civilized people." I definitely doubted this happy adjustment and as definitely disagreed with its being called "civilized."

Like Yelena, her brother Andrei had remained a faithful Communist. A historian, he had gone through a great deal of ideological persecution throughout the years. He had a definite interpretation of history which he was unable to adjust to the constantly changing convulsions of the official line and regularly had to pay the price by being fiercely attacked by the press. Unlike many other historians, who had during the purges paid an even harsher penalty for their views, he had never been arrested. He accepted the necessity of paying a price for his views as an inevitable part of the "period of adjustment" in which he felt they were still living. To him, as to several other Communists I talked with, all past, present and future wrongs and errors are inevitable, transitory ills which do not shake their belief in the future.

But among all the Communists I met, Yelena and Andrei were the only ones who believed, as all Communists believed in the earlier days of the Soviet regime, that the millennium was very far away. They thought that their children and grandchildren would still have to make a great many sacrifices for the sake of the future. This was certainly contrary to the prevalent attitude that the time had now arrived to reap the results of past sacrifices.

They were sincerely convinced that no other form of society, and certainly not capitalism, could create a satisfactory life for humanity. But they certainly did not approve of all that went on around them—Khrushchev's thundering and rocket threats; the Soviet people's concentration on material achievements. Yelena and Andrei and their families are good and gentle people, as honest and pure and selfless as members of an idealistic religious sect. I don't think there are many of their kind left.

The visit to Yelena was followed by one to a young woman, Nadya, the daughter of dear friends who had both died in Siberian exile. When the old dilapidated building in which she lived was torn down, she was assigned a room in one of the new housing projects in the famous Southwest of Moscow which grew out of wilderness only a few years ago. It could have been a room in an American apartment house had it been equipped with a built-in closet. It was not, and Nadya was saving to buy a wardrobe. She had plenty of time to save the money since she was far down on the waiting list for what she wanted—a modern Scandinavian model which the Russian factories had only recently begun to produce. Meanwhile, Nadya kept her clothes hanging on the wall or spread out on a chair. There was no other place for them because there were only two rooms in the apartment—the second, quite a large one, shared by a family of four—besides the common kitchen, bathroom and toilet.

Nadya's room had German chairs and a German lamp, a Czech lounge chair, a Finnish table, bookcases designed by her and made to order by a neighborhood cabinetmaker in his after-work hours, a good-looking Scandinavian-style Soviet coffee table. Everything was light and modern. The bathroom, kitchen and toilet were spotless. Nadya told me that it had taken her some time to teach city ways to her neighbors, new arrivals from a Kazakhstan village, but she had obviously succeeded. I met the neighbors, good-natured, friendly people who seemed to be very proud of their new way of life even if learned under the strict tutelage of my demanding friend. The kitchen had a good gas stove, hot and cold water, plenty of cabinets. The latter do not come with the kitchen and are bought by the tenants. Nadya and her neighbors had their own worktables, which were covered for the night with clean lacy cloths.

Several more reunions followed, reunions which I had planned while still in New York. As in the past, I spent hours with Margot talking of things having little connection with Soviet problems, like the latest fashions and antique furniture, and listening to her, exactly as in the old days, bursting out into anti-Soviet diatribes between questions about the latest hairdos in the West. Daughter of a Russian father and a French mother, Margot was still teaching French, was still unable to get out of the dingy room she had lived in for thirty years, was still unable to create some kind of satisfactory personal life, and was still fighting the 1917 revolution with great vigor. How this woman survived all the purges is an enigma to me.

Scatterbrained, with a mercurial temperament, passionately adoring elegant clothes which she had never in her life possessed, not afraid of anyone, not even of the secret police during the worst years of the purges, Margot was the only truly flamboyant person I knew in Moscow. She had not changed a bit, at one moment hurling a torrent of abuse at the Soviet regime for being what it is, at the United States for not having overthrown the Soviets long ago, and almost in the same breath at the Soviet seamstresses who didn't know how to sew, at the house management for not taking care of the garbage, and at the Moscow climate. She was still full of ideas on how this or that or the other thing would speed the overthrow of the Soviet regime. All this sounded like 1920 rather than 1960. She certainly was not typical of any segment of Soviet society today but a fascinating phenomenon she had remained and I was delighted to see her again. And even though everything she said was hugely exaggerated and politically unsound, she may reflect the feelings of some of the other older people who as a rule don't speak up and whose voices I could not hear.

The next reunion was with Larissa, who used to be the secretary of one of Moscow's foreign correspondents. I found her too in her old apartment in the same small room she had shared with her boy after his father had left her. We used to do translations together and often, when my boys and their friends made my own apartment too lively, I used to work with her in her room.

There was, however, little of the old Larissa left in the white-haired bent woman who opened the door. Her eyes filled with tears, she clutched one hand to her heart and with the other almost pulled me into the room. One glance around showed me the reason for the shocking change in her. On the dresser stood her son's picture, draped in black gauze with bunches of immortelles around it. Larissa caught my glance. "My life was finished on May 13, 1943. I don't know how to live and why I live." She didn't say much more except to tell me in hardly audible words what had happened on that May 13 and how many long months later she learned of his death by torture when he refused to give the Germans the information they wanted. "And that was the end of everything." She did not ask a single question about our family, and I was glad about that. This was the one time when I would have been reluctant to talk about my sons and their families.

Again and again I heard the same sad refrain when I talked to women about their lives. So many started with the simple words: "My husband . . . my son (or sons) . . . was killed in the war." One of the hotel chambermaids said in a terrifyingly quiet voice: "My husband was killed in the first year of the war, my only son in the last. Now I am all alone." She was a gentle woman and I never heard a complaint from her about her tragic lot. Very few complained, maybe because their tragedies are shared by so many others, maybe because they all work so hard that they have little time to feel sorry for themselves.

The next day I rang the bell of the apartment where Varvara used to live. Someone opened the door and pointed to her room. I had seen her last in December, 1938, when she was dashing off, as usual in a mist of secrecy, to some undisclosed part of Russia. She was an epidemiologist and was always being sent on trips to cure, to prevent, to lecture on epidemics. Since this was one of the many subjects that were taboo in the Soviet press, her work was "top secret." Varvara had been left a widow at twenty-two, with a baby boy, while in her third year of medical school. That same year she joined the party, and between the many duties the party imposed at that time, her strenuous medical studies, and later her work there was precious little time left for the boy. During the rare leisurely moments we had together she would never fail to express her regret that she was not a good mother to her child. Nevertheless, he worshiped her and paid her the great compliment of being interested in her profession from childhood and of himself becoming an epidemiologist. He now had a wife and two children and they all lived together.

I remembered a slim chain-smoking brunette who hardly ever permitted herself to sit down and was constantly dashing around trying to get into a twenty-four-hour day the activities of at least forty-eight hours. I remembered her endless telephone conversations with colleagues, using words I had never heard, or interrupting a very personal talk to bury her head in a volume of Russian, German or English. She had mastered the latter two languages by herself in order to read whatever she could get hold of on epidemics written in those languages.

When I knocked and heard a gentle "Come in" I was sure that I was at the wrong door. Gentleness was not one of Varvara's characteristics. Her voice was always full of hurry and impatience. I walked in. The snow-white bent woman with a well-filled-out matronly figure, changed as she was, was definitely Varvara. She did not at once look toward the door because, as she told me later, she had expected a neighbor with her sewing machine, and I had a moment to watch her. She was sitting at a table covered with mending bits and ends, holding in her hands a little girl's dress. Her eyes were on a paper covered with words and figures—as I found out later, a shopping list—and her foot gently rocked a cradle holding her brand-new grandson. She finally turned her head, dropped the little girl's dress, and the cradle stopped rocking. She had had no idea I was in Moscow and it took us a while to recover. Her first coherent words were: "Have a good look at me! What you see before you is a new Soviet product: the Grandmother!"

And that was all she was now and all she had been for the four years since she had retired at the age of sixty, five years after her legal retirement age, to devote herself to keeping house for her son's family. Varvara had a good pension which, combined with the two other incomes, was providing them with a satisfactory life. Forgotten were Varvara's books, professional excitements, life outside the family. Her one and only profession now was to be a grandmother, and she would rather talk about her and my grandchildren than about anything else, she assured me. I doubted that, because at the dinner table she avidly listened to the occasional remarks her son made about his work.

Throughout the following weeks other meetings followed, and then came repeated visits with, as well as search for, friends who had changed addresses, names, spouses, and through friends finding other long-lost friends or making new ones. Every reunion was a great joy but the greatest joy came from finding alive those who, I was sure, had long ago died in prison or exile, and from seeing that they were leading wholly satisfactory lives.

Our talk was devoted largely to family matters, to simple everyday things—the bringing up of children, relations between husbands and wives as well as between the generations, discussions on love, death, the purpose of life, on art, literature—as they would be anywhere in the world. Did we talk much about politics? Of course we did, almost constantly. But not necessarily in the pure sense of the word and in pure political terminology. In Russia politics is the very essence of life. Whether we talked about love or food or summer resorts or a new pair of shoes or children, politics was our sometimes silent but more frequently not so silent partner.

Politics reaches into every niche and nook of life in the Soviet Union. It isn't at all what we call politics. In Russia one does not have to talk about taxes or elections or a party platform or foreign relations to be talking about politics. There an individual is an indivisible part of the state and the state is an indivisible part of him. Whether one wholly accepts or rejects it, this is an undeniable and, for the time being at least, an unalterable fact of life. And no conversation, not even on a subject that would seem to us as remote as the sky from politics, is without political undertones. My most intimate talks with friends on purely personal matters gave me as much insight into Soviet changes and present trends as any purely political discussion did.

CHAPTER THREE

Marya, the Returnees, and Khrushchev

One day I went to see the old dilapidated two-story house in which we had lived for three years. Our quarters there had been unbelievably crowded. The nine rooms, one tiny toilet, one small bathroom, and one primitive kitchen without a stove or hot water, were shared by seven families consisting of twenty-three adults and children. We were among the privileged ones, since we had two rooms. That we were five in those rooms, including our maid, did not seem a calamity to our neighbors, some of whom lived four and five in one room.

I walked and walked around the picturesque pond on to which our windows had looked and where there used to be rowing in the summer and skating in the winter, and where to the delight of the children Red Army soldiers trained their service dogs. Our house was not there any more, neither were any of the other old houses on the block. In their place stood several four-story buildings with wide windows covered with elaborate draperies and curtains. No one had curtains in the days when we lived on that street. The pond had always been picturesque but in the past had no embellishments except its natural beauty, magnificent old trees and a few swans. Now there were wide walks around the pond, and between the walks and the water there was young grass and a beautiful display of irises, pansies, peonies and tulips as well as thousands of seedlings of annuals. Along the walks were comfortable benches with people playing chess and checkers, gossiping, reading, meditating.

In prerevolutionary days this had been a neighborhood where high officials lived; and today I still saw sitting on the benches a few old men and women who could have come out of the pages of prerevolutionary Russian novels. Their clothes and looks were more than simply old-fashioned; they definitely belonged to a long-gone page of history. I tried to eavesdrop but had no success. They were talking in low voices, sometimes even whispering. Whatever they were saying was not meant to be heard by an outsider. Whenever I sat down on a bench near them even a whispered conversation stopped dead.

There were not many of these historic relics. The hundreds of others in the park were exactly like the hundreds and the thousands one found sitting on park and boulevard benches all over Moscow. And their conversations were the same and they were not conducted in whispers. They talked about the high cost of food, a child's cold or school marks, plans for vacations, neighbors, hopes for a new room.

I sat on a bench from which I could take pictures of the children on the playground and felt quite sentimental. I was thinking of the people with whom we had lived so closely for three years, sharing sorrow and joy, gossip and tragedy, the quarrels of children and adults. Where were they and which of the "they" were still alive? I moved to a different bench to take pictures of a little boy who was urging his grandmother to join him on the seesaw, which after a great effort she accomplished. And on this bench I got my answers.

Next to me an elderly woman was feeding an orange to a blonde little girl, and in the same words and with the same intonation which every Russian child under any regime has heard and will probably go on hearing kept urging her: "Eat, my darling, eat, Katinka, it is good for you. You will grow big and strong, eat, my little pigeon." She cast a smile at me, looking for approval of her sentiments from an obviously fellow grandmother. Then came a hesitant "Marya?" from me and an anything but hesitant shout "Markoosha!" from her.

Marya was one of my old neighbors whom I very much wanted to see. During the years we had lived in the same house Marya had more trouble than anyone else. She had husband trouble, job trouble, maid trouble, bedbug trouble, lover trouble, robbery trouble. She had an adorable little blonde daughter, Vera, who used to play with our boys and who once deeply upset them by insisting that no papa and mamma ever stayed together, that papas and mammas always keep changing, and that their own papa and mamma were not going to stay very long with them and they would have either a new papa or a new mamma. Little Vera was talking out of her own unfortunate experience, which she shared with many other Russian children of that era.

To digress for a moment: my children were attending kindergarten at that time and few of their playmates there or the many children in our house lived with both their own parents; it was either with mother and her new husband or with father and his new wife. I don't remember the divorce statistics but they were frightening. Family life had been totally disrupted in the chaotic years after the revolution and hadn't even by the thirties returned to a normal pattern. There were many reasons for that. As a result of stringent laws, divorce had been almost nonexistent in Czarist Russia; consequently, the rush to be free of unwanted ties was tremendous when immediately after the revolution these laws were abolished.

Free love was a slogan never proclaimed by the Soviet government but enthusiastically proclaimed and accepted by many who saw in the loosening of marital and sexual ties one of the great attractions of the new regime. The penny-postcard divorces, by which a person, either man or woman, was simply notified that he had been divorced by his mate, made this kind of freedom available to anyone who wanted it, whether it broke the rejected partner's heart or not, whether there were children involved or not. The general turmoil, with every law or custom of the prerevolutionary era discarded, and no new postrevolutionary norms, laws and customs yet established, was reflected to an enormous degree in the relations between the sexes. The picture began to assume a less violent pattern within the decade after the revolution but the results of it were felt well into the thirties. Now, however, family life is completely normal and there is little trace left of the earlier turbulence. There are of course divorces and there are remarried couples living with the children of one ex-partner as there are in the United States and anywhere else. But they are now rather the exception than the rule.

The Katinka of the playground was the child of that blonde little girl Vera who had so alarmed my boys. Vera was now married to her second husband, Katinka's father, having lost her first husband in the war before their daughter, Mashenka, now sixteen, was born. Their life was harmonious and peaceful, filled with family and work. Both were biologists. Both were party members. Unlike Vera, her children had a completely secure and protected childhood. They also had in Marya a doting grandmother, of which the revolution had deprived little Vera—and not by death or geography. When we knew them, Marya's mother had visited her occasionally but following the spirit of those days Marya had not wanted her child to be influenced by a "counterrevolutionary," even if it was her own mother. The old lady would cross herself whenever a word that she considered unholy was mentioned in her presence and she had to cross herself quite frequently in the company of her daughter's friends. But Marya, like the other grandmothers of her generation, is what is called in Russia "a product of Soviet society." These are people who have spent a life in honest labor, not like some of their own parents "exploiting the toiling masses" and worshiping a "nonexistent God." Consequently, they are considered fit to be around their grandchildren.

When our old house was torn down, Marya told me, some of our old neighbors were moved to new buildings in the same neighborhood and most of them still live there. She urged me to go back home with her and spend the day looking them up. I had to rush off to a luncheon appointment but not before a date for two days later was set for dinner at Marya's with her daughter and family, and afterward a tea with the old neighbors she could get hold of.

She was highly successful in this endeavor and there was standing room only. Everybody was eager to bring me up to date on what had happened to them since we parted in 1933 when our family moved to another apartment. It was among my most delightful, unexpected evenings and it was followed by two more in the apartments of other old neighbors.

The person who won my heart was Vera's older daughter, Mashenka. She was sweet, serene, and at peace with life. From her mother and grandmother she had heard many tales about the Fischers, and always sat open-mouthed watching me, as if, her mother teased her, she expected me to say and do something extraordinary, something no one she knew had ever said or done. She was quite disappointed that I spent so much time listening with obvious interest to people talk about all the boring things she always heard people talk about. But her ears would prick up when I was asked questions about that fabulous land America, of which she had heard such wonderful and horrible things.

Once, the only time I happened to be alone with her and urged her to ask me questions, she said: "Please, tell me about American girls of my age." I thought of some I knew, nice girls every one of them, but worlds removed from Mashenka with her unrouged lips, her almost babylike innocence, her ignorance of dating and popular hits and joy-riding and the many other things that are important to our 16-year-old girls. Then I remembered Mashenka's interest in music and I blessed Leonard Bernstein. I delivered an enthusiastic talk on his concerts for young people and on the many 16-year-old American girls who attended them. I stretched out my account and there were no more questions.

Mashenka was preparing a gift for me, a reprint of an old snapshot showing several children, including her mother and our boys, playing in the yard. The picture was not ready by the time I left. They did take my address and promised to send it "when the times are more felicitous." Will I ever see it?

One of the greatest joys of my visit to Moscow was seeing again friends who I was certain had perished in Siberia. One of these was Simon, a member of a family who before the revolution had filled the Czarist prisons and during the purges those of the Soviets. He was the last survivor of his family, and, despite t.b., had miraculously overcome the rigors of many years in Siberian mines. In the old days when several members of his family were still alive and at least one of them without fail in prison, our family helped out with food packages during the short period when the authorities permitted such packages to be sent to prisons.

Simon's mother was a woman who in my memory will forever remain a saint. When we were getting ready to leave Moscow in 1939 she was going through an especially difficult time: Simon was in exile, she was crippled by arthritis, every other member of the family had some misfortune, and there simply was not enough money for food and fuel. But she did not want me to leave without a present from her, though she could not spare a penny and had sold or given away nearly everything she had. She did, however, discover something she still possessed from the old days, a good linen bed sheet. That was her present to me. I was to take it to a dressmaker to have her cut out a dress for me, after which she with her aching fingers embroidered it in an old Russian design. This dress remained for many years one of my most prized possessions.

Like several other members of the family she perished in the war. She died a bundle of bones and nerves, up to the last moment sharing her only crust of bread with anyone who was hungry. She had other children besides Simon and the others had their share of prison and exile too, but most of her love and heartache was for him. He was the youngest and had been ailing since childhood; she had no hope of ever seeing him again, and she didn't. I well remember the day this normally reserved woman came to our house, completely distraught. She had received a letter from Simon asking for a drug which a doctor, a prisoner in the same labor camp, had mentioned as a miracle drug for t.b., which had been discovered in the West. She came to us after she had pleaded unavailingly with several doctors and pharmacists to get it for her. We wrote for it. It could not have reached him till a year after he had written the letter. By that time we were in the United States. But it did reach him. It is hard to find words to say how it felt to hear about it from him in Moscow so many years later, drinking tea with lemon and eating strawberry jam made by his wife.

To sit with Simon in a pleasant room in a new building and to meet his wife and young son was something that by itself would have made my trip to Moscow worthwhile. During my weeks there I had occasion to speak to many "returnees," or "rehabilitated persons," but most of what I learned about them was around Simon's hospitable tea table to which, after our first strictly private reunion, he would, whenever I came, invite his friends who had been in prisons and camps.

To me the inconceivable thing was the quiet, almost unconcerned way in which most of them told their stories. There were some disagreements among them. For instance, a few said that everyone had returned from exile except those who had been shot or who had died a natural death. Others said that there were still a number of political prisoners in the camps and that some arrests, though not many, were still being made. None of them knew of concrete cases but they repeated rumors which I had heard from other sources. Some said that the process of rehabilitation was speedy, without any delays or red tape, and that the government was making an honest effort to correct past wrongs as smoothly as possible. Others said that some appeals for financial compensation, for living quarters or for jobs were still pending and not moving.

There was also some disagreement about whether Khrushchev was the only one responsible for the rehabilitation of political prisoners. Several said that it had begun before he was in sole charge of the government, but the majority were definitely of the opinion that immediately after Stalin's death Khrushchev had considered it one of his very first tasks and had lost no time in setting about it. When I asked whether at that time Malenkov was not the one who made decisions, the answer was that Malenkov did make many and good decisions, but that they were mostly without a basis for practical achievement, while Khrushchev, a practical man, made only promises he knew he had the power to keep, even before he assumed complete control. Though quite ready to discuss the question of return and rehabilitation, none of these men liked to dwell on the years spent in prisons and camps. Some of them made it plain that they preferred not to say anything at all about them. But even those who were not so categorical said little and preferred to shift the conversation to their miraculous return to normal life.

At first, immediately after the trek back from the camps and prisons began, some memoirs were published, long-prohibited novels and poems by exiles appeared again (to be sold out literally in hours), reputations were officially rehabilitated. But now the tide has turned again and the authorities consider it wiser to let bygones be bygones. One hardly ever sees anything on this subject in print these days.

Once two men, each of whom had spent seventeen years in Siberian exile, clashed in an argument. One was now a 100 per cent patriotic Communist who in high-flown language kept proclaiming his loyalty to the regime and explaining the purges in general and his own exile in particular by "inevitable historical process," a term I kept hearing whenever there was no truly logical answer to an argument. The other scoffed at the "historical process" and heatedly swore never to forgive the lost years of his life, the broken family, the unfinished education, the ruined health. But he ended his outburst with "but that is all I can do about it, nothing else. This is the only motherland I have on earth, and this is where I want to live and die."

One of the men told me that up to 1941 his exile in a Siberian labor camp, the separation from his family and his sense of injustice, since he knew himself totally innocent of any crime, were overwhelming and quite as hard to bear as the physical hardships. However, after the beginning of the war, he was ashamed to admit, he as well as some others of the younger age group felt relieved because even in exile they were safer than they would have been in the front lines, and life in camp began to seem less harsh. Among other things, this same man mentioned that exiled Chinese, mainly students, worked in the camps, usually as cooks and laundrymen.

I was shown the certificates which the amnestied and rehabilitated received from the government upon their return. It is a plain piece of paper saying briefly that no infringement of law was found to have been committed by So-and-so. This certificate was shown and talked about sometimes with indifference, sometimes with sarcasm, and only rarely with the kind of fierce indignation one would expect. In most cases the relief at being returned to life outweighed everything else. Their attitude reminded me of survivors of concentration camps whom I had met in Germany during my work there after the war. Many of them, like the returnees from Soviet camps, were full of zest for a life that had been miraculously restored to them. On the other hand, among both groups one found some who could never forget nor forgive.

I had the impression that the majority of the returnees were politically unorthodox, as a result both of their personal experiences and of having lived for so long among people who, having little to lose, talked much more openly than people did elsewhere in Russia during those years. No doubt many of them pretend deeper orthodoxy and loyalty than they sincerely feel, but then it is easy for them to behave in a cynical way. They had been given the proper training in cynicism.

Once I heard a woman, who had no bitter words to say about the sixteen years torn out of her own young life, tell the story of another with tears of pain and outrage in her eyes. She spoke of a friend who was called in by the authorities to receive posthumous rehabilitation letters for three people, her entire family—father, mother and brother, every one of them shot in 1937. Usually such certificates were given out during the working day but this woman was called in after office hours when no one would be around in case she became too emotional. The precautions were superfluous. She controlled herself, and her hands shook less than those of the official who handed her the rehabilitation certificates. I had known her parents and I had played with her when she was a little girl. Her father had been an ambassador in Western Europe in the twenties when I worked as an interpreter at international conferences.

What my "rehabilitated" friends had to say about Khrushchev reflected an opinion I heard voiced many times. After decades it is now firmly established in the minds of the Russians that any change in their condition, whether good or bad, is the result of an order from above. Since the government at present obviously means Khrushchev, he is given sole credit for the improvements of the past years, and particularly for the lifting of the terror. When I asked what happened to people accused of crimes nowadays—and the Soviet press is full of reports of graft, mismanagement, speculation, dishonesty, inefficiency—I was told: "Nothing terrible," or "Hardly anyone is being shot now." People read the reports of crimes without the horror they formerly felt when it was an open secret that once a man was officially accused of a crime—however small—he most probably was no longer alive. Today the culprits are reprimanded or discharged or demoted or sent to outlying regions, or in more serious cases imprisoned.* (I was interested to learn that, whereas in the past when arrests were an integral part of Russian life and an important topic of conversation, now they are rather kept a secret. A member of one family I saw several times had been in prison for a year, but I learned of it from their friends; no member of the family mentioned it to me though I had known them quite well in the past and had asked them about the arrested man. I have no explanation for this changed attitude, which I was told was quite general.)

Moreover, Khrushchev reaps constant praise for the removal of

---

* This is drastically changed now and death penalty for speculations has become commonplace again.

another nightmare of Stalin's era, when families, friends and co-workers of a person charged with a crime—and usually it was an imaginary one—were held responsible with him; and the where-abouts of the arrested person was sometimes not known until the notice of an execution or natural death reached whatever member of the family had remained free. This, it is said, no longer happens.

People are deeply conscious of how much better things are. "Wouldn't you want to stay here now?" a question often asked of me during my visit would have been unthinkable coming from the same people at the time I left in 1939. The question then usually was "Why do you live here when you can live abroad?" Most people could not understand then why anyone who had the choice would choose to live in the Soviet Union.

Not only the relaxation of the terror but the rise in living stand-ards is so important and so absorbing that few are willing to pon-der the whens and whys. When I asked whether immediately after Stalin's death, before Khrushchev took over the reins, the trium-virate (Malenkov, Kaganovich, Khrushchev) was not out to do the same things, I met only a look of blank disinterest. The people I talked to were not much concerned about what was really going on in the Kremlin during those days, and who was for and who against more heavy industry or more defense or more consumers' goods. All they knew and all they were interested in was that since Khrushchev had definitely become the top man their daily wants were given more attention than ever before; that was all that counted.

I once asked a woman who was critical of everything done by the government in the Stalin days a question I had asked several others: If Stalin as well as many other Soviet leaders of the past like Trotsky, Zinoviev, Bukharin, Beria, Malenkov, Molotov, etc., etc., etc., had proved to be wrong couldn't it be that someday Khru-shchev might be proved wrong too? This woman, who was fiercer in her attacks on the past than anyone else I talked with, staunchly de-fended Khrushchev. She definitely wanted no change; she wanted him to stay, not out of love for him, she said, but because she felt safer with him than with anyone else. She had no doubt that he was going to stay in power.

"He is very shrewd," she said. "He would forestall any attempt against him; he has been through too much of that kind of thing himself. And the people wouldn't stand for anyone else right now; they are on his side; he has done a lot for them."

Since this was a very cultivated woman who spoke a refined, literate Russian, I was interested to know whether Khrushchev's manners and language affected her breed of Russian.

"It did at first," she said, "a great deal, even though heaven knows we had not been spoiled by Stalin's manners and language. It still shocks me at times as it does others, but this is really of no consequence. People see results and this is all that matters."

A number of other people who admitted that at first they were quite contemptuous of Khrushchev's roughness, rude manners and uncultivated language have now made peace with him. Among the foreign journalists in Moscow I heard the same talk about a struggle in the Kremlin between Khrushchev's adherents and opponents that we see reflected in the American press; but I hardly ever heard it spoken of by my Russian friends. The few who did mention it were vague, and admitted that they had no idea what was really going on in the higher strata, but said they doubted that Khrushchev could be in serious trouble. To them, as to everyone else I talked to, he is definitely the man who sees to it that they have more of what they want to have.

Several times, however, I did hear that, though Khrushchev lacks the megalomania of Stalin, he may be acquiring a taste for the "personality cult." His name is mentioned more and more in the press ahead of those of the other members of government rather than in alphabetical order, as it used to be. The press is full of letters of praise and adulation and he is thanked for anything good that happens anywhere. More and more frequently he is quoted next to Lenin on pronouncements of political theories, a quite disturbing symptom to some Russians. But I heard young people laughing off these fears when the older generation, remembering too well how the Stalin-worship began, expressed their concern.

To me the deep belief in the benevolence of Khrushchev's intentions means that most people will unquestionably accept whatever he decides about anything. A very intelligent young woman told me that, should Khrushchev tomorrow tell them that they had to sacrifice their present soft life (this is how many Russians view today's standard of living), eat less, wear less, work more, they would follow him unhesitatingly.

"If we were to be told today that the production of shoes had to stop or that butter would not be available any more, I for one wouldn't even ask why and I would certainly not grumble."

She sounded enthusiastic and sincere and, though I doubt that she reflected the sentiment of all the people, there are without question many like her. Khrushchev is a great manipulator; he knows his people and he knows the right strings to pull at the right time and in the right way.

A not very orthodox Moscovite who had much fault to find with Soviet domestic policies said that should there be a free referendum today at least 90 per cent of the people would give a definite yes to Khrushchev and the Soviet regime. As was my custom, I asked several more people the same question and the answer was always the same, with a slight variation in the estimated percentage. Some added that, of course, in the past, especially in the thirties, the answer would have been a different one. And a few others said that they would vote for Khrushchev, though they don't by a long shot agree with everything he does, because someone else would be so much worse.

These latter were people who had preserved a certain capacity to think for themselves and were searching for ways to improve what they thought was wrong. There are probably not many such people around but even these few were by no means anti-Soviet or pro-Western or ready for any kind of anti-Soviet activity. They were above all else Russian patriots. They would like to see the Soviet regime democratized, they would like to improve and to modify it—

but certainly not to overthrow it. By no means did they seem to me likely material for counterrevolutionary subversive activities.

Despite the generally favorable feeling toward Khrushchev, there are plenty of jokes about him going around Moscow, not all of them kind.

Here is a sample: An American doctor tells a visiting Russian in the United States that he has invented a method of reviving corpses, even those who had been dead for some time. The Russian, not to be outdone, boasts that the Russians have a runner who runs twenty-five miles a minute. Some time later this American doctor visited Moscow and offered to give a demonstration of his method. Khrushchev was informed about it and asked what to do, since they certainly could not produce a man who could run twenty-five miles a minute. "Oh, yes, we can," replied Khrushchev; "just watch me in case he revives Stalin."

CHAPTER FOUR

Meeting with Niura

Aside from old friends, I also tried to hunt up some of the chance acquaintances of the old days: a young actress I had met in a doctor's waiting room and become friends with; parents I had worked with on the Parents' Council in the boys' schools; people I had spent summers with in a suburban bungalow; a seamstress who had made dresses for me. For none of them did I have a telephone number. Telephone books are a great rarity in Moscow and not knowing the fate of the people I was looking for I preferred not to ask for information which, by the way, is promptly and efficiently given. I simply went to the old address I remembered and knocked at doors or rang doorbells. A few had left Moscow, others were dead, some had moved to addresses unknown. But not once was I simply turned away from the door when the people I was looking for were not there any more. There was always someone who tried to be helpful. Not once was I met with suspicion or unfriendliness. It is true that during those weeks the authorities had not yet started to warn the public against American spies who came to the Soviet Union under the guise of tourists.

Once when I was sadly leaving a house after having learned that the entire family of the jolly Armenian mother who had been my colleague on the Parents' Council had been wiped out by the war, a voice called out, "Don't you remember me?" She was an old neighbor of my Armenian friend. The first short encounter was a preliminary to a dinner, with neighbors dropping in afterward. At first I was reluctant to accept the dinner invitation. I had in the past met this woman only a few times and not at all during the last years of my stay in Moscow; at that time people were afraid to be associated with foreigners, so I used to meet my Armenian friend in a museum or movie rather than visit her at her home. Her old neighbor laughed off my doubts: "We live in different times today, we are not afraid of foreigners as we used to be."

I wonder what she is saying now. But whatever she says now, that evening in her house was full of give-and-take and added a great deal to my understanding of Soviet life. During that evening, too, as so many times before and after, people were eager to get me into a corner to tell me their personal stories. Their desire to recount their tragic pasts reminded me again of the refugees in postwar D.P. camps in Germany. Like the Russians, they were delighted to find someone from the outside world who would listen to them. They wanted to talk about their past misfortunes but they could not get the ear of those who had gone through the same hell. If they started, the person they were talking to would interrupt either by saying he had had enough of these stories or by starting to tell his own. And now in Russia, as earlier in Germany, I, fresh from the outside world, was ready to listen to accounts of their past agonies without interrupting them to tell my own.

My Armenian friends were not the only ones no longer alive. That is why so many of my first moments of reunion were full of sadness. The list was long of those who had died—on the front or from hunger, in concentration camps (German) or labor camps (Soviet), or during the blockade of Leningrad. The tales of those who were hurriedly evacuated from Moscow when it looked as though the Germans were going to enter the city were harrowing. With hardly any possessions at all whole families, including the ill, the aged and infants, were put on trains without food, water, blankets, toilet and sleeping facilities, and sent to faraway corners of Asiatic Russia where the local population frequently met them with nothing but hostility. The evacuation of schools and organizations was carried out efficiently but, as so often in Stalin's days, the individual was ignored. Many evacuation stories were told me, but none stands out in my mind so vividly as the story of the potato soup.

A family of four was forever scrounging for food. One day a local peasant gave them several potatoes and a pinch of salt in exchange for a pair of shoes. They did not know when another such windfall would come their way, so they ate only one potato a day, made into soup for the four of them. Their youngest daughter was unable to take the starvation diet and only three of them returned to Moscow. There, like so many others, they found that their apartment had been looted. They told me that they were lucky at that, for others found their houses destroyed by bombs. Out of nothing this family, like many others, had to create a new life. And they did. This story was told to me in homey surroundings, around a table laden with food, with laughter interrupting even the sad tales, with neighbors telling their own stories, with the younger people going off for fun in the park.

Incidentally, during that evening the story of my white bathrobe was told. When we were leaving in 1939 and I was distributing my possessions, an old woman living in this apartment was recovering from pneumonia. It was a cold winter and she had a long walk from her room to the bathroom and kitchen. I left my warm terrycloth bathrobe with her. She died soon after that and her daugher-in-law inherited the robe. Whatever made her pack it when she and her family were hurriedly evacuated from Moscow she never understood. She left behind many more essential belongings. However, in the midst of their long journey she came down with typhus and was taken to a primitive hospital in a small Siberian town. It was cold and drafty in the hospital, and she was certain that without the bathrobe, which she never took off during her entire hospital stay, she would not have recovered. The "white bathrobe" has become a legend in her family; it is still in use and the owner of it baked a cake for me in its honor.

After a time I succeeded in finding almost everyone I had expected to see, with the exception of one very important person, our
former maid Niura. She had been the mainstay of our family for a
long time; without her the last years in Moscow would have been
even more unbearable than they were. An old friend told me that
she had remained to work as a janitor or elevator operator in the
apartment house where we lived during our last six years in Moscow.

One of my very first visits was to this building. It would have been
anyway, even if I had not been looking for Niura. A pilgrimage to
this house is a sentimental custom of every member of the Fischer
family on a visit to Moscow. It is still in a state of constant repair,
as it was within less than two months after it was built, and there
are always workers swarming around the courtyard.

When I asked at the management office where I could find Niura,
I met with the only rude treatment I received throughout my Moscow stay. I was not able to supply the woman in charge with Niura's
surname, having forgotten it. "We have plenty of Niuras around.
Without her surname I can't be bothered," she barked. I tried to explain who I was and why I wanted to see Niura. She cut me short:
"I am not interested in who you are. I have work to do," and she
got busy shuffling papers on her desk.

That was that. I dawdled around the entrance hall leading to our
old apartment and talked with a number of women going in and
out of the house with shopping bags. But none of them had lived
there in our time and all in a friendly way confirmed the fact that
there were a number of Niuras working in the house and without
her last name they could not help me.

(May I digress for a moment? Niura is really not a name in itself.
It is a derivative of Anna; she could also be called Anya, Niurochka,
Niusha, Anichka, Annochka, Niuta, Aniuta, Niussya, among other
names, and be easily recognized by a Russian as Anna. Just as a
Russian would know that Kolya, Nika, Nikolasha, Kolinka, Koliusha,
Kolka are the same as Nikolai. Or that Alik, Sasha, Sanya, Shura,
Shurik, Sashutka, and many more are Alexander. That Manya,
Masha, Manichka, Mashutka, Marussya, and many more are Marie.

This may explain the difficulty that non-Russians often have in reading some Russian novels.)

My disappointment in not finding Niura was great. Twice more I made an attempt, with the same result. And then, less than a week before I left Moscow, with days overcrowded with the many things I still wanted to do and people I wanted to see, I telephoned a friend to confirm an appointment. Her first question was: "Has Niura phoned you?"

During my third visit to the house in search of her I had noticed a tiny old woman standing at some distance from the group of women I was talking to. I felt it useless to approach her, since she didn't look like a person who would welcome a conversation, and she definitely did not ring a bell of recognition in me. But I did in her, it seemed, and as it happened she knew the woman I was telephoning to on this particular morning and that we had been friends in the past. She had telephoned her and asked whether she had seen right and whether it was possible that I was in Moscow. And so she found out that I was looking for Niura, and gave Niura my telephone number. Poor Niura kept calling me but since I was hardly ever in my room and the hotel did not take messages she never reached me.

My careful schedule of that morning went up in smoke. I dropped everything I had intended to do, grabbed my camera, and in a very few minutes a cab took me to Niura's door. Though by this time I had had a few quite dramatic reunions, ours was certainly one of the most sentimental. No photographs I showed her of my sons as grown-up men with wives and children could convince her that George and Victor, the two small boys she used to take care of, were really these grown men. A friend of hers, also called Niura, who in the old days spent all her free time with us, happened to be there, and the three of us talked for hours trying to catch up on the twenty-one years. From time to time "our Niura," as we used to call her, to distinguish her from her friend, would interrupt a sentence or stop listening, and, with tears in her eyes, throw her mighty arms around me and hug me.

Niura now lives in her own room supplied by the house management. It it filled with fresh flowers and plants, with pictures, furniture and knickknacks in quite good taste. The room is very clean and well kept, the curtains are gay, the floor well waxed and covered with a colorful rug. Niura is in charge of the automatic elevators, is well paid, and earns extra money baby-sitting, apartment-watching, housecleaning. She showed me her elaborate wardrobe and was delighted when I told her that mine could not compete with hers, especially in the cost and number of coats.

Niura had never married but seemed to be thoroughly pleased with life. She has many friends and they get together on Sundays and evenings for a meal and a drink, a dance or an outing. Of all the people I met Niura is the only one who has no bad memories even of the war years. She had stayed in Moscow, worked very hard, but never starved and always had a roof over her head. She lost no one who was close to her. The one regret she has is that her belongings, many of them things we gave her in 1939, were stolen during the short time she was sent to work outside of Moscow. But it was obvious that she has since been able on her own to surround herself with everything she needs for a contented life. All that was left from her days with us was a picture of Lenin as a child, which has a prominent place on her wall.

We were far from talked out when we decided to pay a visit to her aunt Pasha, about whom I had written in *My Lives in Russia*.

There was Pasha . . . a handsome woman in her fifties, who spoke a beautiful Russian folk language, rich in idiom and images. In a deep melodious voice she liked to tell stories of her childhood, of the old landlord and of his wife who had seemed like a fairy to the little peasant girl. Pasha's stories were a mixture of reality and superstition, of past and present. She grew up in fear of God, of the landlord, of rich people, of the priest, and of the czarist police. When I met her in 1932, she still lived in the world of her old fears. . . . I saw her gradually losing one fear after another until they were all gone except her fear of God which never left her.

Like Niura, Pasha had changed little, only aged a bit. I found the same handsome, kind, hospitable, wise, slowly and gracefully moving woman. Her large room, shining with cleanliness, was in a half-basement but she hastened to tell me that she expected any day to be assigned a new room. There was a decree by which everyone living below the first floor was to get out by a certain date and the date was approaching. Unlike Niura's, her room was furnished in an old-fashioned way, with large heavy furniture, bright paper flowers, a large bed piled high with featherbeds and tremendous pillows richly covered with crocheted pillow cases. Everything that could be was decorated with doilies and antimacassars, all embroidered or crocheted by Pasha. She had been getting an adequate pension since her retirement from her school janitor's job, also a pension for the military service of her late husband, an excellent shoemaker and a notorious drunkard. She commented matter-of-factly that after his death life had become much easier for her. Not only was she better off financially, since money was not being thrown away on drinking, but, as she said in the simplest words I ever heard a woman use on the subject, she found it pleasant to sleep all by herself in a clean bed not soiled by a drunkard.

Pasha's other niece joined us later, and the red velvet cloth with the silk fringe covering the large round table in the middle of the room gave way to a snow-white tablecloth which in its turn soon disappeared under an unbelievable display of food and drinks, including delicious homemade wines and liqueurs. Many of the foods were those she used to spoil us with in the past: homemade preserves, pickled mushrooms, and several kinds of marinated fish.

My day was a ruin of broken appointments and of plans that it was impossible to carry out any other day, but it was worth it for the great delight that seeing them gave me and for what I learned from them. They were thoroughly satisfied with their lives. No doubts tormented them. There would have been no sense in my asking them my usual questions about the purges or Stalin or the cold war or East-West relationships. These women had not the slightest interest in anything except what was happening in their own lives and in the lives of the people they cared about. Suppose Stalin had made mistakes, suppose Khrushchev made some? Who didn't? And who cares? would probably have been their reaction. It had nothing to do with them.

This was the only intimate, prolonged conversation I had with people who had always earned their living through manual labor— Pasha's niece and Niura's friend both worked in large factories—and it was as if words like "government," "party," "politics," "human rights," "East-West" had suddenly disappeared from the Russian language. If I had talked with these women during my first days in Moscow I might have seen something sinister in their total lack of interest in the political scene and suspected that they were afraid to speak in front of a foreigner. But by now I knew better. They were totally absorbed by their daily lives, even though for a short moment they might be aroused by something like the U-2 incident, for instance, just as many of our own people are momentarily shaken out of their absorption with their everyday lives by a presidential election or an international crisis.

By the time we said good-by the day was nearly gone and the only appointment I could keep was with another friend I had despaired of locating. When also by sheer luck I finally succeeded in getting in touch with her I was for one of the few times during my stay in Moscow confronted with someone who only after a long struggle with the fear of decades had mustered the courage to call my hotel and invite me to her home. This woman, Natasha, was almost sixty, one of the few survivors of the older generation of an exceptionally numerous, highly intellectual, brilliant family which before the revolution had been very wealthy. The purge had taken many of her contemporaries, both relatives and friends. The war and the Leningrad blockade had accounted for even more, and the health of the remaining few had been so undermined by sorrow and privation that they were dying off rapidly. Very few of her generation remained—honored scholars, retired scientists, aged long before their time. The picture became rosier when she talked of the younger generation in her family. They were all doing work in which they were deeply interested and, like most other young people I met, were little concerned with the past. Completely loyal, patriotic, not one of them dreamed of going abroad as Natasha and many of her contemporaries had in the past when life at times seemed more than they could bear.

I am sure there must have been people besides Natasha who were afraid to get in touch with me, who could have seen me and did not. I have heard many stories about Russians who would not be caught talking with a foreigner. My personal experiences should not be taken as a general rule. There were other little incidents that warned me that all was far from perfect on this front. I once made an appointment over the telephone to visit an old friend whom I had not yet seen. She opened the door, we embraced and, since she had obviously had no qualms about calling me at the hotel and inviting me, I said while walking with her through the hall to her room:

"I never dreamed all these years in America that I would ever see you again."

She paled and literally dragged me into her room:

"For God's sake, never mention 'America' out in the hall. Suppose a neighbor should hear you."

On the very eve of my departure I saw someone else I had long since given up hope of ever seeing again, Mikhail, whose wife had been one of my closest friends and who had died several years ago. Mikhail's work took him out of Moscow frequently, necessitating a constant change of address, and none of my friends was able to locate him for me. But on the day before I left he had an appointment with a dentist whose sister knew someone who knew me. Knowing Mikhail had a personal reason for being interested in visitors from abroad, she casually mentioned me to him without being aware of our past friendship. The chain reaction following this casual remark brought us together for a miserly hour on my last day in Moscow. Our entire conversation was devoted to a private problem that weighed very heavily on him.

After the revolution, he told me, a young brother of his had fled the country. They had never heard from him again and Mikhail and the other Moscow brothers and sisters assumed that he had long since died. They had no idea even in what country he had settled. But several months ago a letter had come from him postmarked California, where he had lived for the last forty years. After he left Russia, he said, he had decided for the sake of those who remained there never to write to them and to disappear forever from their lives. But, encouraged by the glowing reports about Russia and the tales of Russian-Americans who had visited their relatives in the Soviet Union, he had decided first to find them and then to visit them. He wrote to all the addresses he remembered until one of his many letters had reached a sister. Happy as they were to discover that their brother was alive and that he was coming, they were faced with a tremendous and dangerous problem.

During the decades that they had been out of touch, new generations had grown up in the families of the brothers and sisters he had left behind in 1920. They were young people who aspired to higher education, to important jobs, to party membership, to travel abroad. Throughout all the years whenever they had to fill out an application for any of these privileges they had negatively answered the question "Do you have any relatives abroad?" Having a relative in the West was a black mark. Some said no because they honestly believed that the uncle of whom they had only vaguely heard was long since dead; some because they knew that otherwise their applications would be refused, and in any case they never expected to hear from him again. The very youngest generation had not even suspected that there might be a relative of theirs somewhere in the outside world. Three members of the family had classified jobs and, if their premeditated or unconscious lie was discovered, they would face even more serious trouble than the others.

How it ended I will probably never know. The brother was to arrive the day after I left Moscow, and I can only hope that the joy of the reunion was not followed by too much sorrow. In the course of several previous conversations I had learned that this problem had confronted other families too. Even those who had corresponded with relatives and friends before the purges ceased writing then and many never re-established contact. And, as in Mikhail's family, the young generation had, as they thought, honestly declared in their study and job applications that they had no relatives abroad, only to be suddenly faced with a refutation of their statement in the form of a happy uncle or aunt or cousin from the West.

CHAPTER FIVE

Conversations with Some Chance-Met Strangers

Of course I enjoyed most seeing and talking with old friends, but also deeply rewarding were conversations with chance-met strangers. For instance at the theater one evening the woman who was sitting in front of me turned around during the first intermission and asked:

"Do you like the play?"

I didn't and said so.

"Neither do I," she said.

Following this short exchange a conversation took place which I would not have missed for anything. Once more in my life I was taught not to rely on people's appearance or on my ability to judge people at first glance. She had a plain face with not a single expressive feature, straggling hair knotted in a most indifferent fashion; she was built on square heavy lines, dressed in an ill-fitting mouse-colored dress, and was obviously not in the least interested in the impression she made. But she turned out to be, among all the people, I met, one of the best read and had a most live, keen mind.

Her great loves in life were theater and poetry. She was a born Siberian, the daughter of an old Czarist exile, loved Siberia, was

51

quite condescending about Moscow theaters, and assured me that in the larger Siberian cities the theaters now were much more interesting and daring than the world-famous Moscow theaters which, as she put it, sleep on their past laurels. Since I was at that time reading with great interest one of the numerous Soviet novels depicting the excitement of building up Siberia I could not ask her enough questions about it. She reflected the great enthusiasm of the new life there. She was full of a pioneering spirit and, while admitting the life was difficult in many respects, sounded thoroughly sincere when she said that she wouldn't exchange the hardships for any Moscow comforts. (To non-Moscovites Moscow seems a paradise of comfort.) Her feeling about Siberia had in it nothing of the "old" Siberia, Czarist or Stalinist, the Siberia of prisons and eternal snow, the Siberia that was a symbol of human suffering. To her Siberia was the Land of the Future.

Her husband had a technical job in a factory there, and had been sent on a mission to a town not far from Moscow for several months, and she could hardly wait to return to Siberia. Soon her husband, who had left for a smoke, joined us. He too was a stocky, plain-looking man, but, like his wife, full of life and interest and friendliness. Soon the three of us were throwing questions and answers around. We chatted all through the long second and still longer third intermission, and stayed behind in the theater till every light went out. Like so many others, they asked endless questions about the United States and assured me of their friendship for the American people. As a very young man the husband worked with American engineers during the first Five-Year Plan and said he could never forget those years of common enthusiastic endeavor or the friendly, easygoing relationship between the Americans and the Russians.

All through the performance, as soon as the lights went out, he would take her hand and so they would sit, hand in hand, till the lights went on. We parted good friends, exchanged addresses and promised to correspond. I intended to write to them. Subsequent events, however, have changed my mind. But I shall keep their address written by her on that evening's theater program.

The couple readily answered all my questions except one. I asked them what I had asked many others, whether the way love was often pictured in Soviet fiction, a way which would be too Victorian in a Victorian novel, truly reflected Soviet reality. For instance, I had just read of a couple who, after a prolonged courtship, finally exchanged a chaste kiss. Until then an occasional holding of hands had been the highest expression of their passion. My theater friends blushed, smiled, and changed the subject.

This question interested me because I found a great discrepancy between what I heard and what I read. I heard much about passionate love affairs, about marital infidelity, about illegitimate children, about women chasing other women's husbands, men chasing other men's wives, all so familiar in non-Communist societies. But their books and magazines described love in terms too ridiculous for our times. My blushing theater couple had provided no answer, but a few days later I got a more expressive reaction to my question.

As often happened when I sat alone at a table in a crowded hotel dining room, the waiter asked me if I would mind if he put several people with me. I was always delighted to meet new people, whether they were Russians or visiting foreigners. On that particular day four young Russian women, all of them good-looking, intelligent, and extremely well groomed, were my companions. They were participants in an international conference with a most complicated scientific name which turned out to be "plastics." After having touched on various subjects, important and unimportant, I asked my question on love in contemporary Soviet fiction and whether the description of it was true to life. A burst of gay laughter was the collective answer and they sounded as if they knew what they were laughing about. No additional explanation was necessary in their case.

We talked a great deal about our respective press and even with these young women, seemingly so intelligent and well read in two foreign languages, I had a hard task explaining that our newspapers are not really paid slaves of Wall Street, that if editorials do reflect the attitude of the newspaper owners, the columnists express their own opinions, which are often completely at variance with the editorials and with the opinions of other columnists on the same page. This sounded incredible to them, but at the end of the conversation two of them admitted they were convinced and that it was a great revelation. Again, as happened so often, I was troubled after this conversation. Was I right in disturbing these people and telling them things that contradicted everything they had ever been told before? Suppose I did change their thinking? How could this help them, in view of their total inability to change the climate of their lives?

Another encounter that I cherish was with a young woman, Galina, who was the daughter of an old Leningrad friend whom I used to see on her regular visits to Moscow. Galina was a baby then and never accompanied her mother to Moscow. The mother was dead now but Galina knew my name from her mother's stories. As one of those strange coincidences which at times happen, Galina worked in a chemical laboratory with a young woman, also the daughter of an old friend of mine. Soon after my arrival I had met this young woman and she mentioned the name Fischer in Galina's presence. The result was my meeting with Galina in one of Moscow's many open-air cafés.

The cafés are a feature of Moscow life that I thoroughly enjoyed. They are wonderful places at which to watch people, and to me symbolized Moscow's more relaxed way of life. Unlike French and Austrian cafés, which fill up at certain times of the day, the Russian cafés are uninterruptedly crowded from morning till night. And I never ceased to marvel at the extraordinary kinds of food that were consumed at the most unlikely hours. At ten o'clock in the morning, for instance, some people would be eating substantial meals of meat, vegetables and potatoes; others would be having champagne, ice cream, fruit. Never anywhere have I seen such quantities of ice cream and champagne consumed!

As always when meeting a new person I was careful with Galina not to make unnecessary remarks. It paid off. On a table next to ours I saw as the only refreshment a bowl of oranges and a dish of the famous chocolate candy, Mishka. It seemed to me a funny kind of refreshment in a café and I almost said so. I am glad I did not. A few days later Galina invited me to visit her and the first thing I saw in her room was the refreshment prepared for me—a bowl of oranges and a dish of the Mishka chocolates.

My talk with Galina confirmed a great deal of information I had gathered before. For instance, in a few days she was going off on a vacation on her own. I had heard that people did this now in Russia, but all those I had met previously were going on putyovkas (passes issued by organizations for a place in a rest home or sanatorium) from their unions or their places of work. The going on one's own is a new development in Russia. The local populations in the Caucasus, in the Crimea, on the Baltic Sea, or wherever there are woods or water or mountains and wherever there is a room to spare, sublet rooms to vacationers from the big cities. This, of course, is "private enterprise" and the press occasionally brands those who sublet rooms as "speculators," but the authorities close an eye to it. It relieves the tremendous pressure for official assignments to resorts. The question of food is solved by the open farmer markets and by eating places run by the government all over Russia. Galina had spent the preceding summer in a rest home in the Crimea but did not get a pass this year. So she was going on her own and she knew many others who were doing the same thing. This too may sound like a trivial development. What is so exceptional about a young girl's going to a summer resort for her vacation, renting a room and eating in a restaurant? But it is not trivial in Russia because it has not been done for a long long time.

From Galina I also heard one of the many versions of Stalin's last months of life. The details differed in the various accounts but they were all alike in one respect: according to each of them, Stalin was supposed to have been stark-mad with fear of assassination and convinced that doctors plotted against him by refusing to help him. One story was that in his villa outside Moscow several rooms of the same size and shape had been furnished exactly alike. He slept every night in a different room and no one ever knew which one it was. The only other person living in the villa was his cook, who took care of him and brought his food whenever he rang for it. The cook never entered these rooms unless summoned. At the end of one day, when Stalin had not once rung for his meals, the cook called the members of the Politbureau. When they arrived they found Stalin on the floor, unconscious. He never regained consciousness.

Another version gave the same details about the rooms and the cook, but added a number of bloodhounds which wouldn't permit anyone on the grounds except Stalin and the cook. In this version the members of the Politbureau found Stalin raving mad.

In still another, roses were included. Stalin was said to have developed a passion for them during his last years. He took care of them himself, was interested in developing new varieties. There wasn't much I could find out about members of his family. It is not that the Russians were secretive about it. They honestly did not know anything about them. One woman told me that his daughter Svetlana works, if I recall it correctly, as a textile engineer. Twice in the last years her name had appeared in the regular bulletins of her organization, once when upon her request, according to the bulletin, she was transferred to a less responsible job and the second time when, again upon her own request, her name was changed from Stalin to Dzhugashvili, which was Stalin's real name. What was categorically denied by everyone I asked about it was that Stalin had ever been married to Kaganovich's sister, although their marriage had often been mentioned in the American press.

Though Stalin's name and image arouse anything but merriment in people, many anecdotes about him still circulate in Moscow. One that I heard from Galina was that during Stalin's regular party interrogations (which were a milder form of the purges) a party member was asked whether he had ever wavered at any decision Stalin had made. What with the constant reversals of Stalin's general line, this was a tough one to answer. After some fast thinking came the answer:

"I loyally wavered with every wavering of the party line."

The absence of these constant interrogations, which were one of the scourges of the Stalin period, was often mentioned to me as proof of the extent to which things have improved since his death. Party members are still questioned closely about their loyality to the party line, but these grillings are child's play compared with what they were subjected to in the past. And the duties of an ordinary party member are far less arduous than they used to be. When soon after my arrival in Moscow I made a dinner date with some friends I asked a young Communist member of the family how he could be sure he could make it, because in the past a party member was never sure ahead of time whether he would be free on any particular day or evening. How could he know that at the very last moment he wouldn't be told that he had to make a speech in a factory or attend a meeting? There could be no "no" to a party order. No time, or sickness in the family, was no excuse.

My young friend assured me that it was very different now. He was not a professional party man and his duties, less numerous now in any case, were scheduled well ahead of time and only rarely interfered with his private life. With the exception of professional party workers or some individual enthusiasts, he said, people were not encumbered with party duties and could live normal lives. I heard the same answer from Galina and several other people.

Professional Communists, those who are employed in the party apparatus, I was told, work as they used to in the old days. Their time belongs to the party. They may be summoned at any time of day or night to solve an urgent problem, to be reprimanded for an error, or to save a bad situation. They are the salaried employees of the party and are at its beck and call. They may be sent away from their families for any length of time. Their lives do not belong entirely to them.

None of the party members I met were professional Communists. They pursued their own professions and were members of the party cell at the place where they worked. Though they still could be called on to carry out special assignments for the party, they could plan their leisure and their vacations with about as much certainty as anyone else in Russia. Their lives were not much different from the lives of their nonparty colleagues, and infinitely more normal than the lives of nonprofessional Communists were in the past.

All the Communists I met talked openly and in great detail about their work with the exception of two who, as I found out, worked on what we call "classified" jobs. One of them was the son of a man who many years ago suddenly broke his relationship with our family because he was assigned to a classified job and was not permitted to associate with foreigners. Now, though his son would not of course talk about his job, just as his American counterpart would not, he felt completely free and relaxed about seeing me and entered into all kinds of heated discussions.

American tourists with whom I talked in Moscow about Communist membership had the wrong impression that Soviet citizens do not want to be members of the party, since comparatively few join it. A couple of decades ago, the party had about three million members; today it has about seven million. This is a very small percentage of the Soviet Union's large population. But the reason for it is that, though joining the party today is easier than it used to be and the government wants to see people prominent in their fields join it, it still is a highly restricted organization. One has to go through a great number of interrogations and investigations before being handed the card that, though it requires fewer duties these days, gives one many advantages and much prestige.

CHAPTER SIX

Sightseeing

As the emotional impact of the first days of reunions began to subside I regularly devoted some hours every day to sightseeing, often revisiting places with which old memories were connected. Part of my first Sunday, a beautiful sunny day, I spent in the zoo where my boys and I had come to know all the animals well, especially the young ones. The Moscow Zoo has a beautiful nursery for baby animals, one of the greatest attractions for Moscow's children. The zoo has been enlarged since I saw it last and the crowds on weekdays as well as Sundays are enormous. Hard as I tried I was unable to get close enough to my old favorite landmarks to get decent photographs of them.

On that same Sunday, early in the morning, I watched the great exodus from Moscow. The city is surrounded by a green belt of woods and meadows and by rivers, ponds and lakes. Whole families, dressed in their Sunday best, little girls with huge white bows in their pigtails, everybody loaded with bags and nets and baskets of food and drink, with water toys and balls and sports equipment, were heading for the country, in cars, on buses, on subways, on bicycles. I saw them again late in the evening, with armfuls of lilac and mock orange, with sleeping children on their fathers' shoulders. There was about these Sunday excursionists an air of relaxation and easy enjoyment which I did not remember from the past.

Even if I had not intended to visit the famous Agricultural Exhibition of which I had heard and read so much I would have had to go there. I had to do it in order to be able to answer yes to the question every Moscovite asked me in the course of every conversation: "Have you seen the Agricultural Exhibition?" It is a most impressive show. My knowledge of agriculture, however, doesn't go much further than a smattering of flower gardening. But I did admire the beautiful layout of the exhibition grounds as well as the colorful national exhibits, including those showing the home industries of Kazakhstan, Uzbekistan, Armenia, Georgia, and the many other Soviet republics. The Industrial Exhibition is a newer addition to the same grounds and no less impressive in its scope and wealth of exhibits.

Though I went there on an early weekday morning, the crowds were dense, which made it easy for me to eavesdrop. The visitors were largely out-of-towners with some Moscovites on vacation or on their weekly free day. They were mostly families or groups of friends or excursionists on a guided tour. Their comments on what they saw expressed obvious pride and enthusiasm. I heard no criticism, which some of the massive ugly statuary certainly deserved. The grounds of the two exhibits are magnificent. The numerous fountains, some of them truly spectacular, flowers, lawns, trees, lighting, comfortable benches everywhere, the many eating places, the little open buses taking visitors around, make for a delightful day. The exhibition is a permanent feature and Moscovites are immensely proud of it.

There has always been in Soviet Russia a certain identification among her more loyal citizens with every improvement that is made. I remember from the past the excitement over a new building going up or another street paved or a new park opened, not to mention the pride and joy over the building of the first subway line in Moscow. Now this sense of identification is infinitely stronger and almost every person I met in one way or another showed his deep personal involvement with the improvements around him, which in his mind are symbols of the general march forward.

How many New Yorkers by contrast would express pride in the modernization of a railroad ticket office? Most people would not notice it and those who did would probably react with a quip. While I was in Moscow the ticket windows at one of the railroad stations had recently been rebuilt and I met several people who had made special trips to the station simply to see them, afterward describing them with genuine pleasure. Many times I heard Moscovites mention similar improvements with a definite sense of personal gain. Government actions and everyday changes are closely intertwined. I met much less of the "we" and "they" than there was in the past, "they" being the equivalent of our "bureaucrats" or "Washington," only more so.

Moscovites are almost unanimous in their patriotic attitude towards the Gorki Park of Culture and Rest (for short, Park of Culture). I found the park little changed, only there was more of everything. More flowers and flowering trees and benches and people and eating places and entertainment. I was never there in the evening but was told that I could name any kind of entertainment and the park had it. A professional pianist told me that she goes there for good serious music while jazz lovers congregate there for their favorite entertainment.

I discovered the same shady quiet spots with comfortable lounge chairs for those who want to read, meditate and be quiet. In the old days I used to spend hours there after having parked my boys in the children's sector of the park. The eating places are much more attractive now, each decorated in a different way, each out to attract more customers than the competition. Though they all belong to the same organization, or trust, they depend on their individual financial success for attractive bonuses and other material advantages.

Everywhere, of course, are stands with ice cream, fruit, soft drinks, sweets, buns, patties, as well as children's toys. There are shooting galleries, outdoor and indoor dancing, there are military participation shows for young people, there is every kind of entertainment that Coney Island offers. There are lectures on a great variety of subjects, there are theaters—opera, musicals, comedies, drama. There are large exhibition halls and the year round all of them are occupied and visited by enormous crowds. There were two exhibits in the park I would have liked to see—an art show and a Yugoslav exhibit. I did not succeed. The waiting lines were a mile long, or so they seemed, especially at the Yugoslav exhibit. Later friends told me that any foreign exhibit draws crowds.

The pride of Moscovites expressed itself in all kinds of ways, and particularly in their pleasure in possessions not available in the past. Once a young man triumphantly showed me his fountain pen. It was an excellent Parker pen manufactured in China in the expropriated Parker factory. When I said that I did not think this exactly a Soviet achievement he didn't seem to get my point.

"Had you ever seen this kind of pen in Moscow before?" was his response. The fact that the pens were now available to them made it a Moscow triumph.

With more justified pride people talked of the many vacation camps which surround Moscow now and which, I was told, are spreading all over the country. Near rivers and lakes, schools, factories and organizations have built camps for their members equipped with comforts bordering on luxury. At the disposal of the campers are tents, boats, eating areas, bicycles, sports equipment, games of every imaginable kind, fishing gear. All entertainment in these camps is planned and carried out collectively but most Russians whom I asked about it didn't seem to mind being constantly in groups and doing everything in groups. Some did not even understand what I meant when I asked if at times they would not prefer to be alone. The younger people, trained in crowd activity from nursery age on, have with few exceptions lost the desire to do anything on their own. Hardly anyone I met, young or old, knew the luxury of a room of his own.

Probably the greatest boast of the Moscovites (at least of the

older ones; the younger ones take it for granted) is the subway.
I so shocked my friends by my lack of interest in it that I tried to
avoid the very mention of it. They could not understand what I
was talking about when I said that to see sculpture and painting
I am used to going to a museum and not to riding in a subway.
They are so conditioned to these underground museums that a
functional subway seems almost barbaric to them. Nevertheless,
they had a right to be proud, not only of their subway but of their
entire transportation system. I hope I am not going to hurt anybody's feelings if I say that I wish our New York transportation
was equal to Moscow's. Buses and trolleys have large clear numbers, as well as the destination, on the front, and clear detailed
routes on the sides, and the same information is given on a sign
at each stop. There's no necessity, as in New York, to strain your
eyes in an attempt to decipher the murky number on the bus, and
then pay your fare only to find out that what looked like an obvious 3 was a dusty 5. And no need to ask the driver whether the
bus goes up this or that street. The very wide streets, avenues and
squares have underground passages with large maps and signs and
detailed descriptions of the various entrances and exits.

This may not sound important enough to include in a list of
achievements the Russians point to as proof of the government's
concern for the people, but it is evidence to them. After decades of
having been told that socialism is being built solely for the people
and seeing hardly any sign of it, they are beginning to feel that the
promise is being kept. And this makes them feel optimistic about
the future.

My lack of interest in the Mausoleum also shocked some people.
They felt that I must go see it, a feeling I did not in the least share.
Many years ago I saw Lenin lying there and I had no desire to look
at him again, and I certainly had no desire whatever to look at
Stalin, even at a dead Stalin. Instead I was glad to share the
anecdote about Tito's visit to the Mausoleum: not wanting to look
at the face of his enemy Stalin, he walked through the Mausoleum

with the eye on the side of Stalin's coffin tightly shut and the one toward Lenin open. Tito would not have this problem today, since Stalin has been removed from the Mausoleum.

One visit I did not have to be urged to make was to the Lenin Library. With its endless number of rooms for study, not to mention the tremendous treasure in books, it can favorably compare with any great library in the West. The one difference is the card catalogues. They are truly teasers, listing a great number of books that are available only to a chosen few. Among these are Soviet political books of an earlier day which the public is not supposed to read. There are many books and magazines published in the West, in original languages or in translation. All of them are marked with a few letters which Soviet citizens well know mean it would be wiser not to ask for those particular books and magazines.

I went on a regular tour of the entire library but spent most of my time in the Children's Room. Soviet children's books are very colorful, and a display of them in itself is a most attractive spectacle. But besides the books, the children there have at their disposal a choice of raw materials from which to make toys, dress a doll, build a house or a machine or a plane. Before they leave they have to tell the librarian what they have done while in the room, and if they have been reading they tell her what the book was about. I did not think that I liked this idea when the librarian told me about it, for it sounded like a duty, but after I had watched the children animatedly interrupting one another, full of eagerness to tell in as much detail as possible what they had done or read, I realized that there was no feeling of compulsion involved in it. Outside the performance was repeated for waiting mothers and grandmothers. The library was obviously a source of great joy and stimulation to the children.

Soon after I arrived in Moscow I heard that on the site of the former Cathedral of the Saviour, which was razed in the early thirties, an event still deplored by many Moscovites, a new project was being completed—a swimming pool of huge dimensions. It was supposed to be the largest in the world, a notion which has a tremendous appeal to the Russians. I wanted to see it as I wanted to see everything new in Moscow. But this site was also on the list of my sentimental journeys.

Before the cathedral was torn down and before the foundation was laid for the planned monumental Palace of the Soviets, Stalin's stillborn brainchild, his answer to the Empire State Building in New York, there was a playground in front of it. We lived then within walking distance from the playground and I spent a great deal of time there with my sons.

When I read in the papers that the pool was finished and that the first swimmers had used it I rushed over to take pictures. The newspaper item was, to put it mildly, more than slightly premature. Workers were swarming all over, huge trucks blocked the entrances, and there was not a drop of water in sight.

Still another of my sentimental journeys was to the old Narko-mindel (Foreign Office). Many memories were connected with it. The kindergarten my boys attended was in that building. So was the Foreign Office library in which I had spent so much time doing research. None of my old friends of the Press Department, where in the old days so many of the jokes circulating in Moscow originated, were now alive. It was sad thinking of the past, of all the people one used to know there, who disappeared during the purges. The Moscow correspondents of today, when the relationship with the Press Department is totally impersonal and bureaucratic, cannot imagine what it was like then. The jokes, the poker games, the easy camaraderie are hard to visualize. No doubt, there were plenty of difficulties and conflicts and red tape then too but compared with now it seems to have been a truly easygoing setup.

On this same stroll I saw a building that had no sign on it. A militiaman was guarding the entrance. I asked him what building it was. He carefully looked me over and quite sternly asked: "And what do you want to know for, citizeness?" I suddenly realized that I was in Moscow where one does not ask questions about a building that is not identified. I squeezed out a smile and said stupidly, "I am an out-of-towner; I thought it was a museum." (It had less resemblance to a museum than a railroad station has.) His reply, "This is no museum," reached me as far away from him as my feet could carry me. Later in the day a friend to whom I explained the location of the "museum" burst out laughing. It was a secret police building. Once more I blessed my accentless Russian. A foreigner interested in that kind of building would not get away so easily.

Another day I went to the pet shop where we used to buy food for the various pets we had during our Moscow years. The shop was still there and the long line was still there. Either there are not enough pet shops in Moscow or there is a shortage of food for dogs, cats, birds, fish. As in the old days, I found this line the friendliest of all. Yet with the exception of goldfish in one apartment I never saw any pets in any of the homes I visited. And I saw very few people walking with dogs.

Next to our old pet shop there was now a watch-repair shop. This is a great innovation in Moscow. In the old days there were not too many watches to repair, but now there are watch-repair shops everywhere, even in parks and hotel lobbies, and, judging by the waiting lines, they all seem to be quite busy.

The watch situation was one of Moscow's great mysteries to me. Looking at the numerous displays of watches in the jewelers' shops and in the department stores, I recalled the first postwar years during the Russian occupation of Germany, when ury (distortion of the German word "Uhr" for watch) was the battle cry of the Russian soldiers. They paraded in the streets with several watches on their wrists. For watches they were ready to attack brutally and even to murder. Whether the satellite countries are responsible for the enormous variety of watches now available in Moscow or the Russians themselves have caught up with watch production I am unable to say. No one I asked could give me an answer. People don't seem to be interested in the whys and hows as long as the product is there.

As soon as I began my sightseeing trips afoot I became acquainted with the purely Moscow way of crossing streets. There are plenty of green and red lights at crossings. And where there are no lights there are signs showing where it is safe to cross and where cars have to slow down. I cannot image that anywhere else in the world people display such a total obliviousness to signs. I am not exaggerating when I say that, though I watched sometimes while the lights changed several times, I never once saw a Russian pay the slightest attention to them. All a Russian does is to look at approaching cars and whenever he thinks there is a chance to slip through he runs. I saw pregnant women, old women with small children, invalids do it. I asked people for an explanation but never received one because they couldn't understand why I thought this strange. Why should anyone look at those fancy lights when they could see for themselves whether a car was coming or not? I soon felt quite foolish standing all by myself at a crossing waiting for the light to change, and learned to surge with the crowd, cars or no cars.

Incidentally, I was amazed at how many people in modest circumstances owned cars—many, that is, compared with Moscow before, not with the United States today. Buying a car is a very expensive project, and they cannot be bought on the installment plan. I asked several families how they had managed. One family of three wage earners bought theirs after planning for two years. They had all taken evening jobs, saved on clothing and food, and forgone vacations. Another family, not wanting to wait for two years, borrowed the money and were paying it back, also by working at night and generally economizing.

There was little left in the center of Moscow to remind me of her shabby looks in the twenties and the thirties. All around I saw efforts to glamorize things that in the past received either no attention or only the most indifferent treatment. For instance, movie houses are decorated with bright posters which, though far from being as daring as ours, are infinitely more daring than in the past.

Store window displays in Moscow used to be an accumulation of dust, cobwebs, flies, and most unattractive objects not available in the stores anyway. I still heard derisive remarks by tourists about Moscow's window displays, which they did not find very elegant. I would not either if I compared them with New York's Fifth Avenue. But I found them close to glamorous when I compared them with those cobwebby eyesores of the past. All of them show some attempt at beauty, and I saw several that showed definite artistic imagination and excellent color combinations. I heard many passers-by comment on them with great pleasure. To them these displays meant more than something that was merely pleasing to the eye. They were another confirmation that life was becoming easier and more relaxed. If time, goods, money could be diverted for the sole purpose of giving pleasure to the eye and urging people to buy, what other conclusion could they draw?

CHAPTER SEVEN

The Family Bond

Though I was warned against generalizing, by far the great majority of the families I saw throughout my stay were extremely close knit. "A family bond is a holy bond," I heard several times.

This was a far cry from the years when one of the aims of Soviet society was to make family relationships subject to the infinitely higher loyalty to state and party. At the regular party investigations, not to mention during the purges, the charge often was simply that the person in question had been in contact with members of his family who happened to be under a party cloud. During the big purges, regardless of whether family ties were close or not, the parents, siblings, and children of those arrested were considered guilty too; many of them also were arrested, and some even shot, for no reason other than relationship to the accused. To a certain extent this had begun to change even under Stalin. In 1953, I was told, the families of the doctors arrested in the Doctors' Plot were as a rule not involved.

At present the trend is definitely toward a glorification of family bonds. One hears constant talk about it whenever Russians consider it their duty to enlighten foreigners. Once during a sightseeing trip our young guide, a girl in her early twenties, delivered the usual sermon on the importance of the family in Soviet life.

She was right about the present status of the family. But she was not telling the truth when she assured the tourists that from the very first day of its existence the aim of the Soviet government had been to strengthen the family unit and make it the basis of Soviet society. I had a private talk with her after the tour. She had been sincere. She truly had no idea of the total disintegration of family life during the first years after the revolution, when divorce and remarriage and a new divorce and a new remarriage, as well as no marriage at all, were the accepted pattern of conjugal life, when children tragically floated around on the debris of the adults' messy relationships.

Communal housing and kitchens were pushed hard by the government and by the party's women's organizations. Women were told to get away from their children and homes and become useful members of Soviet society. Being bound to one's family meant to follow the pattern of the decayed bourgeois societies. Our young guide had not the slightest idea that it was largely the resistance of the individual to communal living that eventually reversed the trend. She was convinced, as many other young people were, that the present pattern of family life was solely the result of the Soviet government's "concern for the people." I did not try to influence her by hammering into her the numerous facts of which she was ignorant. I don't think I would have succeeded. She would hardly have accepted the word of an American tourist against what she had been taught since early childhood. Besides, the purpose of my trip was less the formidable task of changing the Russians' minds than of trying to find out what they were thinking, and in this I definitely got further by asking questions and listening to answers than by listening to my own speeches.

A young man was shocked when I told him that my sons were living at a great distance one from the other and met only rarely. "Why couldn't they, since as you say they had the choice, find work closer one to the other?" he asked. "Brothers are brothers and they should be closer with each other than with anyone else in the world, the way I am with my brother." When I mentioned as delicately as I possibly could the totally different earlier attitude of the Soviet government about family ties he cut me short. That was nothing but capitalist propaganda, he retorted, like everything else the West has invented to blacken the Soviet Union. Was there any use for me to say more? Would he have taken the word of one living a 15-minute subway ride from Wall Street against the word of his government? It was quite clear that no history book dealing with the Soviet past mentions anything that is contrary to the present party line, however much it has to falsify the past.

In the twenties and thirties the Soviet government did not encourage children to listen to their nonparty elders. It was assumed that parents and grandparents brought up under the Czarist regime could only give the young wrong ideas. Now the young generation is encouraged to respect and listen to their elders, for, as "products of Soviet society," today's parents and even many grandparents are considered safe. And where the crowded living conditions did not interfere too much with human relations I found young people had infinitely more respect for their elders than before. I heard young daughters and sons discussing personal as well as professional and economic problems with their parents and listening to their advice, which I don't remember their doing in earlier Soviet days.

Also, I found the parents much less reluctant to talk in the presence of their children than they used to be. The parents of today's young parents had to be careful what they said before their children, who were taught to be constantly on their guard against counterrevolution and were encouraged to report any suspicion of anti-Soviet feelings. The nightmare of parents being publicly denounced as enemies by their own children is part of Soviet history. Today's parents are full-fledged "children of the revolution" and are regarded as such by their children.

Nor is courtesy any longer considered "a bourgeois fancy." A number of my older friends told me how happy they were that they could now teach their grandchildren good manners without fear of being accused of harboring counterrevolutionary ideas.

In one field of family relationships I found a familiar situation. Even during my short stay I came across some only sons who had been definitely spoiled for marriage by their adoring, clinging mothers. In general, the in-law problem exists in Russia as it does everywhere else, but with the more serious complications posed by the crowded living conditions. Either the older generation, as the more experienced and wiser in the ways of living, or the younger, with stronger nerves and more stamina, must make an effort at living peacefully together (and in that case usually succeed) or life can become sheer agony. I knew a family consisting of mother, daughter, son-in-law and grandchild, living in two small adjoining rooms, sharing cooking and bathroom facilities, and never, the old and the young, exchanging a word. Because the mother had made no secret of her thorough dislike of her son-in-law, mother and daughter had become enemies. The grandmother was not permitted near her granddaughter. It was a frightening thing to watch.

I met a young couple whose marriage was ruined because the son would not hurt his widowed mother, who lived with them. (He was an only son.) She felt it her duty constantly to inform her daughter-in-law of her defects and offenses till life became totally unbearable for the younger woman. A romantic couple who had started on what could have been a happy life together had applied for a divorce. Even after the divorce the three will be obliged to continue living in the two rooms they occupy now. "I hope at least that I won't have constantly to hear what an awful woman I am," the young wife said, her eyes red from crying.

A young man whom I knew as a devoted son, husband, father, with the reputation of being a perfect son-in-law, once after a good dinner with plenty of vodka, confided that it was very hard for him to play the role of the perfect son-in-law which he didn't feel like at all. He was sure, he said, that he would have been one if only his mother-in-law had not had to live with them. Grandmothers are desperately needed in households where both parents work but not all are able to surmount the problems created when three generations live together. One hears few jokes about mothers-in-law.

It is not a laughing matter in Moscow.

Divorces are officially frowned upon but this does not prevent people from getting them. After years of postcard divorces the law became extremely strict in the thirties and to get a divorce was a project of magnitude and expense that few could afford. Now again divorces are easier but one still encounters much red tape. Nevertheless, the necessary and endlessly complicated procedures, though not too pleasant, did not seem to me more objectionable than many of the unsavory practices and false oaths that some of our own citizens have to engage in to obtain a divorce.

When I first heard someone use the phrase "He is a very wealthy man" it sounded like an anachronism in the Soviet Union and I did not pay much attention to it. But I heard it again and then again until I finally realized that once more these words had become part of the Russian vocabulary. When I showed my interest Moscovites were delighted to enlighten me. Yes, there were people in Moscow with a great deal of money. They spend it on expensive co-operative apartments, on antique furniture, paintings, jewelry, on food and drink, on entertainment, on elegant clothing bought in exclusive salons. In the past I had known writers who earned much money and spent it lavishly but I don't remember that people used the word "wealthy" when talking of them. Now there are many more people with large incomes and they have become a distinct group.

My curiosity was aroused and I was most pleased when an occasion presented itself for me to spend a day with one of these "wealthy" families, one that is considered to be in the very highest stratum of Soviet incomes. The head of the family is one of the top Soviet scientists who, besides drawing a big salary, has received several large money prizes for his discoveries and has a steady high income from his writings. The family occupies a four-room apartment in a co-operative building, for which they paid a large sum. When I told them that this sounded much like the capitalist West they seemed rather flattered than insulted. The rooms were full of antiques and paintings, on which, according to what

I had been told, the wealthy Moscovites spend most of their money.

The furnishings of the apartment were magnificent. Some of the paintings and the most valuable pieces of furniture had been protectively covered for the summer since the family was spending most of its time now at its luxurious dacha. With true Russian hospitality the hostess had the coverings taken off for me. If I had any doubt that this family was "wealthy" I could not doubt it after one look around. Whenever I admired a painting, an unusual object of art or a magnificent drapery, the refrain was:

"Oh, this is nothing, you should see what we have on the dacha."

This dacha, as I understood from a friend, is not really the ordinary summer cottage but rather a country estate where the family spends weekends and vacations all year around, and where their most important entertaining takes place. They have two cars with two chauffeurs and domestic help in the country and in the town apartment. The way this family lives would be luxurious by any standards anywhere. I found, however, that their kitchen, in which our two elaborate meals were prepared, and their bathroom were not up to even our most modest standards. And despite their obviously unlimited means and the help of the chauffeurs and cooks, shopping, or having a coat made, a sink replaced or a couch repaired quite obviously was for them too an enervating, complicated, time-consuming process.

I spent the daytime hours with the older women of the house in the same chitchat I would have engaged in anywhere with women who don't work, who devote their lives to home and family and are not interested in much outside. Later in the day, when the head of the family and the married children, who wanted to meet me, were there, the atmosphere changed. World problems, books, theater and art were discussed. Despite the fact that there was nothing the younger generation could not have and do—aside from travel abroad—they followed their own professions as seriously and devotedly as any other young people I met. They—a son and a daughter—had their own apartments, and soon expected to have their own cars. They were well dressed, they had no difficulty in getting tickets for an important theater première or a Van Cliburn concert. They probably will not be sent out of Moscow to a job in a faraway place if they don't want to go. They were brought up with governesses, and the married daughter has an English-speaking governess for her child. But it was obvious that they were all deeply interested in their work—the daughter and her sister-in-law were both doctors—and they certainly did not belong to the jeunesse d'orée as, I was told, many of their contemporaries in similar circumstances did. I sincerely regretted that they did not, because that was my only chance of meeting any.

Though this family had all they wanted and needed in Moscow, they told me that when they were permitted to go even to a satellite country they felt like paupers. The foreign currency they received for such trips was very little. On their last trip, to a health resort in Czechoslovakia, they took along Russian cigarettes, sweets, the famous hand-painted boxes, Ural semiprecious stones, and used these for tips in hotels and restaurants.

Originally it had been planned for us to spend the day at their dacha; the two senior women of the family were to call for me at a certain hour and I was to wait for them in the lobby. Since it was pouring rain, they changed the plans and tried to reach me on the telephone. I had meanwhile gone down to the lobby much earlier and sat there reading newspapers and talking with people. The ladies did not reach me till much later when I returned to my room, having given up hope of ever seeing them again. It was simply impossible for them to have a message delivered to me.

This was only one of the many mixups that occurred because hotels in Moscow do not take telephone messages. If you expect an important call you simply have to sit tight and not move from your room. I gave my friends certain hours when I would definitely be in my room, but I constantly heard of calls I missed involving appointments in Moscow or trips to the country or a theater visit, and by then the chance was lost.

But, though many Russians still seem not fully to understand the purpose of a telephone, it is, of course, not as bad as it used to be. I remember once in the past telephoning an organization for information, and being told in a very irritated voice:

"You must come to the office. We don't give information over the telephone."

When I persisted the operator said:

"Telephones are not meant for information."

When I asked what she thought they were meant for she angrily hung up. This I think could not happen today. Telephones have finally been accepted also as instruments of information.

But people in general seemed to have a very casual attitude about telephoning and about keeping appointments. On my last Sunday in Moscow, a very important day because there were many things to do and people I could see only on Sunday, I had an appointment to go with friends to visit a family in the country whom I very much wanted to see. It would be my only chance. I was to meet my friends at 9:30 A.M. in front of their house and a car was to take us to the country. As I was leaving the hotel, sure that everything was all right since no one had called me to change the place or the hour, I decided at the last minute to telephone my friends to make certain they would be downstairs when I arrived. The voice on the other end said matter-of-factly:

"I am so glad you called, the trip is off. K is not feeling very well."

My last Sunday was totally spoiled since by that time all the other people I wanted to see had already left the city. It never occurred to my friends to pick up the telephone and let me know.

Similar situations came up more than once. An appointment at two or five or eight did not always necessarily mean two or five or eight. To be half an hour or an hour late even for dinner was not of consequence. To have to hold up dinner never ruffled a Russian hostess—she was used to it. There is a difference, however, and on the whole, I admit, people are more punctual than they used to be. A cavalier attitude toward time, I was told, was strictly a hangover from the past when to be late was expected and legitimate. People used to stay at their jobs as long as their superiors required or as long as they themselves did—and that could be up to any hour of the evening or night. This changed soon after Stalin's death, when strict hours for the end of the working day were decreed. For some time, I was told, people actually had to be made to leave on time. The habit of staying around after the official end of the working day in case Stalin himself or some other superior official should telephone and expect an order to be carried out, regardless of the hour, did not disappear overnight. To the delight of everybody, this is a thing of the past. These days an employee would receive a reprimand instead of praise if he were found in the office after working hours. But the ingrained habit of irregular hours and the uncertain amount of time one has to spend on shopping and additional after-work jobs do not make for strict schedules.

CHAPTER EIGHT

How They Live

If I had not had the past for comparison, the present state of house-keeping, housing, and shopping, in Moscow, would have seemed appalling to me. But remembering the pitch-dark, bitter-cold winter mornings when at 5 A.M. women bundled in whatever warm clothing could be found in the room—whether belonging to a husband or to a child—stood for hours in the hope of being early enough in the line to get a pint of milk or a loaf of bread (a hope not always fulfilled) life today seemed heaven.

Nevertheless, I found the great majority of my old friends living in the same overcrowded old-fashioned apartments they were living in when I left, sharing primitive kitchens and bathrooms with several other families. In many cases I found the same old neighbors and in all cases wives and husbands of those I had known as children had with their own children taken over whatever space there was for an extra bed or dresser. The preparation of a meal was the same complicated affair it had been twenty and thirty years ago. In some cases I found the younger generation had taken over the same old family kitchen quarrels. It sounds unbearable, but it doesn't seem so to them and I heard fewer complaints now than in the old days.

The answer to how it is possible at all for several families, sharing one kitchen with one four-burner gas stove, to prepare the usual three-course dinner lies in mutual understanding and mutual accommodation. Where these exist the problem can be solved. Everyone knows the working schedule of everyone else and all adjust themselves. A woman who stays at home cooks her meal earlier in the day so as to leave the burners free for those who come home later. In appreciation of this, when she has to warm up a dish prepared earlier the others make no difficulties. When one family expects guests the others take this into consideration and in one way or another it always works out. I asked about this several times when I was served an elaborate meal prepared in a four-five-six-family kitchen. The answer was always the same: we accommodate each other and work out turns in cooking, especially since not everyone works and eats at the same hour.

But where there is warfare preparing a meal can be hell, as I remembered from old days when one woman might put a cupful of salt into the soup of a woman she was feuding with or put the burner out or raise it so that the food was completely burned. One day we had as guest an important writer, for whom our maid was preparing a very special soup. For one moment she left the kitchen and a neighbor, an embittered, envious person, seized the chance to pour the soup into the sink. This still happens, I was told, and it still causes hysterics and fights and ulcers.

One friend who years ago was bitterly resentful of her living conditions no longer complained despite the fact that she shared the same space now with her son's family. She explained it this way: in her younger years she still remembered the niceties and comforts of her childhood home and could not accept the wretchedness of her Soviet household. But her children had never known any other life and accepted it matter-of-factly. As for herself, her memory of an easier life had by this time completely faded. She had meanwhile gone through the agonizing years of privation, or purges, and of a war during which she lost one of her three sons.

Now all this was in the past. The recovery after the war, more correctly since Stalin's death in 1953, she added, was close to miraculous, the amount of home construction so tremendous that they might soon be able to move to new comfortable quarters. Both sons were married, had good wives, good children, good jobs, and were looking forward with hope to the future. And so was their mother.

This conversation was repeated with variations throughout my stay. Always I tried to keep in mind my resolution not to stress the shortcomings of the past, not to talk too much about the old political terror, and not to forget that once upon a time I went to Russia of my own free will and that I subjected my family and myself to exactly the same hardships about which a million and one words have already been written.

These hardships have certainly not been exaggerated; indeed, it seems to me that even the most hostile descriptions of Soviet life have underestimated them. And still I had lived in such apartments in Russia for many years, had suffered every misery and indignity that this kind of crowded existence can inflict, and I think of those years as happy rich years. Why and how? The answer is that there were compensations of a magnitude that transcended the short-comings. What were they? They lie in a very short word: hope. Even in the darkest days of the purges many people—by that time, though still in Russia, I was no longer one of them—believed that it was but another dark page, even if one of the darkest, in Russian history, a page which they expected to be turned, as others in the past had been turned. How much more does hope sustain them today, when they seem to hear distinctly the rustle of turning pages.

The pages turn thunderingly for them above all because of the many new apartment buildings going up and of the food and department stores stacked with riches unknown for decades. The agony of the war and the renewed Stalinist terror after the war are so much more recent in their memories that even among the older generation there is little mention of the years preceding them. The thirties have been digested and came up in conversations only when I asked direct questions.

The prewar past when mentioned at all was used most frequently to draw a comparison with the present and the future. And what seems to some Americans a situation still in great need of improvement and certainly not good enough to shout about in delight looks very bright in the eyes of the Russians.

Nevertheless, except for the tiny stratum of truly affluent people, Russian everyday life still lacks a thousand and one things that have become so much a part of our own lives that doing without them would seem unthinkable. But Russians do without them and do not even seem to miss them. For instance, to wash for dinner one family trekked through crowded halls and kitchen to reach a dark corner where a primitive cold-water washstand served twenty-two people. In another family the predinner handwashing took place in their only room with the three members of the family (plus guest) helping one another pour water over a small basin. Never having had any other facilities, they thought this a normal way of getting cleaned up before dinner. Despite the inconvenience of their arrangements, never once throughout the many lunches, dinners and suppers with Russians did I see either an adult or child sit down without washing his hands.

On several occasions friends invited me to visit them in their dachas outside of Moscow. These are summer cottages, usually set in woods and near a pond or lake or river. There are luxurious government dachas in choice locations and with all imaginable comforts, for members of the government and those in high managerial, scholastic and other important positions. But who knows? One may not always have the kind of job that entitles one to such a dacha. Even though people these days do not expect to lose their heads together with their jobs, they would certainly lose the right to the dachas. Therefore those who can afford it build their own. They are of course built on government land, since all land is state property, but people are able to buy (sometimes in a legitimate way but not necessarily) building materials, and with the help of friends or the after-hour labor of workmen manage to build their own cottages. Others not lucky enough to possess their own can often rent from people who are ready to share theirs with summer tenants or from absentee landlords who are willing to sublet their entire dacha, which they have frequently built for the sole purpose of exploiting it financially. This is not exactly according to Communist theory but human nature frequently proves stronger than this theory.

The dachas have changed a great deal since the years when my sons were young children and we used to rent one for the summer. There is still a great deal of primitiveness, especially in the more modest dacha settlements. There is a lack of decent roads and of a food and water supply, though these are constantly being improved. But most of them have electricity now and some Muscovites even bring their refrigerators out for the summer.

However, unless one rents the same dacha year after year or is lucky enough to own one, and thus can keep at least some of the necessary furniture and household equipment there permanently, there is still the same old nightmare I so well remember. One has to hire a truck—in the old days it used to be a peasant cart drawn by horses—which, since everybody moves to the country during the same two or three spring weekends, is a project on which people begin to work in the middle of the winter. The truck takes all the furnishings and necessities for three to four months' living, since the cottages as a rule are sublet completely empty. The cart in the old days and the truck now rarely arrive at the appointed hour, and bundles and boxes have to be reopened to get out the necessities for a nonscheduled meal or to put a child to sleep. It is a day that, as in the past, is still awaited and spent in agony. In the fall, when returning to town, the ordeal is repeated.

Since food supplies for most dachas have to be brought in from either the city or a neighboring village, and few services making life more comfortable are available to the average dacha dweller, life for most of the adults is far from a bed of roses. And again, as in the past, I heard people vow that never but never would they go through this torture again.

The reason for all this is the children. On a dacha they can safely run around, soak in the sun and fresh air. There are summer camps run by the various nurseries and kindergartens for the children enrolled in them, but far from all children are. When they reach the primary grades, the majority of children go to camps run by their schools or their parents' organizations. But since many camps work in shifts, they are only a part-time summer solution. Though Moscow has many excellent playgrounds and a great number of organized excursions and other entertainments for children, those who can possibly afford the money and the energy to leave the city would not think of exposing their children to the Moscow summer which, I bear witness, is infinitely easier to take than the summer in New York, Chicago or Washington.

Dacha life now did not seem as relaxed and carefree to me or to my older friends as it had in the past and I wondered aloud whether it was because we were older. The unanimous answer was: the difference was not so much because of the years but because then we all had maids. After work hours and on weekends we used to have leisure for swimming and sun-bathing and games and mushroom picking in the woods without all the worry over the shopping and cooking and cleaning and laundering in the maidless households of today. As a rule we shared a cottage with one or two other families, and each of us had a maid. The young families of today are to a great majority do-it-yourself families helped by a grandmother. This gives them little time for the leisurely pleasures we had enjoyed.

Some pleasant hours were spent on dachas with old friends reminiscing about the enchanting evenings when we enjoyed the nightingales, the scent of flowers and linden blossoms, and the games we used to play. One family remembered my favorite game. It was a simple one. Within a limited number of minutes—the fewer minutes the more fun—we had to write out all the famous names we knew beginning with any chosen letter of the alphabet. We used to have fierce arguments about who was famous and who was not. A chemist would passionately insist that a name he mentioned, one none of us had ever heard, was that of the most famous chemist in the whole world; so would a doctor or a botanist or a mathematician.

And here we were talking about it with those who twenty years ago would have been asleep in their cribs and who now, when we tried our hand at the game again, were throwing at us, the older generation, names that I at least had never heard. Nor did they know many names without which mankind's culture seems unthinkable to me. But we had great fun.

Among all the improvements since the war nothing means as much to people as the amazing amount of home construction. It gives them a confident feeling that after all the nightmarish years they are finally moving ahead, that the old, overcrowded, dilapidated houses will soon disappear altogether. To be sure, there was much criticism that the new buildings were being put up in too great a hurry, that the construction was shoddy and wouldn't hold up. Nevertheless, everywhere I found people delighted with the new apartments, defects or no defects, and the reason was readily understood. Again going back to my own past experiences, I remember well our happiness when after years of living in a typical overcrowded Moscow apartment we moved into a new house. On all sides we were warned that the house would soon begin to fall apart, which it promptly did. However, this in no way dampened our joy and delight at being all by ourselves in a new and clean apartment. And that is exactly the way people who move into the new Moscow houses feel these days.

The great majority of new buildings look alike but fortunately are without the ornate decorations which will go down in at least Russian history as Stalin's wedding cake ornaments. They are very functional and if they are poorly constructed, as most people, Russians and foreigners alike, agree, it is not noticeable to an untrained eye like mine.

A footnote to this: a very dear Moscow friend has been working for many years on Soviet construction materials. I was greatly pleased to read one day in the *New York Times* that, though Soviet construction was faulty, Soviet research and achievement in building materials was on a high level, and this is exactly what my friend had devoted her life to.

The new housing developments are generally of four or five stories, to save the expense of an elevator. On the ground floor there is usually a large food store, possibly a clothing store, an electrical appliance store, a shoe-repair shop, a beauty parlor and barbershop, a book and stationery store, a laundry. In the very latest developments, however, the shops and services are in separate two- or three-story buildings. This is a great improvement, for having the many shops on the ground floor, as well as the polyclinics, nurseries, post offices and the like, gives rise to much noise and confusion. The newer developments are supposed to be little cities in themselves, even more so than the present ones. They have everything that is required for complete living. I was in one that had three different kinds of schools, several nurseries and kindergartens, a large hospital, two movie houses. All of them, of course, the very newest and the plain new, have large playgrounds and plenty of indoor and outdoor recreation facilities for adults too.

Apartments are as popular a topic of conversation in Moscow as the weather is in New York, and I had to describe innumerable times the exact location of every piece of furniture and kitchen equipment in my own modest New York apartment. I was glad that I was unable to transfer feet into cubic meters, so I got away with the size of it without arousing too much envy and incredulity. I certainly did not try to boast but I couldn't help it if to them it all sounded unbelievable. The young people, though also interested in some details of the apartment, were most impressed by the fact that I could simply lock it and go away on a trip of my own choosing any time I wanted to.

In many apartments I noticed that an effort had been made to bring comfort and beauty even into overcrowded rooms. In one of the kitchens, which in the old days had been a jumble of ill-assorted pots and pans and kerosene burners and broken-down tables, I saw now six good worktables—one for each of the six families living in that apartment—covered with clean plastic cloths.

Everything was in good order, and over some of the tables brightly shining utensils were hanging in attractive patterns. Here and there pictures had been pasted on the walls, and the floor was scrubbed clean. Cleanliness is not easy when six families share one kitchen with one gas stove and one cold-water faucet. The younger women of the apartment were very proud of their achievement.

Another day I was enchanted by the room of two young sisters who had performed a miracle of good taste and charm out of literally nothing. Their door opened into their parents' rooms, a jumble showing not the slightest effort at order or taste. In another apartment two women lived in adjoining rooms. One of them had long ago given up any attempt at beauty, defeated by the clang and clutter surrounding her. The other had come back to Moscow only a very few years earlier after eighteen years in exile. Her joy at returning expressed itself in colorful embroideries and immaculate cleanliness. With the financial compensation she had received upon her return from Siberia she had bought furniture and decorations in as modern a style as she could find in Moscow.

She told me how in the miserable drafty barracks she had dreamed of just such a room furnished with modern pieces, about which she had read in a magazine that had found its way into the barracks, never expecting her dream to become reality. In our conversations we never got far from the topic of decorations, but it gave me deep joy to see with my own eyes what one so rarely sees: an apparently unattainable dream attained.

Most often, however, the apartments I visited reflected the taste of decades long gone. For a short time in the twenties there had been a spark of modern daring in the designs sponsored by a group of young Soviet artists, but it did not have a long life. Stalin's atrocious old-fashioned taste, his admiration of things he had envied in his childhood, as well as his heavy fist, took care of that. But even today, watching the crowds in Moscow stores, I realized that mass production cannot indulge in great refinement if it is to cater to the taste of a majority whose roots are still in villages and hamlets.

I was told that the United States exhibit made many women conscious of the advantages of simplicity, of the desirability of eliminating unnecessary objects in a room. Once, after having described at my hostess' request the arrangement and decoration of a typical American apartment, I started to suggest that she too could easily improve her own rooms by—when she interrupted me and declared with great pride: "But we are living now exactly the way you describe!" Whereupon she enumerated all the cumbersome furniture and useless knickknacks she had got rid of after her visit to the U.S. exhibit. Her rooms still looked pitiful to me, but I had once more slipped into the mistake of comparing Moscow with New York instead of with Moscow.

I visited friends in an apartment with a ravishing view on the Moscow River. The gentle intellectual old couple loved the view. On summer evenings they sat on a tiny balcony overlooking the river and the sparkling golden domes and lights of Moscow, listening to the sounds of river boats and distant music from the Park of Culture. And every evening was marred by the drunken brawls of their neighbors in the next room. It had been going on for years and there was nothing they could do about it, for, no more than divorce, drunken neighbors were not a reason for being assigned new "living space." For a long time they had been pasting little notes alongside many other little notes, all reading "Room to exchange," in shop windows, on walls of buildings, anywhere they were permitted to do so. I saw such notes attached even to trees. They were usually handwritten, sometimes typed, slips of paper offering two rooms in two different parts of Moscow in exchange for two in the same apartment or vice versa, or one large room in exchange for two small ones, or simply one room in exchange for another.

Often they indicated nothing more than a change of job and a desire to live closer to work. Sometimes it meant that two people, each lucky enough to possess his own room, were getting married. But very often there was heartache behind them: a divorce or two generations who could no longer live together in peace. Though there is much greater concern for the individual in Russia today than in the Stalin era, there is still shockingly little consideration for situations in which human unhappiness could easily be alleviated by an exchange of rooms. The wall of bureaucracy is still very solid.

I was constantly amazed at the way people accepted the bureaucracy and whatever orders emanated from it. A house that I visited several times was being repaired. The staircases were dilapidated, some steps completely broken, part of the railing missing, the halls dimly lit. Walking down (elevators only take one up, not down) was dangerous and there had been several accidents involving old people and mothers with babies. None of these defects, however, was being repaired; only the *exterior* of the house was being renovated.

None of the people living in the house to whom I mentioned this as something we would consider thoroughly unacceptable seemed to mind. Wasn't the safety of the people living in the house infinitely more important than how it looked on the outside? I persisted. But they had been well trained to accept the fact that these things were decided for them and not by them. They were not exercised about it because they knew there was nothing they could do.

Once when visiting friends I found the entire apartment in a pleasant uproar. Grownups and children rushed out to announce the glad news: their toilet had been repaired! This toilet served eighteen people. When I first saw it decades ago the toilet seat was loose; in time it disappeared altogether. The floor was splintery and the walls were crumbling. Bits of newspaper substituting for toilet paper were sometimes piled up in a corner, sometimes not. A tiny naked electric bulb on the very high ceiling added a sad touch to the general desolation. The only relief was an occasional clever verse penned and pinned up by one of the eighteen tenants.

I was as delighted as my friends to hear that the new Soviet era had entered the forgotten spot. But when I was triumphantly led to behold the great change I was shown one newly patched and painted wall; nothing else had been touched. I did not have the heart to say that I did not see much cause for rejoicing and joined everybody in a gay celebration.

I remember this party very well. As at many others, the conversation roamed over a wide field. Among other things we talked about painting. Marc Chagall's name came up. The older generation remembered him well but only one of the five younger people present had ever heard of him. I mentioned that George had wanted a print of one of Chagall's paintings for his study and that I had got it for him. One of the young men burst out laughing. "I only wish I had George's worries," he said. His own life was so thoroughly occupied with his full-time day job and part-time evening job, and with the whole complicated business of living, that the leisurely selection of a picture for one's room was beyond his imagination. Then the idea sank in that I was talking of George's study. It meant that George had a room for himself to work in besides the family bedroom, living room, kitchen. He didn't laugh any more. The idea simply overwhelmed him.

CHAPTER NINE

Shopping in Moscow

My hotel was in a new neighborhood on a wide boulevard flanked by trees and flower beds and by rows of new buildings. As in similar neighborhoods, the ground floors housed stores and services. Several times I tried to get acquainted with these stores but had to give up because I could not push my way through the crowds. My chance came on a fine sunny Sunday morning when most Moscovites were out in the country. All Moscow stores are open on Sunday; some close on Monday but many are open seven days a week, till 8 or 9 or even 10 P.M. On that particular Sunday I could have bought anything, even the newest dance records, without standing in line. I studied prices and qualities, and was amazed, considering the high prices, how well Moscovites eat and how comparatively well they are dressed and shod.

I wouldn't even try to get into a comparison of their prices and ours or into a discussion of the comparative incomes to make their prices comprehensible. Many times, with paper and pencil, I sat down with Russians trying to figure out U.S.–U.S.S.R. incomes and family budgets and prices, and not once did any of us come up with a sensible answer. All I can say is that rents in Russia are so low that they play no role whatever in a budget, that prices in stores are very high, and that people keep buying furiously despite high prices. Taxes also are very low; the government is able to get its income in a much simpler, more direct way. It has even promised to abolish taxes altogether in the not too distant future. I asked someone well acquainted with the workings of the Soviet system why they had not already been abolished. Since all the income and profit from industry and commerce went to the state in any case, it didn't have to depend on taxes for any of its functions.

"That is true," was the answer, "but the state cannot free too much money at one time. There are not yet enough goods on the market to absorb the money, and people will be dissatisfied. As more goods are produced, taxes will gradually be completely abolished. Not before." This was the only conversation about taxes that I had in Moscow. People simply do not give the matter a thought.

Moscovites, however, do not buy everything in sight as they did some years ago and as out-of-towners still do. At least some of them have learned to appreciate design, good quality, attractive looks, usefulness. They are turning their backs on clumsiness, shoddy materials and poor workmanship. This creates problems the Soviet government was not faced with before. In the past, anything factories turned out was grabbed, and the high production figures were the pride of managers.

The public, especially the young generation, now clamors for light new furniture, for more elegant clothes and shoes, for more graceful home decorations, more attractive and efficient kitchen utensils. The press openly talks about the struggle between the old and the new. I am not able to judge heavy industry, but it was obvious to me that light industry has been slow in catching up with the times. This is partly because of a certain fear of anything new, a fear strange in a new revolutionary society but instilled so deeply in the Stalinist period that it is hard to get rid of.

Also it is so much easier to "Fulfill the Plan" if one continues to turn out, for instance, the time-honored huge clumsy wardrobes, which nobody wants now, than to design and produce the new ones, since, for a time at least, this would mean a slowdown in production. Few factory managers want to risk being path-breakers if it means not fulfilling the plan—though this is not so frightening a prospect as it was under Stalin. The worst a manager of a plant not fulfilling the plan can expect now is a reprimand or demotion, in exceptional cases an arrest but not a bullet. People are very conscious and appreciative of this difference.

The criticism I usually heard about the poor quality of dress materials or furniture or shoes came from the more sophisticated Moscovites. They, however, constitute a minority even of the Moscow inhabitants and certainly of the Soviet population in general. The majority still seems exhilarated simply by being able to buy, a pleasure of which they had been deprived for many years. But lately, I was told, even they have begun to show signs of having learned to distinguish between good and inferior quality, and to reject what they don't like—which will mean more headaches for the authorities.

Though food, like everything else (with the insignificant exception of the kolkhoz market produce), is produced and sold solely by the state, there is competition between the various food companies. They have much more leeway than in the past to follow their own initiative in packaging and displaying their goods. For instance, I saw cheese stores which showed great taste and variety in displaying many different cheeses each packaged and labeled in a different, often quite ingenious and attractive way. Ice-cream companies try to attract consumers with bright packaging, colors, and a great variety of flavors. So do confectionery concerns. There is an enormous variety of canned fish, meat, vegetables and fruit, of jams, jellies and preserves, all of them alluringly presented to the public.

During our Moscow years we had a choice of lighter or darker gray bread; now there are endless varieties of bread from the whitest white to pure black, as well as all kinds of rolls, biscuits, pastries, cakes, cookies. One can buy live fish and poultry; one can buy cleaned or uncleaned fish and poultry, packaged or unpackaged, half frozen or completely frozen, even roasted chickens (not barbecued). But despite the great variety it is not always possible to buy the particular product you want, and always you must spend a long time waiting in line.

Much has been written about the inefficiency of shopping in Moscow. To buy meat, for example, women first stood in a long line waiting to get to the meat counter; then came the choosing of the cut, the weighing of it, and being told the price of the purchase. Then they stood in a second line at the cashier's, then finally with the cashier's slip they went back to the first or, in some stores, to the special wrapping counter, after standing in a third line. There are always these three lines in all stores. It seemed to me a tiresome and inefficient procedure, until suddenly one day it struck me that it was exactly the same routine I went through at Macy's meat counter, without ever thinking it time consuming. The difference lies in the word "efficient." In Macy's the salespeople are numerous, experienced and fast. The cashier works speedily and does not use the ancient abacus to figure out the change. The wrapping service is handled by more numerous and more efficient hands.

My Russian friends all offered the same solution. There must be more of everything—more stores, more goods in the stores, more store personnel. There was also talk of self-service supermarkets of which they had heard and in which the Soviet authorities were greatly interested. But above all there should be fewer out-of-towners filling the stores and buying up what was meant for the Muscovites. They stream into the big city by train, bus, plane, boat, with pockets full of money, crowding the stores and buying foodstuffs, rugs, china, silver, stockings, dress goods, hats, shoes, rainwear, chairs, radios, TV sets, and whatever else is sold. However, the situation is improving. I was assured now that the cities and villages outside Moscow are more amply supplied.

Food supplies keep pouring into Moscow. But, whether they pour in irregularly or the distribution is faulty, the supply is obviously erratic. One day Moscow will be flooded with fresh cucumbers or scallions or chickens; then for several days none of these items can be found anywhere. I saw women with their string or plastic shopping bags rushing around and asking one another whether they had seen this or that. Anyone who had one or another of the scarce products sticking out of her bag could hardly move through the crowd of women all eager to know where she had bought it. The reply usually was "the kolkhoz market." The longest lines in Moscow stores were those at department store counters with huge signs "Goods Being Sold Here at Lower Prices" (sales, in our language). Only rarely was I able to find out what was on sale. The lines were too dense for me to get to the counter, and few in the crowd could enlighten me. They did not care. What difference did it make to them whether it was blouses or stockings or sweaters or a bed sheet, lamp shade, hat, or handbag. They, most of them out-of-towners, would buy it anyway. More demanding Moscovites are rarely seen at these sales, which, they said, seldom offered anything worth buying; it was only when the stores wanted to get rid of unsatisfactory merchandise that they put it on sale.

I was told that very few days after the future currency reform was announced on January 1, 1960, the Moscow stores became stark empty, and rumors began to fly that they would remain empty for the rest of the year until the change went into effect. This did not happen. The stores were empty only because Moscovites as well as non-Moscovites became panicky, descended on them and bought up everything in sight. It took a little while to replenish the shelves and, though I occasionally heard complaints that they had never been fully restocked, I found them extremely well stocked as compared with the past.

In spite of the almost compulsive buying, however, one still hears people speak of "organizing" a winter coat or a good pair of shoes or a piece of furniture. It needs careful figuring to buy them and much pinching here and there as well as an extra evening job for several months. I heard a great deal of talk about it in middle-income families and could well imagine the sacrifices entailed for those of lower incomes.

The largest Moscow store, GUM, called by Americans the "Moscow Macy," is opposite the Mausoleum at the Kremlin wall, and I have seen people come out of the Mausoleum and enter GUM, while others preferred a visit to the dead leaders after shopping. GUM has been described by many travelers to Moscow and I agree with those who called it unnecessarily huge, illogical, hard to shop in. In the Czarist days GUM, under a different name, was also a sprawling shopping center consisting of several narrow buildings connected by colonnades. It is now somewhat modernized but there are still the dozens of separate shops on the three floors, some glassed in, some half covered with a kind of light roofing, others completely open. The colonnade-walks separating the buildings have several stairways and there is an unending stream of shoppers and onlookers going up and down the hallways and the stairs. The sights and sounds of this perpetual giddy surging of crowds make one's head go round and round. It certainly did mine and probably many others' since most Moscovites I talked with said they wouldn't dream of doing their shopping at the central GUM.

"That's not for Moscovites" is their proud comment. They prefer the smaller GUM and the specialty shops to Moscow's No. 1. I was forever amazed at the amount of money people spent in this particular store on luxury articles considering the high cost of items like food, clothing and shoes. (Even more amazing, in view of the high cost of necessities, is the money lavished on weddings, funerals and expensive tombstones. I was frequently told, even by people I met casually, like cab drivers, how much a wedding in the family had cost or what a beautiful tombstone had been erected for a father or a wife. The sum mentioned was completely out of proportion to the family income. It reminded me of the Sicilian peasants who, poor as they are, go deeply into debt for an elaborate wedding and even more often for an extravagant funeral.)

Moscovites in the upper-income brackets—the highly paid writers, artists, scientists, scholars, high government officials—ignore all the GUM stores and similar shops. They are the habitués of the famous antique and commission shops, they get things from abroad, for them are the best ateliers de modes and shoe salons. The average Moscovite, however, still has to spend a greal deal of his time and money and energy for the necessities of life. But I did not hear too many complaints. Their measure of comparison is not New York or London or Stockholm, and not the way of life of a famous Soviet writer or scientist or internationally known musician, but their own life of only a few years back; and their optimism is being nourished by the steady improvement they see from day to day.

This I kept hearing whenever I voiced even a hint of criticism. I once saw a long line of women queued up to buy unbottled milk at stands unprotected from the sun and dust and flies, and I commented on it to friends. The answer was that these women still happened to live in old houses and had none of the conveniences of the new housing projects. When they all moved into the new houses, as they soon would, they too would enjoy home milk delivery as well as all other advantages of modern living. The answer bore an undertone of rebuke. Whether people talked of milk delivery or the end of terror, they sounded confident that life for them had taken a turn for the better.

After my return to the United States I was frequently asked whether there is any private enterprise or private initiative in Russia. Definitely no and definitely yes. Officially, there is none whatever, with maybe the exception of street-corner flower markets and the free farm markets. Unofficially it flourishes under a variety of names and activities: speculation, bribery, graft, favor, consideration, patronage, pull, inside track. It can be completely on the level and legal; it can be completely dishonest.

I knew a highly paid woman engineer who had expensive tastes and was always very well dressed. Knowing her high income from her job and writings, this seemed to me only natural. Then one day she told me the inside story of her ample wardrobe. Between job, writing and family she has no time for shopping. But she has good "connections": a highly placed friend in the Shoe Trust, another is the head of an atelier de mode, and still another is the wife of a satellite consul who often goes abroad. Among these three, without ever entering a shop or standing in line, the lucky woman is supplied with everything she needs as far as her wardrobe is concerned. She reciprocates with a hard-to-get plane or railroad reservation which she can procure through her ministry, a fur coat or a dressy outfit loaned for a special occasion, a theater ticket for an important première. All this is completely honest, no cheating is involved, and the valuable time of a valuable person is saved.

There are many such cases which involve no material gains or losses to the government. But there are also many where somebody gains and makes the kind of profits that are prohibited or involve illegal favors. Store employees whisper the secret of scarce, newly arrived items to professional speculators. The speculators also have connections in warehouses, factories, ministries, and wherever else they can glean useful advance information. This information is rarely given out of friendship. Cash or favors are expected in return.

A speculator not lucky enough to have the proper connections roams the streets and watches the stores, often throughout the night; he observes where shoe shelves are being emptied, additional hangers are being brought to a coat department, long-awaited new toys are being put on display, summer or winter goods are being replaced, new records are being delivered by truck. At each such sign he takes up his post long before the general public discovers the newly delivered treasures. Of course, the speculator has helpers, since it would be too obvious if he bought too many items at once. Besides, scarce goods cannot be bought in bulk. Members of his family, friends, or if he is a large-scale operator, paid assistants join him in the predawn vigil at the store. Though the stores seem quite well supplied, it is easy for the speculator to dispose of anything for which people have to wait long hours in line, especially if the goods in question are of better than average quality.

Several of the people I met buy either directly from speculators or are helped by information from friends. The first is a purely commercial and illegal enterprise, the second a friendly service. When I was once unable to find the kind of peasant doll I had set my heart on for a grandchild, a friend telephoned a cousin who worked as a saleman in GUM. He got hold of the particular doll in one of the GUM stockrooms and set it aside for me. There was no graft and no favor involved, only a friendly service.

There are other forms of private enterprise too. Many seam-stresses, shoemakers, beauticians, as well as doctors, teachers and lawyers, work on their own after their regular hours. Some of them, very few indeed, declare their private income and pay such special, exorbitant taxes that they are quickly taxed out of every penny of this private income. The majority, however, work "in the dark," as far as the authorities are concerned, openly if living among friendly neighbors who will not report them, in secret if neighbors are unfriendly.

The fields in which people can exchange one good deed for an-other are numerous. To build a summer cottage, to get a son or daughter into an institute to which appointments are in great de-mand, to avoid being sent on a job outside of Moscow, to get an apartment in a new building, to get the necessary supplies for a plant one is in charge of, to get a soft job for a relative or friend, to get a ticket for a Van Cliburn concert or the première of a new ballet, to get a plane or train reservation—for all these and many more a good friend or a disguised or undisguised "middleman" is greatly in demand. Those in high positions have plenty of oppor-tunities to be of service, naturally expecting the service to be recip-rocated when they in turn need a favor. At times, these services come very close to illegality and, when discovered, the erring person is punished as a lesson to others. The occasional punishments, I was told, do not seem to lessen the friendly wrongdoings. The new wave of death and prison sentences of this last year has brought great changes in this attitude.

There is one type of private enterprise, however, on which the authorities cast a benevolent eye. Georgians mainly, but also others from the warmer regions of Southern Russia, bring to Moscow (often on passenger airlines) sackfuls or crates of early vegetables, fruits and berries. They pay a trifle for a stand in the open market where collective farmers sell their private produce, and they return home with a considerable profit. The prices they charge have no limit, and the Moscovites will save on anything else to indulge in the fresh fruit and vegetables of which they are deprived during the long winter months. Friends of mine, none of them in well-paid positions, were at great sacrifice paying between $2 and $2.50 (at the then favorable tourist rate of exchange) for one pound of cherries or strawberries. This season is limited, however. As soon as the local berries, fruits and vegetables ripen in the north the Caucasians stop commuting to Moscow and the Moscovites pay normal prices for their local produce. Russians assured me that this custom would disappear soon. In the near future, they said, the government will have organized the proper shipping of perishable foods and thus be able to supply the Moscovites the year round with fresh fruits and vegetables.

CHAPTER TEN

The Women

Though shops are comparatively well filled, transportation infinitely more plentiful and efficient than in the past, and the feeling of fear and insecurity has subsided, everyday life, especially the life of women, is not an easy one. Whereas in past years not only professional women but many women factory workers had a maid to take care of the household, only few can afford a maid today. The wages now demanded by domestic workers, plus their upkeep, are much too high for the average family. Besides, few of the young girls who come to Moscow from the villages these days after graduating from school, with factories and offices clamoring for them, would be satisfied with the uncertain working hours (which no law defines) of a domestic or with a dark corner in a communal kitchen as living quarters.

Without domestic help, the task of organizing family life is not simple. The refrigerators which some Moscovites possess these days are so small that even for these lucky ones it is necessary to shop daily; for most working mothers this means after work and frequently after a long bus or subway ride, and precious time spent standing in line. When the mother finally gets home, relieving an exhausted grandmother, there are still the children to take care of and in some cases the evening meal to prepare. She does not have time, patience, nor nerves left for a pleasant leisurely evening. And in the older apartments there is the added exacerbation of the primitive cooking, dishwashing and laundry facilities, and the never-ending sounds of people behind the walls and in the halls.

I was forever amazed to see how despite all this so many women find time for reading, a movie or theater, or for a supplementary job. Yet sitting around the tea table in animated conversation I would forget the grueling day my hostess had had because she herself seemed so completely to have forgotten.

In case it sounds strange that I have not mentioned men in talking of all the heavy burdens women carry, the reason is that as a general rule Russian men don't help much in carrying them. They feel that a man's place is not in the kitchen or in a line of pushing women, and most of the women to whom I broached the subject agree. Men do, of course, take care of necessary mechanical repairs in the household and help in the heavier work, like carrying wood or coal, and sometimes lend a hand with the children. And I discovered that the many conversations Russians had with young Americans during the Youth Festival in 1957 and during the United States exhibit in 1959, in which they learned about the way American husbands help their wives with domestic chores, were definitely beginning to show results in the younger households.

Some of the young women I met, busy as they were, took the time not only to read but also to collect clippings from special women's magazines and general illustrated magazines: recipes for baking and cooking, medical advice, household hints. The women's magazines devote a great deal of their space to fashions, and they even have personal columns. It isn't exactly what we would call a column for the lovelorn but they do have occasional comments on problems of human relations, written from the most Victorian point of view with a dash of Marxism added. The fashion magazines lack the elegance of *Vogue*, to be sure, but they are infinitely more attractive than what was offered as a fashion magazine some years ago. Most clothes seem to be copies of what is being worn in the Western world, but the models wearing them are slightly on the fuller side. Noticeable in both the fashion magazines and the Moscow streets is the variety of colors and tasteful matching or blending of colors. This attention to color schemes is quite new, since until recently Russian women had no choice, but bought whatever they could find in the stores. Every model in the fashion magazines, unless she was wearing a house dress, was shown gloved, generally in the then-fashionable shorties. And I often saw women on the street wearing gloves which used to be quite an unusual sight in Moscow in the summer. Indeed the appearance of women has enormously improved and I saw many who could easily have blended with a well-dressed crowd on any American street. I had proof of that when on my first day in Moscow, dressed in my new elegant white knit dress, I was twice mistaken for a Moscovite and asked for street directions. This mistake was made many times later, but it could not have occurred in the past when a foreign dress was recognizable from afar.

One evening I saw some women leave our hotel for the Bolshoi Theater, and without hearing them talk it would have been hard for me to tell whether they were Russians or foreigners. They wore the same elegant evening attire, their slippers, jewels, bags, gloves matching their gowns to perfection. They were all beautifully coiffed. Of course, these women are a most insignificant minority even in Moscow and hardly exist outside of that city, with the exception maybe of Leningrad and Kiev. It was easier to tell the difference between a Russian and a foreigner by looking at the men. Even if a Russian was wearing a well-cut suit of good material a little something would betray him—the shoeshine, the tie, the haircut. It seemed to me, though, that the Russians have an ambiguous attitude toward women's make-up. The stores are well supplied and sell all kinds of beauty aids, especially lipsticks, and many women use them. At the same time one often encounters a puritanical attitude about make-up and I heard from several young women that their husbands wouldn't stand for their using lipstick and powder. Formerly one could easily recognize a Russian woman by those ugly tight little curls the hairdressers gave her. Now one sees these frizzy hairdos only on the older peasant women. For the most part, the hair styles are not much different from those of well-dressed New Yorkers.

Some of the Moscow hairdressers are excellent but one word of warning to future women tourists in Moscow: don't eat anything salty before going to a beauty salon—there is still only one glass to drink from, and no paper cups. Neither are there paper cups at the kiosks and stands dispensing soft drinks. The Moscow beauty parlors make definite appointments, but I have seen women walk in, whisper something into the ear of the person in charge and be taken out of turn. Why she and not another depends upon whose wife or daughter or sister she might be. And it doesn't have to be high up in the hierarchy at all. A few rungs above the beauty parlor manager does the trick.

Once there was great excitement while I was waiting for my turn in the beauty parlor. A high school girl had come in for a hairdo for her graduation ball that evening. She had longish straight hair and wanted it done in a style that the hairdresser assured her could not possibly be managed with her kind of hair. The girl agreed to follow the hairdresser's suggestions, but soon an aunt of hers sailed in, cast one look at her niece's half-finished hairdo, and broke into a torrent of abuse. That was not at all the hairdo the family wanted the girl to have; it must be changed, she insisted, intermingling her outburst with the suggestion that the hairdresser scrub floors instead of attending to people's hair. Her angry recriminations continued until the hairdresser lost her patience and replied in kind. After the aunt had flounced out, a number of hotel employees descended on the hairdresser. Since they spoke in subdued tones I could hear only a few words here and there: ". . . but realize the trouble she can make for you . . . she is going to complain about you . . . what do you care how the girl will look in the evening? . . ."

Since the same young woman attended to me after the high school graduate I heard the whole story. The aunt was only the supervisor of one of the hotel's minor departments and not Khrushchev's right hand as her haughty behavior had suggested. But it was obvious that even her not very elevated position in the Soviet hierarchy put her on a rung higher than the others, and she would never forget it and, what is more important, never let the others forget it. It didn't seem to arouse anyone's resentment, it was such an indisputable fact of life.

Indeed—if I may digress for a moment—I never am as conscious in the United States of the division between classes as I was in Russia. Everyone I talked with about it confirmed it, many with great regret. The gravitation of people to their own kind was most obvious. Everyone is part of a definite, circumscribed group and feels at home only among others of the same educational level, who have the same way of speaking, the same interests and tastes. This, of course, is true everywhere including the United States. But in the Soviet Union, forty-three years after the revolution which had proclaimed the beginning of a new era, I had expected a much greater leveling off, a much deeper realization of the equality that had been heralded as one of the main aspirations of the revolution. Many of those who have maids still address them as they used to in the old days with the condescending "ty," the "thou" employed in speaking to someone of a lower class and also, incidentally, to members of one's family or friends.

I had observed this division of classes on my very first day at the airdrome. One of the lesser clerks dropped a paper, and a charwoman bent down to pick it up for him. I was then certain that it was purely accidental. It was not. I soon learned that the woman was expected to do that. Wasn't she a much lower worker than the clerk? I found in Russia that our bourgeois capitalist society has infinitely more feeling for the equality of man than Communist Russia has.

Two days after my arrival while waiting for the elevator I heard one of the hotel guests, a Russian, shout insults at the floorlady and a chambermaid. Both of them tried meekly to defend themselves but were definitely defeated by his loud threats to have them discharged. I later asked the floorlady what it was all about. It seems that he had broken something or other in his room. The maid re-

ported it, as she was supposed to do. That was when he followed her
and let loose the torrent of abuse at both of them.

"But he was in the wrong and he knew it," I said. (I had the day
before paid $5 for a hotel radio which I damaged.)

"What can we do?" they said resignedly. "He is an important man
and he will always be right." I asked who he was. Assistant manager
of a collective farm in Southern Russia, was the answer. Not one of
the more important positions in the Soviet hierarchy but high
enough for these hotel employees who are so much lower. This was
my second example of the supposedly classless Soviet society,
which throughout my stay was often repeated.

Describing the incident to a group of people, I asked whether the
floorlady and the maid could not complain about this rude treatment
to their union. I was met with a rebuff: "That is not what unions
are for. They have more important things to do," meaning, of
course, that their main function was to raise production. It was clear
from their tone that I had proved once more how little those coming from the capitalist world understand what the Soviet system is
all about and what labor unions are for.

Status seekers are not unknown in this classless society either,
though I found none among my own acquaintances. I was told, however, that among people in high circles the kind of fur coat that one's
wife or daughter wore, the kind of trips one took, and the kind of
cars one drove were very important.

Despite their busy crowded days, few indeed were the women,
even party members, who were not interested in everything I could
tell them about foreign fashions, hairdos, ways of cooking, home
decorations, leisure hour occupations. But few of my personal
friends would accept gifts of wearing apparel or cosmetics. A book
(I had no controversial books with me), a roll of Scotch tape, good
quality writing paper, a photograph album, an unusual notebook,
above all a ballpoint pen, but not more than that. And it was not
because they were afraid but because they truly felt that they could
buy whatever they needed in their own stores. Some refused to take
anything at all. In their cases it was obvious that they wanted to

impress on me the fact that they are as well supplied as we are.

This is not to contradict all the reports we have heard from American travelers about the great interest Russian women show in possessing anything from the West. I met a number of these women too and I easily got rid of many of my belongings. I even could have sold them had I been inclined to do so.

The younger women listened with fascination to my accounts of young American women, intelligent, well educated, who had many children and happily devoted their lives to their homes and families, and perhaps did useful community work. The amenities of this existence seemed to appeal to them but the final reaction usually was: "Oh, no, I wouldn't want to stay home and do nothing but housework and take care of children." I wondered whether this deep dislike of a life devoted exclusively to the family stemmed from the unattractiveness and difficulties of Russian home life and housekeeping.

They do dream of and talk of modern apartments, of easy shopping and home delivery, of modern efficient cleaning and cooking devices, of freezers and precooked foods. They visualize excellent nurseries, kindergartens and schools within walking distance of their homes, and well-organized ways of freeing the parents for evening recreation. They admit that all is far from right on the women's labor front. Women must be taken out of heavy construction jobs, they must not be assigned to nightwork, they must be supplied with more efficient tools for work (street cleaning was most often mentioned), their family status must be taken into consideration when work hours are set, and so on.

But to give up their work and their duty to society—as some said, to deprive society of what they, women, could and must contribute to it—was something they would never do. It is true that almost all the young women I met were professional women: doctors, engineers, lawyers, architects, economists, teachers, scientists. Even if they wanted to stay at home, they said, for any length of time, they could never catch up with the changes and advances in their professions. I told them that our professional women had the same problem when they started raising a family.

Women in the middle- and high-income groups work because this is the Soviet pattern of life; and it is obvious that they never give it a thought unless one asks them directly why. Some of the cab drivers to whom I talked said that their wives had started to work because everything cost so much, but most admitted it was because there were so many things to buy now, whereas the temptation was less in the past. Perhaps in the reactions of the Russians to their material betterment lies one of the major answers to the future development of Soviet society.

A certain wistfulness would come into women's eyes when, talking of our daily lives, I would describe an unhurried predinner cocktail, a quiet evening of reading and listening to good music, the easiness of shopping for a pair of stockings or a roast for dinner, a leisurely weekend trip with food available wherever one went. This was very different from what they were usually told about the never-ending mad rush of American life. They could never understand why rush if you could order things on the telephone or by mail, if you could get anything you wanted without standing in line, without fearing that what you wanted might be gone by the time your turn came. My description of our mail-order catalogues sounded like a fairy tale to them. So did the delivery (and nondisappearance) at one's door of newspapers, milk and rolls.

And what appealed greatly to the women was our institution of baby-sitters, which is unheard of in Russia. Recently there has been a drive to get the Pioneers to volunteer without pay, of course, to help families with shopping or in taking care of children or invalids, but it is not the same thing.

As a rule, however, I tried to impress my listeners with our spiritual values, with our freedom of choice, for instance, which the Russians are thoroughly conscious that they lack. I elaborated on the more materialistic side of American life only if asked definite questions about it, or if people provoked me by sneering a bit too much at it while boasting in the same breath that in a very few years they would overtake us and be far ahead. My question why work so hard in order to achieve such obviously undesirable aims was usually followed by someone's repeating for the *n*th time the well-known story about overtaking and pants. This as a rule helped bring the conversation to a harmonious end before it exploded in an East-West controversy. The story concerns two men who were boasting about overtaking the United States. "It won't be long now," said one, "till we have caught up with them and overtaken them." "Let us stop at the catching-up point," cautioned the other, "otherwise the Americans will see that our pants have no backs."

Whenever the subject of nurseries and kindergartens came up the same problem I was faced with over thirty years ago was mentioned. There are still not enough of them and they are not always easily accessible. And there still exists the question of what to do on finding a sign on the school door: "Closed for quarantine because of whooping cough . . . measles . . . scarlet fever . . ." These signs appear somewhat less regularly now than they did in my time. But now as then the mother has to take the child back home and, if there is no grandmother or friendly neighbor around, she has to take a leave of absence without pay for the duration of the quarantine, though it no longer means losing her job. In the past absence or lateness was not excused and sometimes brought severe punishment.

In conversations with young mothers I found that, like their American counterparts, they know that the essential need of a baby is love. Therefore many of them, some even stanch Communists who otherwise strictly follow the prescriptions of the party, prefer the less efficient but tender care given by a tired grandmother to the perfect physical and educational advantages of a nursery where individual affection is not always possible. Their feeling about this does not, however, change their conviction that they must carry a full-time job, even though it does make their lives more complicated emotionally as well as physically.

Many women told me with pride that they had regained some of the earlier privileges that Stalin abolished. They again have the right to the longer vacation before and after the birth of a child, as well as to a longer period without pay if they want to stay home until the child is ready for a nursery. Abortions are once more legal and though they are somewhat restricted by law it seemed to me, from all the stories I heard, that any woman on one pretext or another can get an abortion under strict medical auspices and does not have to risk her life in incompetent hands under unsanitary conditions.

Once when I visited friends I was invited to meet a neighbor, a mother who had just come home from the hospital with triplets. I was delighted. I had never yet seen triplets. The family was still living in their single room but expected any hour to be moved into a new two-room apartment of their own which the authorities had assigned to them immediately after the birth. The babies had a nurse, whom the authorities assign to every set of triplets until they reach nursery age. The government also supplies the cribs and whatever else a newborn baby requires. These helps are provided only for three babies or more. Twins do not qualify.

I have not seen any statistics on marriage age but was told that young people don't marry as early as ours do these days. Student marriages are much less frequent in Russia. In all the cases where I inquired the young people had married in their early or middle twenties; the under-twenty marriages were rare exceptions.

Pregnant women go through an intensive preparation. They read books on natural birth, they attend lectures, they are taught exercises and proper nutrition. Unless they have serious medical reasons for not nursing their babies, they all do. Young women among my friends were interested to hear that American women go through much the same preparation. But what always caused great hilarity was that many American husbands attended the lectures together with their pregnant wives. When I mentioned that I knew of cases where the husbands stayed with their wives until the very moment the latter were taken to the delivery room I felt that my stock as a truthful person fell alarmingly low.

To draw any general conclusions about how Soviet women feel about this or that, as I have often been asked to do since my return, is as impossible as it is to draw a general conclusion about anything else. Only a few days before I left I spent a couple of hours with two women who disagreed emphatically on every subject touched upon. One was fiercely against everything the Soviet government has ever done, is doing, and will ever do. The other always was and is for whatever it has ever done, is doing, and will do.

The first one said: "The currency reform means only that everything will be even more expensive than it is now. Whatever we had before, occasionally even excellent cloth from England and France, totally disappeared as soon as the reform was announced. It will appear again on the day the new currency is introduced and will cost us twice as much as before. . . . Devoted Communists? Don't make me laugh. These birds if they ever existed, which I doubt, disappeared long ago. . . . Rehabilitation? Only those who were ready to re-enter the party and lick the boots of whoever is on top received high financial compensation, good apartments, well-paid jobs. The rest live in even greater misery than before. . . . Trotsky? Of course I knew he was murdered. And you don't have to tell me who did it."

The other woman said: "I can hardly wait for the day of the currency reform. Everything will be less expensive. . . . I live among party members and they are as devoted to the party and ready for any sacrifice as they ever were. . . . I knew many people who were jailed or exiled, but they are all back, and every one of them, whether they joined the party or not, is taken care of as far as financial compensation, rooms, medical care are concerned. . . . No, I never knew that Trotsky was dead. But, then, what difference does it make to us?"

Incidentally, my question about Trotsky had been prompted by the fact that during my very first days in Moscow I had been shocked to hear from two older Communists, both of whom had known Trotsky personally and had worked with him during the first years after the revolution, that they did not know he was dead and (sincerely or not—I will never know) definitely doubted that he was assassinated by Stalin's agents. If they did not know of Trotsky's death, how about others? Throughout the rest of my stay I asked the same question of as many people as I could. "By the way, whatever happened to Trotsky?" I would say casually. Most people had no idea and did not care. A few knew he was dead. Those who knew he had been assassinated and the circumstances under which it happened were people who had been in exile, who as a rule were the best informed. They had picked up a great deal of information on the outside world from prisoners of war and other foreigners who for some reason or other found their way to the Far North and to the labor camps.

Another topic on which my two women friends violently disagreed was imports from abroad. The first insisted that the only things the satellites (she unashamedly used the expression, the only person in Russia I heard do so) sent to Russia are goods they do not want for themselves. The other just as energetically insisted that they were getting excellent imports from Czechoslovakia, Hungary, East Germany and Latvia.

This conversation was interesting to me chiefly because it showed the woman so violently anti-Soviet was unafraid to talk openly in the presence of a devoted Communist. When we were alone I commented on this. She answered with a laugh: "If nothing has happened to me by now I don't have to worry about the future." This was her only indirect admission that in one respect, at least, the situation has changed for the better.

In general I gained one definite impression from numerous conversations with women. Their lives may be busy, hectic and harassed but certainly not empty and boring.

When I came home I brought regards from a Moscow grandmother to her sister, a New York grandmother. Knowing what a comfortable life the American sister lives I tried to describe the life of her sister in Moscow in as careful terms as I possibly could. It was not an easy task unless I wanted to tell outright lies. The 75-year-old Moscow grandmother led a most harassed life; busy every minute, with never a quiet moment for herself, with two exceptionally lively and active grandchildren, her days filled with duties every waking hour and her nights filled with worrying inside and noises outside. The reaction of the American sister was totally unexpected. Instead of a burst of pity, she said with great sadness in her voice:

"How lucky she is! She is needed and she is busy. My children and grandchildren don't need me. Most of the time I don't know what to do with myself."

Incidentally, a subject which came up in every conversation was the 1959 United States exhibit. I heard some enthusiastic reports on it, some friendly criticism, and some expression of downright disappointment. The last came from those who had been hoping to see exhibits of our latest technical advances. Others were disappointed because they had expected something totally out of the ordinary. That the idea behind an exhibit was to show how the average American family lives did not impress them. They had seen German, Czech, Yugoslav, and many other exhibits which had impressed them more. When I pointed out that those exhibits, like the Soviet exhibits abroad, but unlike the American exhibit, usually presented the ideal of the future rather than the actuality of today, they remained unmoved. They were disappointed because they had expected to find in the American exhibit something they could not even imagine in their dreams. Several mentioned in this connection the Indian exhibit and spoke with great fervor of its beauty, exquisite colors and handicraft. They said that they missed at the United States exhibit the aesthetic pleasure the Indian one had given them.

However, a great many people were unreservedly enthusiastic and marveled that the average family could possess all those beautiful things. They loved the fashion shows and the gadgets, and, above all, the guides, who made a hit even with the severest critics of the exhibition. When I asked what they liked about the guides, most people mentioned their pleasant, natural manner. Many of them told me that they were struck by the fact that the guides answered all questions freely, readily agreeing with legitimate criticism of the United States, and in different ways and words explaining the causes and struggles involved in our shortcomings. It was this—the individuality and the absence of a routine jargon in their answers—that most impressed the Russians, who are trained to express ideas in a definite, prescribed terminology.

I also heard from several Russians that they were deeply impressed by the obvious freedom of movement of the guides, by their acceptance of invitations without having to ask anyone's permission, by their liberty to spend their free time without any supervision. In other words, the Russians were genuinely struck by the absence of an American commissar at the exhibit to watch over his herd and give the proper instructions. It would be hard for them to imagine a Soviet exhibition abroad without the customary rigid supervision.

CHAPTER ELEVEN

The Older Generation

One rarely sees an attractive-looking older woman in Moscow, though our women at the same age still look trim and feminine. Men also age before their time but the neglected appearance of women was, at least to me, more noticeable. There are serious reasons for their premature aging.

The war and the immediate postwar years were hard on a generation which had gone through earlier waves of privation and terror. I did not meet one single healthy person among them, and never have I heard so much talk about sickness.

I met some of my dance partners of former years whose children, whom I had known as babies, discovered with amazement that their papas and mammas who now were forever complaining about their ailments were once upon a time young and some even quite dashing. They certainly were far from that now. They all looked so much older than their age. The little over two decades since I had seen them had aged them infinitely more than the years would justify. And I am not talking now of people who had returned from prisons or labor camps.

The Russians talk a great deal about health foods, something I had never heard of in Moscow in the past. The city has several special health food stores in which the items sold bear detailed labels explaining what they contain in the way of vitamins and calories and what they are good for. In several general food stores I saw large charts explaining which kinds of food were good for what and giving lists of foods recommended for specific health needs. At the same tables where in the past one ate exclusively starches, fried foods and sweets one still is served plenty of these but salads, vegetables and fruit are always added.

From the older people, and occasionally from the not so old, I constantly heard that this or that is bad for one's health; for instance, to drink tea and wine at the same meal is very bad. The old gentleman who said this was so earnest about it that I did not have any tea. I also heard that it was bad to eat yogurt or fruit before going to bed, that one should never drink water after fruit, and much more. And there is still that old fear of drafts. I had to fight for my right to sit near an open window on a stifflingly hot day. The draft has remained in the Russian mind the source of innumerable ills.

Since people have become so intensely diet conscious, many a good meal was spoiled by constant talking about it. Everything we ate was discussed and analyzed. What had and what didn't have salt, sugar, fats, acids, starches. My ignorance amazed them. I would say that I avoided starches, sweets and fats, ate most of my food broiled and concentrated on vegetables and fruit, without going into all the details of the whys and wherefores. My older eating companions felt that the whys and wherefores were such an important and interesting part of dieting.

What amused me most was that all the long and detailed discussions on dieting were so often accompanied by heaps of butter, heavy cream, food fried in a lot of fat, tea sweetened with generous amounts of sugar and accompanied by jams and cake. The side dishes of vegetables and salads seemed to give the dieters absolution.

It is a fact that everywhere I went, in the parks, in the very center of Moscow or on the outskirts, in department stores, private homes, people were constantly eating. Hours, place did not matter. The city, especially the center of it, is full of stands selling oranges, lemons, berries when in season, dried fruits, meat and cabbage patties, canned foods, sandwiches, hot dogs, sweet rolls, soft drinks and, the greatest favorite of all, ice cream in many shapes and many flavors. All around these stands people eat whatever can be eaten on the spot.

It is the young who are profiting from what for their elders is still more a topic of conversation than reality. The young people eat less, move about more, go in for sports—the young women are very conscious of their figures and, contrary to their mothers, do something about it besides talk. The old Russian way of praising a woman's looks by saying "She is so beautiful, she is so stout" is as outmoded today as the singing of the Czarist national anthem.

Whenever I had to report on the kind of food I ate at home I got into difficulty. I was unable to explain about broiling. There are no electric broilers in Russia and no top heat in Moscow ovens, and since I don't know the word in Russian (I don't think there is one) this was almost as hard to explain as the U-2 incident. One woman who has a friend in the Soviet embassy in Washington made me write out in English "electric broiler" so that she could ask him to bring her one. One of my great regrets is that I cannot correspond with my Moscow friends and will never know whether this woman got her electric broiler.

I will leave to specialists in the field the details of medical care in Russia. But I can definitely say that having a prolonged illness or a serious operation is not the frightening financial problem that it is in our lives. Several people told me that they had spent a great deal of money on long sicknesses and the postoperative care of members of their families. But they admitted that they had the money for it and preferred home care and their own doctors. Those who don't have the money receive probably less personalized state medical care.

All medical laws, regulations and decrees are vigorously carried out. I heard a fascinating tale of how Moscow went through a sweeping smallpox vaccination drive a couple of years ago.

A Soviet artist upon his return from India died of smallpox. He would not have died if his vaccination certificate had not been a fraud. The Soviet government, like the United States authorities, demand a valid vaccination certificate from all travelers returning from a foreign country. This artist did not want to be vaccinated and procured a fake certificate through a medical friend. Doctors, certain that he had been vaccinated, did not immediately diagnose smallpox. By the time they did it was too late to save his life.

The very moment smallpox was diagnosed everyone who even by any remote chance might have come near the artist during his return trip or after was quarantined. This, gossip had it, required the isolation, in addition to hundreds of others, of two fairly large family units, since before going home to his own family he had paid a visit to his mistress. Within a few hours after the diagnosis the entire city, borough by borough, street by street, house by house, apartment by apartment, was vaccinated with a speed and thoroughness possible only in a country where people wouldn't dream of offering the slightest objection after the government had issued the order.

Before I went to Russia I had read that Soviet statistics on mental illness were lower than ours. I wondered about this. I remembered the tensions caused by overcrowded living, by the fear of being sent to work away from family and friends, by the lack of privacy for lovers, not to mention by the fear of arrest and exile. I found that the statistics were correct. There are fewer mental patients in Russia.

I spoke to a psychiatrist friend about it. I told him that in my capacity as the apartment-elder I used to witness hysterical outbursts in common kitchens, passionate quarrels, fist fights and hair pulling in front of all neighbors including children. Yes, the doctor said, the strain of crowded living still exists. Nerves are frayed, people are high strung and easily lose control over their words and acts. But this is not mental illness, he said. With a change of living conditions most people easily regain their equilibrium. His daily tasks and problems absorb a Russian's every waking minute and leave him little time for brooding over himself. Much research has been done in Russia on physical causes of mental disease, and many of the findings have already been incorporated in actual treatment of glandular defects as well as of the effects of aging.

I heard from several doctors that homeopaths belong to the very top of the income ladder. They practice privately to a great extent, pay enormous taxes for this privilege, and have incomes that painlessly absorb those taxes. People come to them from the farthest corners of Russia—peasants as well as people in high positions. Some of the homeopaths make appointments exclusively by main, for weeks or even months ahead. A young doctor sang for me some limericks dealing with homeopaths. They were not too complimentary and obviously reflected the negative attitude of the more orthodox medical profession.

Since my conversations on health and medicine were mostly with older people, in the course of them the question of retirement inevitably came up. There is a great inner loneliness everywhere in the world for those who upon retirement are suddenly forced into inactivity. But in Russia the change after retirement, because of the primitive living conditions, is much greater than in the United States, for instance. For men it may mean discomfort and emptiness; for Russian women it may mean discomfort but certainly not emptiness. They find a new full-time occupation by becoming professional grandmothers. Many prefer to continue working as long as they possibly can instead of staying at home and coping with the duties and difficulties of raising grandchildren in cramped, inconvenient households. Retirement age is fifty-five for women and sixty for men but no one is obliged to retire and many go on working for many years after the legal retirement age.

Shortly before I left for Russia I heard several stories of American couples, some comic, some tragic, of what happened when, after a lifetime of having spent only weekends and evenings together, husbands and wives were suddenly thrown together for twenty-four hours a day seven days a week. The stories I heard in

Moscow about retirement were exactly the same, only more often tragic, because of the crowded living conditions and the inability to travel. I was told that many men work until they collapse so as not to stay at home and that many marriages have a way of deteriorating after retirement.

Once a man of sixty-three, who had been entitled to retire three years earlier, told me of his own situation which he made sound quite funny. He is a slim man with a soft voice and quiet manners. His wife, whom he adores, is a very large good-natured woman with a trumpetlike voice which she uses incessantly. They live in a small room cramped with furniture and hardly any space to move. He cannot visualize spending the rest of his life cooped up with the Voice (his nickname for her) in that room, so despite a heart condition he continues to work. Taking into consideration the long Moscow winter months when people don't go out unless they have to, retirement is a big problem for him. He will get an excellent pension and will have no financial problems, and he would not mind some leisure after a life of hard work but, as he put it, he chose the lesser evil. There is no Florida or California for him, no hope for a larger room in a new building; no children and grandchildren to devote time to. The only way out for the rest of his life is that tiny cramped room in the crowded apartment.

Another man I knew, a water transport specialist, had offered his organization the following proposal: he would retire on his pension but would continue to work without additional salary for three or four hours daily. This was partly because he dreaded the emptiness of his life and lack of peace in the crowded rooms his wife and he shared with a married daughter. But it was also because he felt that it would be a crime to waste his experience, accumulated through decades. He said that his ministry as well as many others were still suffering from the holes left in experienced cadres by the purges. A little over twenty years ago people in their best creative working years had been cut off like wheat at harvesttime (that is the expression he used) and inexperienced young people were put in their places.

They had to learn in a hurry with hardly anyone to teach them. This man was one of the few who by a sheer miracle had not been arrested then. He has remained one of the great specialists in his field and his retirement will leave a space not easy to fill. But, despite all the pretty words about filling the leisure of the retired as well as preserving their experience, his bureau is unable to make a decision to do something that has not been done before in this particular organization. To be fair, I should add that a few days after I talked to this man I visited an old friend, a chemical engineer. He had retired, was crippled with arthritis, was much older than the water transport expert. But he sat in his room at a desk covered with piles of papers and pamphlets on which he was working. His organization was still using his knowledge and was regularly sending him new projects for his judgment and keeping him informed on all developments in his field. Nevertheless, among the people I talked with the plight of the water engineer was much more typical and the complaint was widespread that the knowledge of retired specialists was not being used.

I met several retired women who were busy doing voluntary community work. They were not what I call the professional grandmothers or housekeepers for a young working generation; if they had been they would have had no free hours for community work. They were usually childless widows or unmarried women. They helped in schools, in recreation parks, on playgrounds, they organized the planting of trees and other neighborhood improvement projects.

CHAPTER TWELVE

The Children

From my very first day in Moscow my eyes and ears were wide open to children. Several American visitors had told me that they found Russian children spoiled, that much too much attention was showered on them. I do not agree. I found them saying "please" or "thank you" whenever it was called for; they seldom interrupted conversations of adults without being called to order for it; they seemed well disciplined in public places. Indeed they seemed to me to show more of the external attributes of politeness in their relations with adults than many of our children do.

I spent hardly a day in Moscow without finding at least a little time to sit on a playground watching children. Rarely did I see younger women accompany them. It was usually a grandmother or another older woman. In a few cases I saw a grandfather.

The boys of course played their own boisterous games while little girls skipped rope, as they have probably done since Creation. Sometimes the boys would be carried away in their excitement. But when they got too objectionable an adult would say: "Aren't you ashamed of yourselves? You are schoolboys, Pioneers." Then the boys, without a retort or even a sullen look, would lower their voices for a while, at least.

Russians shower attention on children, even on those not their own. In parks and on trains a child can always be certain of friendly attention. An American embassy official told me that whenever he travels on a public conveyance attention is centered on his children. He has four of them, which not many Moscovites, because of their living conditions, can boast of. More than once he was asked in astonishment, "Are they all yours?" and genuine friendliness was shown them.

Most of the children I saw were neatly dressed and clean. I often wondered how the cleanliness was achieved, in view of the lack of bathroom facilities, and asked a friend who is connected with children's organizations. She said that the decades of discipline and training in nurseries, kindergartens and schools, as well as the vigorous health and hygiene campaigns and the constant barrage of propaganda in women's organizations and magazines all over the country, have brought definite results. She reminded me, as I was constantly being reminded in Moscow in many other connections, that the children I saw today were the third generation going through Soviet training.

One of the largest Moscow stores is called the "Children's World." It has everything in it a child could possibly need or desire: clothing, furniture, toys of every description, games, chemistry sets, sports equipment, books, as well as ice cream, sweets, soft drinks, sandwiches. I was in the store several times and it was filled with huge crowds, morning, afternoon or evening. There were no more and no less frequent requests for sweets and toys than there would be in such a store anywhere else in the world. The parental refusal that seemed to be the most convincing and quickly acceptable was "I haven't got the money."

How to take care of the children after school when both parents work and no grandparents or other adults are available has always been a great problem. A new experiment which seems to work well and is gradually spreading through all schools is the new so-called "prolonged school." Children stay in these schools from 8:30 A.M. to 6 P.M., with regular meals, a rest period, exercise and walk, classes, homework, and all kinds of extracurricular activities like music, dancing, sports, science, photography, and art.

Since the great majority of young women have full-time jobs and few can afford to keep a maid, those who have no mothers living with them take their young children to the nurseries and kindergartens in the morning and pick them up after work. Some keep their children there throughout the week and take them home only over the weekend. This is satisfactory from the point of view of the children's being well taken care of but very unsatisfactory emotionally for both children and parents. And unfortunately, according to a young woman whom I had asked why her child was not in a kindergarten—and this was confirmed later by some others—the nurseries and kindergartens are not as good as they used to be. In the past, to work in nurseries and kindergartens was the aim of many idealistic young women. Now it has become a "job" and not a very glamorous one at that, often chosen after failure to get into more interesting professions. There are, of course, exceptions—young women who still choose this work as an avocation—but the present exceptions were the past general rule.

To solve the child care problem parents rely wherever possible on the great Soviet institution: the Grandmother. Those whom I knew I watched in their homes and I saw hundreds of them on playgrounds all over Moscow. The children get loving protection but the grandmothers as a rule neither play with them nor entertain them in any other way. They tell them to do this or that, they feed them, they pet them, and they don't let them out of their sight. But playing is something most of them have completely forgotten how to do during the many hard years behind them.

They are physically and mentally exhausted. Their general health and their nerves are not up to playing with lively youngsters. Many times I heard comments on my patience in playing with children. I had the time (and also the nerves) to read to them, to answer their endless questions, to teach them new games. Above all, I let them open my bag and play with its contents. Few Russian women will let a child do that. Decades of being slaves to food coupons (which no longer exist) and numerous identification cards (which still exist), the eternal fear of having one's bag snatched out of one's hands (this still happens though less frequently than before), the difficulty of replacing anything lost—all these have made a woman's bag a precious, untouchable object. The bright shiny things which fill an American bag were an endless delight for the children.

In discussing children in Russia I had several interesting conversations on a question that has always interested me: Do we have the right to impose our own attitudes on children if these attitudes are contrary to those dominating the society in which we live? Do parents in Russia have the moral right to make their children carry on a fight for religion, for instance, when the official attitude is against it, or to take a stand against the official attitude on literature or art?

The first time the question came up was when I talked with a young couple about agnostics in the United States and the problem of American nonbelieving parents in a churchgoing society. Did parents have the right to make their children participate in a fight for a nonpopular cause? I was amazed to discover that some young Soviet parents too were concerned with this problem of nonconformity and how to solve it with children in the rigid Soviet society where dissent in any field is tantamount to a political crime.

The question came up several more times. There was no satisfactory answer. If parents in the United States have difficulty in bringing up children in a nonconformist way, in Russia it is an insoluble dilemma.

I once gave a seven-year-old boy a ballpoint pen and pencil with a picture of the UN building and "United Nations" spelled out in the five official languages. His father instantly and happily appropriated it. "He is much too young to know what it is" was his explanation. This boy was not brought up on fairy tales or on Westerns or comics. He knew the official political slogans, he could recite by heart the American sins against the Soviet Union, he had a rich political vocabulary, but he had no idea what the United Nations was. He had never been told of it.

CHAPTER THIRTEEN

The Young Conformists

Many American travelers have been enchanted with the natural
fresh faces of the young Russian girls. They enchanted me too.
The natural pink cheeks and bright eager young eyes looked truly
young and unsophisticated, and their chatter and laughter sounded
spontaneous. Their voices were high and ringing but not shrill.
Their hair in braids crossed on the back and brought together with
white ribbons at the sides of the head, seemed properly taken
care of, shiny and well brushed. They wore gay cottons after they
had shed, with the end of school, their uniforms. I used to see
them walking up and down the boulevard paths. They invariably
walked four or five in a row, their arms around each other's waists,
chattering away, sometimes singing.

I never saw boys and girls mixing in these walks. When I asked
about it I was told that teen-agers have many activities and good
times together in the Pioneers and Komsomol, as counselors in
youth camps, in excursions, sports, study circles, theatricals, creative arts, but that as a rule they don't pair off for serious dating till
college or, infrequently, during the last year of high school.

On outings I saw them playing games together, rowing, swimming, singing, flirting, then getting ready for the return home—girls
by themselves again. I saw young girls in parks, of maybe eighteen

or nineteen, walking hand in hand or arm in arm with a young man. Some of them looked as if they had come out of the pages of a Turgenev novel. One day a young woman, a former Pioneer leader and now a member of the Komsomol, whom I had questioned about the interests of teen-agers, invited some young neighbors, five girls, to answer my questions. They were lively youngsters, reflecting as a whole the attitudes and views of their elders but eager to hear and to read more than was as a rule offered to them. Interrupting one another, they talked excitedly about their favorite Russian writers and poets with Pushkin, Lermontov and Turgenev high on their list and Soviet writers trailing far behind. They mentioned as their future occupations those of their fathers and mothers, older brothers and sisters—doctors, teachers, engineers (space and electronics preferred), flyers, lawyers. They expressed their deep loyalty to communism and motherland Russia, but their eyes shone when they spoke of possible trips to the West.

There was giggling and blushing when I brought up the question of boys and dating. I must admit that I did not get too far with them on that. It was obviously a subject they would not discuss as freely with me as they did literature and the professions. But it was clear even from the little they said that there was hardly any pairing off for dating, and the idea of a boy's spending a lot of money taking out a girl for an evening was unknown to these girls of fifteen and sixteen.

Talking with this group and with others of their age, I often recalled the words of a 16-year-old American girl who once said to me: "I wouldn't go out with a boy who hasn't got a car. What does one do then, just talk and talk?" This could certainly not have been said by a Russian girl. She likes nothing better than to talk and talk. Indeed my main impression of Russian teen-agers was that they were extremely articulate, used to thrashing out problems that interested them, though these problems were limited in scope; they were boy-conscious but not boy-crazy, and seemed to be devoid of the fears and threats that had hung over the lives of the older generation at their age.

Whatever these youngsters said sounded sincere, but their thinking was restricted and conformist to a high degree. It was, however, a conformity very different from that of our own youth. American youth is conformist because it has chosen to be conformist. It may be a logical upshot of the present mood of American adult society, though in other periods American youth did not necessarily follow the mood of its elders. However it is, American youth could have made another choice if it had wanted to, and by the time I finish writing this book it may have done so. But Soviet youth is thoroughly conditioned through every word it hears, or reads to a one and only way of thinking and living. No breath of fresh air comes through contacts with people who may think differently, from printed words which express unfamiliar ideas, from trips to foreign countries. It is only amazing that there are some nonconformists.

And it must be remembered that, though Russia is an old country and the Russians are an old people, at the present moment the country and the people show at the same time many characteristics of a new young awakening nation. The country is in a great hurry to grow up in a modern way, to build and to learn. In its rush to build and to see concrete results it is unsophisticated and has little time and inclination for decadence, nonconformity, bohemianism, and it definitely rejects them. When I heard young people passionately denouncing modern art, music, avant-garde writing I often wondered whether, while repeating the official clichés, they were not actually following their own instincts and inclinations as well as the orders from above. They are busy building and growing, and nothing that might slow them down must stand in their way. And one moves ahead so much faster on familiar paths.

I had met a number of young people representative of the average Soviet youth. But I was also interested in those I had been hearing about for years—the Soviet jeunesse d'orée or stilyagi or juvenile delinquents or whatever people choose to call the segment of Soviet youth that does not want to conform to the strictly prescribed pattern. I was told that few of these youths were criminals, that many of these young nonconformists were simply rebelling against the drab and the gray, against the avalanche of slogans that in the course of decades have become totally meaningless and even repulsive to some of them. The majority of Soviet youth have learned to live without letting the slogans interfere with their lives. The nonconformists have not. Some of the rebels find an outlet in art or literature, even though their artistic and literary creations rarely leave their creators' four walls.

From time to time a scandal among high school or college students does erupt into the open and appears in *Komsomolskaya Pravda*. But this does not seem to occur more frequently than in many other parts of the world, maybe even less so. There is no doubt that serious scandals do occur. But the Soviet authorities are extremely strict as far as morals are concerned and sometimes what the press calls a "scandal" may mean no more than staying out later than school rules permit or other minor infractions which would hardly cause comment in the Western press. The wild parties one occasionally hears about, I was told, take place as a rule in higher Soviet circles where the young people have money as well as the use of their parents' apartments for orgies.

Those rebels called jeunesse d'orée or stilyagi find their outlet in exaggerated clothing and hairdos, in an external behavior different from the prescribed one, in admiration of everything coming from the West because it is contrary to what they are supposed to admire, in wild dancing, in drinking and sex orgies.

However, I personally did not meet a single young person who would have qualified as a member of the jeunesse d'orée, and my encounter with the purer type of juvenile delinquent was still more disappointing. All I read and heard about them was that, besides indulging in the usual pastime of young criminals anywhere else in the world, the Moscow brand hung around hotels and approached foreigners offering to be their guides, to buy their clothes or dollars, or to be of other assistance to them. My stay was coming to an end and I was disappointed. No one had ever approached me. I probably did not seem a good enough prospect. Finally, a few days before I left a young man came up to me and asked in a funny broken English whether I wouldn't sell my shoes to him. Our encounter was short. I didn't even say no. He was so obviously a plain crook, totally unattractive, that in this one case I broke my rule to talk to anyone who showed the slightest inclination to talk to me.

All the young people I met showered me with questions about the United States. What seemed to impress several of them was that our young people, even in the highest family income brackets, did not shun lowly jobs and physical labor. When I told them that I had known a governor's daughter who worked as a waitress during the summer or that sons of lawyers or doctors frequently worked their way through college, it was something they had never heard of before. The fact that wives of wealthy and highly placed men did not necessarily have domestic help was another revelation. They had a notion of the United States as a place where there are two kinds of people—rich and poor, the first having everything and the latter nothing at all, where the children of the rich go to school and enjoy life, while those of the poor do all the dirty work, without benefiting at all from the "American way of life."

Young Russians, on the whole, have many of the same aspirations and longings that our own young people have, sometimes expressed in almost identical words. A happy family life, children, a good job, ability to buy whatever can be bought (our terminology would be: whatever one wants to buy), and recreation. But they have also, most of them, a deep sense of duty. It is your duty to do what your government tells you to do and to go wherever your government wants you to go, uncomfortable and undesirable as it may be. To them this duty is a synonym for patriotism, for loyalty to country. To go as scientists, engineers or doctors to far corners of the Soviet empire or the world, to live there as primitively as the local population lives, is to do something important for your country, aside from helping the people.

The Soviet government has always masterfully manipulated its people in whatever direction it needed them to move. I well remember how in 1928-1929, when the Russian government embarked on its first Five-Year Plan and needed more politically loyal specialists than the old Czarist professionals, it appealed to party members to enroll in engineering and science courses. The appeal was for One Thousand Communists (they went down in Soviet history as the Thousanders) in their twenties, thirties and even forties to start life all over again. It was done then without any pressure, only with appeals to their devotion to the cause. I knew intimately several of the Thousanders and know that they went back to school willingly and enthusiastically.

It needs more today to inspire the young people who by the tens of thousands go to the virgin lands of Siberia and Kazakhstan to build new industries, new cities, new agricultural centers. There is no doubt that some go out of genuine enthusiasm; but many unquestionably are lured by material inducements which the government has felt obliged to introduce. Some go under party or other pressure, often as punishment for laziness on jobs, for petty offenses, or for breaking the rules of good behavior for young Communists. And even those most enthusiastic about the sacrifices they were ready to make for their country and for world communism, betrayed unmistakably that they would be most reluctant to leave Moscow unless they absolutely had to. I heard several stories of the lengths to which influential parents go to avoid having their sons and daughters sent to those faraway places. I also heard that as a result of the lack of enthusiasm about leaving Moscow more and more young people are permitted to go on short-term contracts with definite assurance that they may return as soon as their tour of duty expires. There must have been quite a bit of pressure brought to bear by reluctant travelers. Nevertheless, the fact that people admit both the pressure and the reluctance, and that the government recognizes them, is certainly a change from Stalin's days when any kind of pressure or reluctance was unthinkable. The Russians rarely forget to point this out.

Several explanations were given for the younger generation's lack of the kind of burning zeal that fired their parents in the twenties and thirties. Some who were children during the purges, but old enough to realize what was happening to their elders, have retained memories of that bad time and, loyal citizens though they are, the effects have never totally disappeared.

The more recent blow, I was told, and one that has contributed greatly to the lack of present enthusiasm, was the exposure of Stalin and the breaking of the image of him under which they had grown up. Today's comparative prosperity and abundance of worldly goods also was given as a reason that some young people divert their interest and energies to more material ends.

I heard it also said that forty-three years after a revolution there cannot be and is not the same enthusiasm and zeal as at the time of its making. Some of the young people I talked with regretted that they did not feel the same excitement and enthusiasm their elders had been filled with during the first years after the revolution. They admitted that they were certainly not ready to go through the sufferings and privations their parents had endured if they could possibly help it. Oh, yes, they would of course in case of war, for the defense of their country, but not otherwise. "We have reached the stage," as one of them put it, "where we can afford to work hard for our country without having to neglect our own lives and our own wants."

Nevertheless, there is no question but that, despite the importance they attach to their own material welfare, the younger people genuinely take great pride in their work and even more in the general achievements of the country and in its having in such a short time taken a leading place in the world. (It was almost impossible to touch on any subject, even one totally unconnected with the Soviet Union, without having some of the younger people assure me that the Soviet attitude on this particular matter was the only thing of real importance. It was next to hopeless to make them realize that other countries do have problems with which the Soviet Union has nothing whatever to do.)

But I heard some of their elders talk with nostalgia of the years when they had had nothing, when they aspired to nothing for themselves, when, as some of them assured me, they were happier and gayer in the midst of nothing than are the young ones of today with their dreams equally divided between first place for the Soviet Union on our planet (and outside of it) and a washing machine, a refrigerator, TV set, car, a cottage in the country.

Of course, in many such conversations the question of the cost of Soviet progress came up. Here are some of the reactions: "Nothing in human history has ever been achieved without sacrifices. . . . No revolution was ever achieved with the consent of all the people, and those who did not consent always had to pay a price. . . . The future generations will be grateful for the sacrifices which were made for them." Once in the course of such a discussion somebody wondered whether, if within the next decade or so life should not become easy and tranquil, all their sacrifices and suffering would not have been in vain. He was literally shouted down by those present. "We have hardly had fifteen peaceful years since 1917, even less than that, without hunger or purges or wars or fears of war, and look what we have achieved" was the essence of the protest. I heard these same words whenever the question of sacrifices versus achievements came up. Another time the question arose whether each generation does not have a duty not only to work with new enthusiasm to consolidate the achievements of the past but to strive for something better. No; with a couple of exceptions the young people felt that the time had come for them to enjoy the fruit of the sacrifices of the past; they were not much concerned with preparing a better world for future generations.

There is now occasionally, very occasionally, detectable in Russia a whiff of fresh air—in a book, a play, a literary discussion. The young seem to take these whiffs in their stride. They find them pleasant but less exciting than do their elders, who during the past thirty years have not been treated to much fresh air.

Occasionally I heard young (as well as the not young) people mention a political, theatrical, literary, artistic event or name that could not possibly have found its way into the Soviet press or radio. I always tried to trace the source of this kind of information, and found that it came either through contacts of students with their foreign colleagues, contacts of scholars and scientists with their foreign counterparts, foreign broadcasts, contacts with participants of the Youth Festival in 1957 and of foreign exhibits, including the United States exhibit of 1959. Any news or information from such sources is disseminated rapidly. It is, of course, only a pinprick in the general lack of information but it does pierce the wall erected around the Russians and influences the thinking of at least one segment of Soviet youth.

I was interested in the reaction of young people when I told them that in the darkest days of czarism poets and writers were permitted to stimulate in the people a craving for freedom, to try to lift them out of the "gray everyday humdrum"—a favorite expression in the Czarist days—into the world of beauty and light and freedom. I have never forgotten the impact our young literature teacher had on all of us by pointing out, in a guarded way since our class supervisor was always present, the passages in literature that would stir us and make us think. On Pushkin's monument in Moscow are some of these words:

> I shall be loved, and long the people
> will remember
> The kindly thoughts I stirred—my music
> brightest crown,
> How in this cruel age I celebrated freedom,
> And begged for truth toward those cast down.*

I once asked several young people what they felt when they read these and similar poems by Pushkin, or "The Storm Petrel," Gorki's hymn to the freedom of the human spirit which had so stirred the young people of my generation. Not one of them associated in any way the suppression of freedom under the czar with present conditions in Russia. As one put it: "Then there was exploi-

---

* From "Unto Myself I Reared a Monument," by Alexander Pushkin, translated by Babette Deutsch. Reprinted from *The Poems, Prose and Plays of Alexander Pushkin*, edited by A. Yarmolinsky, by permission of Random House, Inc. Copyright 1936 by Random House, Inc.

tation of the masses by the ruling classes while now our country is still struggling on its way to a perfect society without exploitation. And during this struggle while imperialist countries are fighting us we are forced for the time being to curtail some of our freedoms."

In other words, the Czarist restrictions were entirely and absolutely bad, the present ones are a temporary historical necessity. They keep repeating this and they may even believe it. Since words have to such an extent lost their original meaning in modern Soviet terminology, some Russians are sincerely convinced that it is they who have freedom and the Western world is enslaved by capitalism. The fact that the very first years after the revolution were much freer, that more freedom was promised after the regime had finally and firmly established itself, and that the suppression of freedom was mainly a brainchild of Stalin, is not a matter of discussion. The reason is simple: earlier Soviet history has been totally falsified, or ignored. The young do not know the real history of their country. A conversation about the twenties or thirties would be interrupted by a young voice insisting, for instance, that "It isn't true that Bukharin was a favorite protégé of Lenin" (which he most certainly was, though in Soviet history books of today he is presented as a villain) or that "It is not true that the Soviet government ever prohibited the playing of Tchaikovsky's music" (which it certainly did in the early Stalin period).

Once when I was telling some young friends about my experiences while working at international conferences after the First World War, I happened to mention Chicherin, who played a most important role in shaping Russian foreign policy during the formative years of the Soviet republic. One lad interrupted to ask, "Who was Chicherin?" I was shocked to discover that few of them had ever heard of him, and knew little about the actual events of that period.

One name they all were familiar with was Trotsky's, and of him they had heard only that he was the black villain of the revolution —which is the way Stalin wanted him to go down in Soviet history.

I once asked some young people how they explained the fact that while Lenin was in Siberian exile he was permitted to bring there his future wife, to get married and to live with her during his term of exile; that he was allowed to be in constant touch with the other exiles; that they could get together for discussions, could correspond freely and receive books and newspapers and magazines, and that he was able to go abroad, though the authorities knew that all his activities would be directed against them. All this every Soviet child and youth knows from Lenin's numerous biographies. I received from some a mumbling, senseless explanation about "Lenin's overcoming all the difficulties put in his path"; others said nothing. The impossibility of finding a real answer did not seem to trouble them; it was as if their minds naturally refused to move on paths outside the familiar ones clearly outlined for them.

The ignorance in every field except their own narrow professions is amazing unless their field happens to be the humanities, the study of which is quite restricted. All they are told of the outside world and their own Soviet past is what the government wants them to know—which is precious little. I repeatedly asked the older generation why they didn't enlighten the younger ones at least about earlier Soviet history. "It would only upset them and shake their faith" was the usual answer. "It would set them against us, they would accuse us of disloyalty. . . . There was enough trouble in the past, let them live in peace now."

I was once in a car with a young man when we happened to pass Lubyanka, the notorious headquarters of the secret police, with its dreaded interrogations and tortures, with prison cells from which many did not come out alive.

"Is there still a prison in this building?" I asked my young companion.

"Prison? Of course not. Whatever made you ask that? There has never been a prison in this building," he assured me in a tone of utmost sincerity.

I later asked his father whether the young man's denial had been prompted by patriotism.

"Oh, no," the father said with embarrassment. "Most young people don't know that part of our past." And again the excuse: "The books and the teachers don't tell them, and why should we disturb them?"

The father should have truthfully added that even now some parents—though infinitely less than in the past—do not feel confident enough to impart this kind of knowledge to their children. However, from other sources I learned that a number of young people do know about Lubyanka and similar items kept from them by their elders. How? When I asked a friend about it, she said with a smile:

"How do children find out all about sex long before we tell them?"

Even with the youngsters, and despite my good resolves, it was not always easy to avoid heated debate when the conversation shifted from small talk. This was caused more than once by their repeated indictments of what they termed our injustice to Paul Robeson, Henry Winston, sick in jail, Howard Fast (at that time when he was still in Moscow's favor), to American Communists on trial and so on.

Their thinking has been so conditioned that neither were they in the least conscious of the idiocy of their indignation over the fact that the United States denies passports to American Communists. They simply brushed aside my point that the Soviet government does not give passports to anyone for travel abroad. I asked about the thousands and thousands of families in the Soviet Union, separated by the war, who were not permitted to join their relatives in the outside world, wives and husbands, parents and children, who longed to be reunited.

None in the room had ever heard of how Khrushchev, during his visit to the United States, had been approached with pleas to permit relatives to leave Russia. Since some of this group was interested in Jewish affairs, I asked about the many older Jews, harassed and feeling totally useless and unwanted in Russia, who were denied permission to join their families in Israel or in the United

States or anywhere else in the world. To my great surprise I found that some of them honestly did not know what I was talking about. It seems that this is a matter which simply is not mentioned outside of a close circle of relatives or friends.

This recalled my own experience in 1938. Not one of even my closest friends knew that I had applied for and been refused permission to leave the Soviet Union. They were told only when I finally did receive permission in 1939 and we were making preparations for our departure. In this respect the situation does not seem to have changed much. Since leaving the Soviet Union is not considered the proper thing to do, the less talk about it the better.

One group of my young friends was especially persevering on the subject of our treatment of American Communists. One sunny day, while sitting peacefully in a meadow at the end of a woods near Moscow, the sound of a creek in our ears, freshly picked flowers in our arms, we got into it again. After listening for the *n*th time to an enumeration of the United States government's crimes against American Communists I asked them:

"Suppose a group of people in the Soviet Union formed a party whose loyalty was not to the Soviet government but to the United States? They publish a paper, they hold meetings, they invariably without any exception, in peace or in war, take sides with the United States whenever there is a conflict between the two countries. What do you think the Soviet government would do to these loyal supporters of the United States?"

One of the young men said with a smile:

"Well, you have a point there."

He was fiercely attacked by the others but it was obvious that they had never looked at it in that light. I don't flatter myself, however, that what I said made a dent in the thinking of even the one who smiled. The influences on these young minds are too monumental for one fleeting thought to have any effect.

During this conversation I learned that they knew nothing at all about the behavior of Communist parties in countries overrun by the Nazis during the Stalin-Hitler pact. Nor did many older people to whom I later talked about it. They had not the slightest idea that the Communist parties in these countries sabotaged the war effort against Hitler, and that the few who dared consider it an anti-Fascist war and lined themselves up with their own countries, like England's Pollitt, were slapped down by the party. This was the kind of news the Russians, both young and old, were totally unable to digest. They pushed it aside as quite unimportant and returned to their attacks on the United States authorities for their treatment of teachers who were members of the Communist party or sympathizers.

"Suppose they do teach Marxism in schools; why shouldn't they be permitted to?" I was asked. They seemed to be very well informed about American teachers who lost their jobs because of their communism; they knew their names and the details of the trials; they knew about their questioning by the government committees, and about their dismissals, and they were most indignant. It used to shock me when this wealth of information would follow a show of total ignorance about highly important world political matters.

When I asked whether Soviet teachers were permitted to teach their pupils about capitalism I was told that, of course, they were; Soviet teachers gave their students all the facts about capitalism, and no one persecuted them for it. I am sure that in some cases this was said with tongue in cheek, but many of them meant every word of it.

I don't want to generalize, and it is true I did meet a few young people who were not satisfied with all the answers they were given, who were searching for their own answers. And I did meet some families where the young trusted their elders and listened to their stories of the past without calling them disloyal. But the prevalent mood, it seems to me, is not theirs.

One fact I was never permitted to forget is that the youth of today is the third Soviet generation, "a product of Soviet society" or "of the revolution." Logically, then, they should be trusted to breathe outside air and to make their own decisions, which they certainly are not. But I met only a few who were conscious of this and still fewer who seriously objected to having their lives thoroughly governed from above. Several told me that they themselves, of course, didn't need this strict guidance any more, that they were so permeated with the Soviet spirit that any direction they would move in on their own would be the right direction. But the people, the great mass of people who had not reached that sublime stage, who could not stand on their own feet, would need this constant proper guidance for at least some time to come. I heard this slightly contemptuous attitude toward "the masses" expressed by intelligent, well-educated people who, it seemed to me, did not seem themselves to mind too much being led by a paternal hand. They called it "party guidance" or "government care for the people."

The extent of this "guidance" was proved to me by questions I was asked like "What did your government say about it?" or "How did you get permission to do it?" when I was telling, for instance, about my trips abroad or about selling our house in the country and buying another, or about how a women's club had organized a literary circle. The constant quizzing about whether the American government permitted us to do this or that made me feel that both old and young accept the leading hand as the one and only way of life.

Despite the thorough indoctrination and thorough loyalty of the young people I met, it was from them that I heard most of the anecdotes that would certainly be called anti-Soviet. Here is an example:

A Russian was asked: "Would it be possible to build communism in the United States?" The answer: "Of course but it would be such a pity."

A variation of the same story went: An Armenian was asked: "Would it be possible to build communism in Armenia?" The answer: "Of course but why not in Georgia?"

Another young man, as loyal a Communist as any I met, told me the following:

An American, a Frenchman and a Russian were discussing the nationality of Adam and Eve in the Garden of Eden. "Of course Adam was an American," said the American; "the first thing he did was to share one of his ribs with Eve. That's what Americans do— share everything they have with others." "Oh, no," said the Frenchman, "Adam and Eve could only be French. They had nothing but love on their minds in Paradise. And who but the French are capable of that?" "Ridiculous!" was the Russian's contribution. "There is no one in this world but a Russian who would have no house to live in, no clothes to wear, nothing but an apple to eat, and insist that he was in Paradise."

I also heard young people openly, without too many ideological undertones, discuss the pros and cons of entering the party, of the duties it imposed and the privileges connected with it, such as advancement in careers, trips abroad, more glamorous vacations. In the past it would have been a difficult task for an intellectual or an artist to become a member of the Communist party. It still is easier for a proletarian. But I was told by a young actress, who was considering applying for membership for its purely practical advantages, that the party wanted a group of ballet dancers she was working with, in order (she thought) to show how thoroughly devoted and loyal every segment of Soviet society is.

In the many conversations with young people, whether we talked about modern art, Hiroshima, the Finnish war, divorces, the rights of man, poetry—and we certainly did roam all over the world and all over human emotions—there was only rarely a reaction or an answer that was the result of original or independent thinking.

There were some lively exchanges among them, even some disagreements, but all their conclusions were based on Soviet teachings and on nothing else. The great majority of the young people I met were a total product of total propaganda. Many of them were attractive and lively and lovable but totally unresponsive to any way of seeing the world but their own. They may listen with interest to tales of the outside world, they certainly want to travel in it, they may look wistfully at some of our possessions, but all this is superficial and does not affect fundamentals. Again and again, after each such exchange I felt and will forever feel the same fear: how easily the pendulum will swing at the slightest command of the Kremlin, and when it does it will bring the end of tourism, of friendliness, of human exchanges and—the ultimate horror—maybe of peace.

There is no doubt in my mind that the Russians do not want war and are terrified at the very thought of it. Neither is there any doubt in my mind that the Kremlin does not want any war as long as its main goal—the spreading the communism—can be successfully achieved by peaceful means or by brush-fire wars. And neither is there any doubt in my mind that if peaceful means fail, the Communist dove may suddenly or gradually, depending on the regime's needs and intentions, emerge as an ugly bird of prey. Whether suddenly or gradually, I believe that the Kremlin will find the proper words and means successfully to transform the present deep and genuine craving of the Soviet people for peace into a mood more appropriate to the changed bird. It has mastered to perfection the words and means necessary for any transformation.

Among the things that interested me greatly was the difference between the attitudes of the young and the old. Some travelers to Russia had mentioned that when people speak of the "bad times" they now mean the years from 1948-1953. I wondered about it before I went. Could the terrible war years have erased and made them forget the years of the purges, the cruelty and terror of which could hardly have been surpassed? The travelers' reports were right. Few Russians speak of the thirties. These years are too far away, too much has happened since, the younger people didn't know them and are not concerned with them. I had left Russia in 1939, at a time when the very air was still full of the purges, when tragic faces pursued one day and night. Today for the younger ones this is a page of history rarely mentioned. It was one of Stalin's errors, something totally unrelated to their life today. Even for those whose families perished in terror it has been pushed aside by the forties and the fifties.

I met hardly a single family among old and new friends and acquaintances who did not count among its members at least one victim of the purges and who did not go through the period that one Russian even in 1960 kept calling "purgatory on earth." He was one of the few who did not forget. It is he who said that the war, of course, was terrible but that he considered it a world-wide calamity, a result of historic clashes, while the purges were purely man-made by Stalin.

But few think—or talk—in these terms. This is a topic of conversation most people would rather avoid. A chance remark here and there made it clear that the purges had greatly influenced their careers and their personal lives. Some were ruined; others found their careers advanced as they stepped into the shoes of those who disappeared. An engineer now in his fifties found himself at twenty-seven at the head of a large organization because every man above him had been arrested. He told me that this happened in innumerable organizations, plants, hospitals and universities. He also said that it did not do the economy of the country much good to lose the best men in every field. He was one of the few who throughout my stay did not clam up when I asked about the effects of the purges. But even this man, who was able to discuss it openly and intelligently, cannot talk about it with his own children. They are not interested, he said; when he mentions the purges they regard him with suspicion when they are in a serious mood or call him "a fossil" when in a lighter one.

At times in general discussion the older generation showed irritation, even anger, toward the younger who take in their stride the progress Russia has made. To those in their fifties the achievements of today are a source of endless wonder. Much less so to their children, who take everything as their due and who want much more of it and very soon too. They are, of course, no less proud and enthusiastic than their elders, but the reasons lie less in the well-stocked stores and new houses than in the strong voice with which the Soviet Union speaks to the world.

Some foreign observers, including Americans, have said and written that the present young generation as it grows older will give

Khrushchev and his successors cause for concern, since they lack the total submissiveness that Stalin succeeded so well in instilling in their parents. I too gained that impression. Never once did I have the feeling that any of the young people looked over their shoulders before expressing their thoughts, even when those thoughts were not 100 per cent party line.

It does not seem possible to me that Stalin's barbarous methods could be revived. Neither do they seem necessary to gain youth's unreserved following as long as its aspirations are being considered. A thirst for decent living and deep patriotism and nationalism are the driving forces through which with clever manipulation—and no one can accuse Khrushchev of lack of this—he can continue successfully to handle them. (If I keep saying Khrushchev without mentioning any possible future Soviet rulers it is simply because I don't venture to look far ahead, and what I see ahead at present is a firmly entrenched Khrushchev.)

What I was looking for among the young people and what I definitely did not find was that New Soviet Man who was to have been created in the Soviet Union—the one about whom endless poems were recited and songs were sung, a man the like of whom the world had yet not seen. I found no trace of him anywhere. Even in the very young I saw the characteristics of Russians as I have always known them. There are still poems and songs about the New Soviet Man, but I wonder whether anyone over fourteen or fifteen has the slightest illusion that Soviet economics wedded to the teachings of Marx will ever remake the Soviet men and women into the artificial image created by the Kremlin. There was a time when some believed it. This belief has been washed away in rivers of grandiloquent words which have totally lost their meaning and, though still being mouthed, now arouse only total boredom.

CHAPTER FOURTEEN

Of Books and the Press

As often as the Russians asked me "What kind of people are the Americans?" I am asked in the United States "What kind of people are the Russians?" A satisfactory answer would require a long study and a long book. I can only reply with a few fleeting personal observations. Those I discussed this with in Moscow as a rule agreed that Russians show little of the middle. They are kind and warm and charitable at their best; they can also be ruthless and inhumanly cruel, as the pogroms in the Czarist days and the bestial excesses of the Stalin regime showed. When the cruelties under Stalin were mentioned, there were always some dissenting voices. Hitler's atrocities were brought up as examples of real bestialities, so much worse than anything Stalin ever did; others would answer that Hitler's savagery did not excuse the cruel methods of the secret police under Stalin.

Obviously what goes on in Russia today and the way the Russians behave has many of its roots in October, 1917. But not all. No history starts only forty-three years back, and certainly not the history of an old immense country like Russia. To know some of Russia's yesterdays helps to understand much of her todays just as American todays cannot be grasped without knowledge of her yesterdays.

For example, the enthusiasm of those who are, out of idealism, devoted to the Soviet regime has, though very different in its expressions and its effects, something in common with the idealism that pervaded many past generations of Russians. To perform useful work, to serve the People, is an aspiration which runs as a red thread throughout Russia's life from the early nineteenth century and is fully reflected in her literature.

There was a short period when this thread paled and many of the young as well as the not so young, disillusioned by the failure of the 1905 revolution lost their zeal. This too was reflected in literature, especially in the poetry of the decade before the 1917 revolution. It was individualistic, egocentric, not at all in the tradition of the older Russian poets, in whose poetry appeals for love of the people, for service to them, for freedom, for self-sacrifice were important themes.

The zeal for improving the lot of the common people, of those neglected and injured by fate, "forgotten by Providence," was part and parcel of old Russia and found its reflection in much of Russian life. One occasionally gets an echo of this concern and of this spirit in Russia today. The Soviet government gives the entire credit to Marxism, to communism, for everything positive that is done and felt in Russia today. I would give a share to Russia's past.

At the dawn of Russian literary life writers and poets were servants of the state, and they existed and created for the glory of the state. But with the emergence of Russia into the Western world came a great change, and new brilliant pages were written into Russian literature. Then, after the Bolshevik revolution, Russian writers and poets, with some notable exceptions, reverted to their old servility to the regime and, like engineers, ballet dancers, machinists, teachers, peasants, football players and everyone else in the Soviet Union, learned to fulfill plans and became masters of the art of skillfully dancing on the tightrope of the constantly changing party line.

Hardly any present-day visitor to Russia fails to comment on how much the people read. It certainly is impressive. But in old Russia too reading was a most popular pastime, and there has always been a tremendous thirst for knowledge. It was, of course, extremely limited because of the prevailing illiteracy of the masses. But those who could read, read a great deal. Even the more popular magazines had yearly supplements of complete works of the great Russian writers: Tolstoi, Gogol, Pushkin, Turgenev, Dostoevski, Goncharov, Lermontov, to name only some of them. There was also kniga-kopeika (book-kopeck), tiny modestly printed paperbacks of short stories or poems by classical writers sold for one kopeck (a penny). People reading books in streetcars, on railways trains, on park benches were a familiar sight even in the old days.

In the Czarist days, when schools were not hospitable to the lower classes, those with a social conscience among the better educated did all they could without arousing too greatly the wrath of the authorities to organize popular lectures and readings of good literature for factory workers. From the moment I learned how to read and to write I was constantly teaching others. So did my mother, so did my older sister, so did everyone else I knew. This was considered a sacred obligation for people who were privileged enough to receive an education. Our pupils could be the cook or the janitor or their children, a peasant child near the summer cottage where we used to spend our summers, or a peasant in the village near which my maternal grandparents lived.

Even in out-of-the-way provincial towns there were small groups of people carrying high the torch of culture. The group would consist of the local doctors, lawyers, druggists, printers, teachers, liberal landowners, liberal judges, and clerks. These people represented the intellectual-liberal element, sometimes with Socialist undertones, in their town. They were the center for educational work among those who needed it, for intercession before the authorities when injustice was done to people who were unable to defend themselves, for reading and discussing the latest literature, for supplying food, money, even hiding places and escape possibilities for political victims of the regime. Today's Russia excludes anything even remotely resembling independent activity in any field, especially in the field of helping victims of the regime.

I was told once of a "clandestine" group getting together to read Pasternak's poetry or the poetry or prose of other writers whose work has no hope of reaching above the Soviet surface. Others get together to discuss what they heard over Western radios or from other non-Soviet sources, or anything else as sinister as that. These groups are limited, of course, to totally trusted friends.

Of course, the puny individual attempts of Czarist days cannot be compared with the gigantic efforts the Soviet government is making to bring books to the people. I remember in the thirties how our maid, who had only recently learned to read and write, diligently fought her way through Tolstoi's *Anna Karenina,* a copy of which she had bought after listening to it for many evenings when it was read over the radio. By introducing universal compulsory education the Soviet government has satisfied an immense dormant urge in the Russian people. The number of people with books in their hands, which so amazes and impresses foreign visitors, is merely proof of the old Russian longing which before the revolution had no outlet.

"Fat" (this was what they were called in old Russia) monthlies, much larger than our *Harper's* or *Atlantic Monthly* carried excellent erudite articles on politics, philosophy, art, as well as short stories or long novels in installments, poetry, literary criticism, bibliography. The present Soviet monthlies, not so "fat" maybe, are in the old Russian tradition and, to a certain extent, imitate the prerevolutionary ones. But, despite the strict Czarist censor, the magazines under the old regime were infinitely freer, richer as reading material, and certainly more nourishing for the soul and mind than the present so much more strictly censored magazines.

Old Russian literature is full of the word "darkness" in many variations, darkness being a synonym for illiteracy. Numerous Russian sayings express this thought. The most popular of these, "Knowledge is light, ignorance is darkness," I first heard at the age of six and innumerable times after that. In 1915 I spent a few months in Petrograd. Russia was then in the midst of war and the Central Post Office used to be full of people looking for someone to write a letter for

them to a husband, a father, a son at the front. And with the request the words "God punished us, left us in darkness" were heard
again and again. The Bolsheviks found a most fertile soil for their
drive against illiteracy.

Though the seeds of the Russians' love of reading were sown long
ago, I was told on several occasions that the avidity with which they
read today has some practical motivations. Some said that they
would probably read less if they had a greater variety of entertainment or some other escape from the cares of their daily lives. For
others the reading of certain books and magazines was a means of
advancing in their careers. And for still others reading was a symbol
of having achieved a higher station in life.

Intellectuals in Russia are not sneered at as eggheads, nor are they
regarded with wary suspicion, as they too often are in the United
States. Indeed, I was unable to convey the American meaning of the
word to my Russian friends, and not only because there is no translation for it. It was beyond their comprehension that anyone would
use a disparaging word when speaking of an educated person. To be
well educated and well read is an advantage in the eyes of Soviet
society. Of course, one must be well read and well educated within
limits strictly prescribed by the current Soviet line. Original thinking and independent exploration of knowledge are looked upon with
suspicion not so much by next-door neighbors as, what is much more
alarming, by the authorities. Soviet eggheads are considered important useful members of Soviet society. They look down their
noses at our equivalent of petty bourgeois, the same species that in
the United States look down their noses at our domestic brand of
eggheads. Teaching is a highly respected profession. Even a teacher
in an elementary school or high school is an honored person, while
college professors belong to the top strata of Soviet society.

The thirst for knowledge goes on unabated. The revolution
opened the dikes, and the torrent shows no sign of slowing down.
Young and old, elevator women, hotel doormen, cab drivers, railway
porters, grandmothers watching children on playgrounds, people on
buses, on park benches, in cafés, are rarely seen these days with-

out a book or magazine in hand or pocket. Lecture halls are crowded, there are correspondence courses of all kinds, and any opportunity to enrich one's mind (or advance one's career) is avidly seized.

Russians display an intense interest in foreign literature, an obvious sign of their longing to have more information about the outside world than the tiny trickle available to them. Some told me that being hermetically cut off from any other access to the West made them grab any available translation of foreign literature. However, even though many expressed regret that not enough translations from foreign literature were available, they seldom seemed to feel frustrated at not being part of this outside world of which they want to know more. To my direct questions I was told, first, that the Western world had negative features which they didn't envy and wanted no part of; second, that they were now well on the way to achieving the positive aspects of this world without acquiring its defects. This may sound like official propaganda and it certainly is. But many who said this sounded sincere and believed it. And that is what matters and what it is important for us to know and to understand.

Despite the tremendous popularity of any literature coming from the Western world, the old love and admiration for Russian classics has not diminished. Though they appear in astronomical editions, they are hardly ever to be found in bookstores, for they are sold out literally within hours if they show up there at all. The only way to assure oneself of the books is to subscribe for them the moment a notice of a new edition and the terms of subscription are published in the press. In all the bookstores one finds long lists of subscription publications with notices of new volumes available to subscribers. There are always crowds around these lists hoping to find the names of current volumes due on their subscriptions. Those who have no subscriptions or delay even a few days after the appearance of a popular book have to wait for several months or even longer until the books they missed begin to show up in the secondhand bookshops.

Moscow abounds in regular and secondhand bookshops, and there are sidewalk tables at which books are sold—all over the city—new and old books, textbooks and novels, books of poetry, science and art —and they are thronged with customers. I spent many hours in bookstores trying to find out who was reading what. I was unable to come to a definite conclusion. In the same store I once saw an elegantly, even frivolously dressed young woman buy a heavy political tome and an elderly plain-looking and plainly dressed woman buy a sizzling secondhand old French novel (in translation). One impression, however, was definite. Fiction, foreign and Russian, and books on science move infinitely faster than do the piles of political pamphlets or, for instance, the collected speeches of old man Kalinin. The former president of the Soviet Union hardly ever wrote a speech by himself and, though good-natured and friendly, he was certainly never known for brilliant and original thinking.

A man once quoted to me from my husband's book, *This Is Our World*. Knowing that he had good connections, I was not surprised that he had been able to get hold of it. Many foreign books critical of the Soviet regime are translated and circulated in Moscow among a very small privileged and trusted group. This man had read all of Churchill's memoirs as well as several other war books written by Western military leaders, some of them highly critical of the Soviet government. He, by the way, told me that the most widely read and best liked foreign writer at the present moment was Remarque. I often wondered at the popularity of certain foreign writers in the Soviet Union. I asked this man why some authors, not especially widely known in their own countries, like Mitchell Wilson, for instance, become so popular in Russia. He answered exactly as a number of other Russians had. "Because they have been translated and others have not. It has nothing to do with their being superior to others." In short, anything translated from Western languages is widely read.

The Russians have always been great admirers of Mark Twain and he was often mentioned to me as their favorite among American writers. And he was in the public eye more than ever after an attack by a critic in the *Literary Gazette* on *The Autobiography of Mark Twain* edited by the American writer Charles Neider.

The Russians have for years been imbued with propaganda about the cruel treatment of Negroes in the United States. The official stress on Mark Twain's protests against this treatment as well as on his criticism of other negative features of American life has added enormously to his popularity in Russia. The attack on Neider's book was based on the fact that it did not cover these—according to the Russians—supremely important themes in his writing. Since Neider was permitted to answer in the Soviet press the attack on his book— and this in itself was a sensation—Mark Twain came up in many conversations.

How could a book on Mark Twain be written without the emphasis on Negroes, etc., etc., I was asked again and again in exactly the same words. I tried to explain that there was so much more to Mark Twain than this; that his criticism of prejudice and other evils was part of his deep hatred of hypocrisy and cruelty and enslavement wherever and under whatever guise he found it. As clearly as I possibly could I implied that he certainly would not have liked what he would have found in the Soviet Union today. But apparently it wasn't easy for the Russians to see how well the shoe fitted.

In one of the many conversations I had about Pasternak a young woman, a loyal Communist, assured me that Pasternak must have had passages in his book which distorted history or which the authorities considered objectionable at the time. The idea that the reader could be the judge of what was right for him to read was too outlandish for her to comprehend. She was one of the few 100 percenters who deplored the shameful way in which the Pasternak affair was handled. But she put the blame solely on the West. She accused the West of sheer sensationalism whenever the slightest dissent came to the surface in Soviet literature.

Like many other Russians, she could not understand the excitement abroad about Dudintsev's novel *Not by Bread Alone*. In that novel the author describes the thorny path of a Soviet engineer who was hampered in his good work by bureaucratic officialdom. She

considered it, as many others did, a badly written book on a subject
which, she said, others had treated much better. She did, however,
reluctantly agree that he happened to be the first to write about a
subject that had been taboo before. No party or high government
official or anyone in a high position had ever been attacked in literature before Dudintsev.

A young man who was present at this exchange sarcastically
asked: "Wasn't our first Sputnik quite a shock to you after you had
so relished a novel about that poor nice Soviet engineer who got
nowhere with his inventions because of those nasty Soviet bureaucrats?"

I met many who complained that they had no time at all to read
fiction, that there was precious little time to read even what appeared in their own field. I frequently saw a young electronics
engineer and never once was he without a pamphlet or article sticking out of his coat pocket.

Those who did find time to read novels often spoke with derision
of the dullness of most fiction. The novels most read and discussed
are those that have at least some passages that deviate from the
official line or that show in some other way a spark of individuality,
a quality lacking in Soviet literature for a long, long time. People
definitely want less of the total black and total white they were fed
for decades. Fortunately, there are novels now in which a party
member does not have to be all lily-white or a non-Communist all
bad. Some of it sounds almost human.

As for the press: for decades now the same bombastic terminology, the same banalities, as well as the same appeals and the
same kinds of pictures have appeared in the Soviet papers. They
seem to bore city people, who for the most part ignore them. In
Moscow one hears plenty of derisive remarks about the Soviet press.
The truth is that this fare is not meant for the Moscow sophisticates.
It is extremely important, however, to the champion dairymaid and
her collective farm when she is shown on the first page of *Pravda*
shaking hands with Khrushchev, to a plant in the Urals, to a new
city in the Siberian wilderness, that their managers and builders are

singled out for praise in its columns and in the press all over the country. But even if not interested in the details of dairy farming and new machinery, the Moscovites will not miss a word of a speech by Khrushchev, knowing the importance to their daily lives of every word of the speech.

Once, when I had dinner in the hotel restaurant the waiter put me right under a radio blasting out a speech. Since there were several free tables, I asked him to put me farther away from the radio or lower the volume. His response was a look clearly informing me that I must be out of my mind. The man making the speech was Khrushchev, reporting on the summit failure, and the waiter, knowing that I spoke Russian, was showing me the courtesy of the place of honor. There was nothing I could do about it. United States-Soviet relations were strained enough without my adding more strain.

I did not regret it. It was interesting to catch every nuance of Khrushchev's voice, the calculated anger and moderation. It was an important speech and I listened with attention, to the great pleasure of the waiter. In the middle of the speech Khrushchev very informally said something like "Now, let's have an intermission, you must be tired and hungry," whereupon the waiter came over for a chat. He spoke of Khrushchev and the situation in general in a highly patriotic tone. This was neither the time nor the place to get onto controversial subjects, especially since, after a few amenities about peace and friendship between our countries, we indulged in a much more lengthy conversation about his children and my grandchildren.

During the next few days without exception every person I spoke with had heard or read (or both) the speech and approved of it. The Russians are always extremely proud whenever they feel that Khrushchev talks as an equal to the West.

Russians also devour eagerly every word of the meager news of the outside world, as well as the few stories with a human interest angle. Literary newspapers and magazines quickly disappear from the stands; so does the Weekly Supplement of *Izvestia*, introduced by Khrushchev's son-in-law, who is trying to give the Soviet Union a new more diversified journalism. Some of the literary newspapers, as well as *Komsomolskaya Pravda* and the liveliest of all Moscow newspapers, *Vechernaya Moskva* (Evening Moscow) print Letters to the Editor, frequently criticizing an article in the paper or someone else's letter to the editor or registering a complaint. These letters could, of course, be inspired by the paper itself as they were in the past—when they were inevitably followed by an investigation and severe punishment of the culprits—but many of the letters sounded quite genuine.

But even if all of them were planted it means that it is now considered a good policy to have diversified opinions on some subjects appear in the press. These could be personal problems, like love, marriage, or the behavior of youth, labor conditions, work efficiency, housing, the poor quality of furniture, mismanagement, and much more. During my stay in Moscow there was much talk about the famous letter to *Komsomolskaya Pravda* by an obviously disgusted reader—protesting the fortunes spent on exploring the skies while there was still so much to do for those on earth. The paper printed several replies strongly in favor of space exploration.

In discussing this letter with my friends I always mentioned that in the United States and in Western Europe there was much criticism of the tremendous amount of money being spent for space exploration at the expense of schools, housing, hospitals, conventional defense. Only a few of the many Russians I talked to felt that perhaps some of the money being spent on space could be better spent closer to home. The great majority, including people who talked very openly with me, did not agree. Oh, no, they said, both kinds of spending created numerous jobs. Besides, it made people proud of their country. This latter point seems to be of utmost importance. However, not once while I was there did I read a letter that took issue with a government pronouncement, and certainly not one on Soviet foreign policy.

Like so many travelers to Russia before me, I was amazed at the great number of quotations the Russians are fed from the United States Constitution, from the Declaration of Independence, from Jefferson and Lincoln. Of course, the purpose of this is not to acclaim the virtues of the American system but to show how far present-day America has veered from her own original ideas. The Russians are also fed a plethora of stories in connection with those quotations. They were told, for instance, about Americans who had refused to sign the Declaration of Independence when asked to by people who wanted to find out to what extent Senator McCarthy had succeeded in intimidating the man in the street. They were not told what it was, and the language in it had sounded too subversive for that period. The Soviet press reprinted this story from the American papers, and people relished repeating it to me. The fact that it was freely printed in our press and the cowardice of the people editorially attacked made less impression on my Russian friends than the story itself.

The Soviet press had also widely circulated a comment from the American press to the effect that the signers of the Declaration as well as others responsible for the creation of the United States would these days be regarded with suspicion by their neighbors, that their ideas would be considered radical in today's America. It is amazing how Russians delight in repeating these stories without ever drawing a comparison with their own press, in which the appearance of similar comment would be thoroughly unthinkable.

Most of the Russians I met believed, if not everything, at least a great deal of what they heard or read. Even those who regularly listened to Western broadcasts more than once defended the totally distorted view of the United States that their government drills into them. When I asked why they listened to the Voice of America if they didn't believe what they heard, some said they listened out of curiosity, others to pick up news they didn't get at home, but they all insisted that they definitely did not listen in order to be influenced by the American point of view. To pick up news they don't get at home is probably the more truthful answer. During my stay I heard, for instance, several reports from Russians who listened with great interest to the Voice's account of Eichman's capture in Argentina. The Eichman story was given only a few words in the Soviet press many weeks after it happened.

In connection with the Voice, I once astonishẹd my hosts. A teacher of English who listened regularly—solely to improve his English, he assured me—mentioned Patterson's victory over Johanssen, adding that he knew it would hardly interest me. The unrestrained delight which I displayed aroused general surprise and amusement. They simply could not imagine my counterpart—a respectable Russian grandmother—shouting with joy over a boxing event.

It seems unlikely that the Soviet press ever misses an opportunity to find fault with the United States. A Russian magazine enumerated films including *The Defiant Ones* which the State Department would not allow to be sent to the Soviet Union. They were films which, as the magazine put it, "may reflect negatively on the capitalist system." The ban was mentioned to me, with a criticism of the State Department and a triumphant "You see?" When I asked: "Let us assume that you had any films showing a negative aspect of the Soviet system, would you send such a film to the United States? Look at *Dr. Zhivago,* with his criticism of a situation forty years old." I received from at least one person that same vague smile which I had met several times and was never able to interpret satisfactorily. I optimistically called it the "you have something there" smile. In other cases a smile in answer to what I was saying was less enigmatic. It was definitely a smile of pity for me for having fallen so deeply under capitalist influence, for not understanding how wrong anything coming from the "enemy camp" is when it contradicts the Soviet position.

What my Russian friends could not understand was that in the United States a book, a play, a picture, a symphony, a speech by the President or any other political personality could be severely criticized in one newspaper or over one radio station and highly praised by another. Inevitably somebody would ask how were the people to know what was right if they heard and read different, even opposite opinions.

More than once almost the exact words of the talk which Pearl Buck had in the forties with Masha Scott (the Russian-born wife of the American journalist John Scott) occurred in conversations in Moscow of 1960. Masha then said:

"We would not find in our country [that was said not long after her arrival from Russia] two completely different points of view in our press, that is, one man says this is true and another says it is not true. How can the people know which is the truth?"

This thought was expressed in every conversation I had regarding the American press.

As a matter of fact, many of the Russians didn't really approve of the press's freedom to criticize. An old friend who loyally and dutifully disagreed with every aspect of American policy and with the American President in particular told me of her shock when one of the Soviet papers printed a caricature lampooning a golf-playing Eisenhower.

"This is going too far," she said sternly, "this should never have been permitted. Even though we must severely criticize Eisenhower for the U-2 and for his foreign policies we should never go so far as to make fun of him in a cartoon."

When I told her that Eisenhower's golf had been a favorite target of American cartoonists for years and that newspapers, radio and TV freely criticized him, her eyes opened wide in astonishment. The questions she asked me in our subsequent conversations showed that this made a deeper inroad on her previous thinking about the United States than anything else I had said. I gained the impression that the United States never seemed the same to her after that.

Another fact that seemed to make a tremendous impression on her (and on a number of others) was that American political figures, writers, scientists, and journalists submit to completely unrehearsed interviews for the press, on TV and radio, and that people of opposite parties and opinions appear together at such unrehearsed interviews and forums. She had never heard of anything like it before and had she not known me as well as she did she probably would not have believed me. But I am afraid I was unable to convince her, as I was unable to convince other Russians, that cartoons and criticism of Khrushchev in the United States papers are not printed by order of the government as those of an American President in the Soviet press are by Soviet authorities.

Russians accept without too much questioning any kind of news coverage, no matter how sketchy or erratic. An event widely covered in the American press was the plight of four Russian sailors who had drifted in the Pacific for forty-nine days without ever a word about them in the Soviet press during the entire time. But as soon as the American press reported their rescue it was given more space than had been devoted to any individuals for years, aside from labor heroes. I asked several people why, though the authorities certainly must have known that a boat with four men was missing, it had not been mentioned before. If it had happened to four Americans, I said, the United States press would have given it the fullest coverage. Why were the seamen received afterward with such acclaim and honor when not a soul, except their families, had been interested in them during those forty-nine days? My questions were answered with indifferent shrugs. Russians are definitely not in the habit of asking and answering this kind of question. The authorities obviously did not find it necessary to report the event before but did so later. That's all. What was there to wonder about and to discuss?

Incidentally, there are no gossip columnists in Russia and people as a rule show little interest in the personal details of the lives of those outside their own little circle. I well remember the frustrations of American correspondents in Moscow when asked for reports on the private lives of Soviet leaders. No Russian could—or would if he could—enlighten them.

This has not changed. In 1960 I found that I knew infinitely more about Khrushchev's family than any Russian I met. The Soviet press never mentions anything personal about them. But few Moscovites showed any interest in the details of Khrushchev's family life which I had learned from the American press. They are deeply interested in every one of his words and decrees because these so greatly affect their lives. But what difference could it possibly make to them what dress Mrs. Khrushchev wore or whether a daughter of his went to a theater or to a museum?

People are obviously starved for a lighter note in their press. More than once young people who read English or French delightedly recounted to me stories of human interest from the London *Daily Worker* and the Paris *Humanité*. They would not believe me when I told them that never before had I heard of anyone's reading the Communist press for amusement. After a couple of weeks in Moscow, starved for any word from the outside, I bought copies of those two papers. In comparison with the Soviet press they could easily win a contest for lightness and wit. And it certainly did not sound like a great compliment to the Soviet press when Soviet readers of the foreign Communist papers expressed the hope that someday their own press would be as lively and entertaining as the *Daily Worker* and *Humanité*. The same hope was once voiced by a middle-aged Communist who regularly reads the Italian paper *Unità*.

The stories most often quoted as entertaining from the foreign Communist press were usually "society scandals," showing the depravity of bourgeois society. But from the way these stories were repeated to me, it wasn't so much our depravity that interested the Soviet reader as the scandal itself, especially if sex was involved, which it usually was. News of sex crimes or involving sex in any way is taboo in Soviet print.

This prudery about sex, which anyone familiar with today's Soviet literature is aware of, is not altogether new, though it is immensely overdone these days. Puritanism was reflected in prerevolutionary as well as in much of the postrevolutionary literature. With few exceptions, Soviet writers were quite puritan in their language even in the days when the government was little concerned with the sexual mores of its citizens, and free love, marriage and divorce were left to the conscience of the individual.

During our years in Moscow we often had difficulty in making the uninhibited discussion of sex, so popular among our American visitors in the twenties and thirties, acceptable to our Russian friends, who rarely indulged in the details of sexology and certainly not in such candid terms and not in the presence of strangers. The present-day attitudes of Russians toward sex and much else are certainly based to a large extent on the pressures and demands of the Soviet regime. But some definitely derive from the fact that they are Russians and, like other peoples, have throughout centuries developed certain ways, traits and traditions.

Nevertheless, as I studied the Russian press I was conscious of a slight lessening of the conformity of the Stalin period. The naïve absurdity of Soviet satire, as reflected in its official mouthpiece, the weekly *Krokodil,* can hardly appeal to an even slightly sophisticated taste, any more than can the drabness of the daily press. However, I found something in both that had not been there before.

The satire at times, still much too rarely, is slightly more subtle. It was even able to arouse in me an occcasional faint smile which I doubt it ever did in the past. Maybe there is hope again for Russian satirists, of whom there were many excellent ones before the revolution as well as during the first years after it. They were among Stalin's first victims, for he was shrewd enough to know the dangerous impact of humor and satire.

CHAPTER FIFTEEN

The Theater

Like books and magazines, Russian theaters before the revolution were for the literate minority and, like reading, theatergoing was a most beloved pastime. I well remember standing in line in deep snow on freezing nights with hundreds of other theater enthusiasts to make sure of a seat high up in the gallery. These were the only seats my friends and I wanted, even if some could have afforded the more expensive and easily procured seats. That was part of the fun as well as of the ideological attitude. A couple of years later the Metropolitan Opera gallery and the many hours of standing in line for tickets reminded me of my Russian theatergoing.

The excellence of the Russian theater is no more a Soviet invention than is the Russians' addiction to theatergoing. Even before the revolution the Russian theater held its place among the most illustrious. It still is good but today the world-famous Russian theaters have an aura of the past. There is less that is daring and new in them than in some of the more experimental theaters in Western countries. Stalin can be thanked for this. After a few years in the twenties, when exciting innovations presaged a place for the Soviet theater among the most advanced theaters in the world, Stalin's heavy hand descended. That was the end of any daring in the drama as it was in poetry, architecture, art, literature, ballet, and in whatever his hand could touch, which was everything. Some of the younger theaters now show a spark of the mid-twentieth-century temper, and it is possible that the Russian theater may again take its old place among the path-breakers. But it will have lost decades which the rest of the theatrical world has meanwhile used for experiment and discovery.

The Russian theatergoers, with I hope some exceptions, do not seem to be disturbed by comparisons with the past or with the outside world. They love their theaters, they fill them nightly, and they make it very hard for visitors to get tickets for good shows. I envied those tourists whose lack of the language freed them of the agony of hearing day after day the voice at the Intourist desk in charge of theater tickets repeat, "I am sorry, I couldn't get you a ticket." They could usually get tickets to the opera or ballet, since the Intourist had standing arrangements with the respective theaters. They did not, however, have these arrangements with most of the Moscow theaters devoted to the spoken word only and frequented exclusively by a Russian-speaking audience.

The exception was the famous Moscow Art Theater for which Intourist had a limited number of tickets for foreign visitors. The reputation of this theater, based on its flawless performances, compelled many a foreigner to sit through an evening listening to an unfamiliar language. I did not go to the Art Theater. I had in the past seen many of its unforgettable performances. But they belonged to the past. I was eager to catch whatever breath of the new I possibly could and went exclusively to the newer theaters.

To get a ticket to the Russian equivalent of a Broadway hit is as hard as it is in New York. And infinitely harder if a play included an allusion or two to situations as a rule not mentioned in public. There was one such play in Moscow while I was there and the Intourist young lady who knew how much I wanted to see this play frankly said one day: "You may get a ticket soon, the play is being cleaned up and then there won't be such a rush for tickets." The cleaning up—the removal of some political allusions—came after I left.

In New York it takes people a minute or two from the noisy street to reach their theater seats through most prosaic, uninspiring narrow and crowded entrances. The mood of the street and the conversations usually continue through the introductory music until the first words are spoken on the stage. In this respect Russia has remained true to its old theatrical tradition. A theater is still called "a temple of art," as it was in my youth. A Moscow theater generates a very definite emotion; you enter it with a specific mood which belongs exclusively to the theater.

Theater has always been and is now one of the great loves of my life, and among the world's theaters the Russian always held first place with me. But this time I enjoyed my Moscow theater visits as much for the conversations with my neighbors as for what I was seeing on the stage. The fact that I came from the United States— a fact I never postponed disclosing for too long—opened a flow of questions and answers on both sides.

The outstanding impression I carried away from my theatergoing was given me by the Children's Theater, which had always been my favorite. I would have gone anyway but I also went for sentimental reasons. I used in the past to take my sons there and I enjoyed the performances no less than they did. This theater had been one of the best in the past and still is. When the woman director who was its inspiration was arrested during the purges, it was a day of mourning for Moscow theater lovers.

Like all Moscow theaters, this is a repertory house. The actors are not accidentally thrown together for one play and there is perfect harmony in their acting. It has an excellent cast of adult performers, many of them graduates of the Theatrical School attached to the theater, which also supplies the child actors. Its repertory is a mixture of classics, fantasy and politics. The last-named has these days little of the heavyhandedness of the past. It is presented with a light touch, easy to digest, and probably more likely to remain in one's mind.

At the play which I saw I sat not far from the seats we had had when my son George once interrupted a performance. The play then was about a German anti-fascist fleeing from the Nazis. Before disappearing into the underground, he came to say good-by to his wife and child. As he was leaning over the child's crib one heard the stamping feet and voices of the approaching SS men. The man kissed the child and disappeared through the window. But this was only the beginning of the play and for the sake of its later development he left his hat on the table. George, then eleven, in desperation let out an agonizing cry: "Your hat, your hat, you forgot your hat!"

The play I saw this last time was called *Kolka my Friend* and was recommended to me by the same George who on a visit to Moscow had seen it a few weeks earlier.

The play was severely critical of the school Pioneer leader, a silly, bureaucratic woman; of a Komsomol leader, son of a father in high position, cold, well dressed, sure of himself and, like the Pioneer leader, totally devoid of any understanding and sympathy for the children; and of his mother, the chairwoman of the Parents' Council (I only hope that during my years in that capacity I had nothing in common with her), expensively dressed, stupid, fully conscious of her lofty position in the Soviet hierarchy, playing to the hilt the role of charitable patroness.

On their side were some of the children, the careerists, the flatterers. On the other side was an assistant Pioneer leader, a truck driver and former juvenile delinquent who had been brought up in a reform school and was now enthusiastically devoted to helping children in trouble. The hero, Kolka, is the one in difficulty. His father is a drunkard, there is no money and no warmth at home. The truck driver, besides bringing a breath of fresh air into the school, is fighting for Kolka who is threatened with dismissal by the three other officials and by the Pioneers because they consider him depraved, a hooligan, a bad influence on the nicer children. Of course, the truck driver saves him at the end.

But before the end about two dozen other children appear, good and bad, every one of them an individual quite unlike the one-faced mechanical group that would have been presented in the past. This seemed important to me. But even more important seemed the total absence of the party line. Though the most positive character in the play was a proletarian, he was a totally unrepresentative proletarian, with dark spots in his past, never using party slogans or bureaucratic terminology, teaching the children to use their own imaginations, to object to whatever they thought was wrong regardless of where the orders came from.

Another phenomenon that struck me was the reaction of the audience, which consisted mostly of school children. They shouted approvingly and applauded the truck driver, Kolka, and the children on their side, and jeered at the trio of villains (who represented some of the evils of present-day Soviet society: the cold indifferent bureaucracy and the new contemptuous upper class), as well as the young hooligans who tried to win over Kolka and who cursed and smoked and stole and who in the past would certainly not have been shown at all unless also severely punished. To represent as villains members of the Komsomol and the elected chairwoman of the Parents' Council is revolutionary enough. But there was more.

I understood from my neighbors, a young couple, both students at the Moscow Pedagogical Institute, that before the play opened it was shown to the Moscow school principals. Many of them indignantly walked out in the middle of the play and demanded that it be withdrawn and certainly not be shown to children. Remarkably, they did not win. When I saw it it had been running for many months to sold-out houses. I went early in order to watch the audience, and saw many organized school groups come with their teachers.

My two neighbors loved the play but the young woman was not sure that it was right for school children. She wondered whether it wouldn't put ideas of rebellion into their heads. Then she sadly added:

"I love the play now. But who knows? In a few years I may change and become as bureaucratic as the woman Pioneer leader."

Her companion loved the play without any reservations, thought that it was a perfect picture of many Communist youth leaders he knew, and presented a situation that, like any evil, should be brought into the open. When the young woman said that she didn't think children should be presented with controversial ideas, different from those they were taught, unless the answers were spelled out clearly, I said that I believed that controversial ideas should be presented to children as well as to adults. They both smiled, and I left the conversation at that.

My theater-going confirmed the feeling I had throughout the weeks in Moscow that I was living in an old-fashioned world. In what I saw there was rarely anything truly imaginative, fanciful, unique, odd, daring. There are magnificent sports spectacles, exquisite ballets, no less enchanting national dances. There are excellent theater performances, outstanding concerts, a few good variety shows, spectacular festive illuminations. But all these have existed for some time without much change. As I listened in vain for exciting new ideas, so I looked in vain for something truly new and different, especially for something daring. One may find it anywhere in the world but not in the Brave New World of Communism.

After a while one had the feeling of having seen it all long ago.

CHAPTER SIXTEEN

Culture Has Many Meanings

The word "culture" in Russia has many applications unfamiliar to us. For example, to enter a theater or concert hall wearing one's coat is considered "uncultured" and is strictly prohibited. It is as hard to explain to American visitors today as it was twenty and thirty years ago why they had to leave even light summer wraps in the checkroom before entering the hall. It makes good sense during the long snowy winter months when coats and boots are wet and heavy, but Russians lack the knack of adjusting easily to different circumstances, and in this case summer weather. To wear even the flimsiest summer coat in a theater is a sign of lack of "culture."

Some of the maids in my hotel unburdened their hearts to me about the uncultured behavior of American tourists. Their main complaint was about men. When breakfast was brought into the room, for instance, an American coming out from under the shower, might appear with a towel around his middle or, just as bad from a Russian point of view, in his shorts. The waitress would indignantly leave the room, taking the breakfast tray with her. I tried hard to explain to them that the towel or shorts were not intended as an insult. But this is one of the arguments I definitely did not win. They had one answer:

"It is uncultured. This is a hotel and not a beach." They took

167

the Americans' behavior as an insult to Russian womanhood.

One woman said that the management once even had to complain to the American embassy since the waitresses refused to serve the "half-naked" men.

Another complaint was that Americans have a way of throwing blankets or pillows or anything else they don't use or are through with on the floor. (By the way, Russian pillows are about three times the size of our pillows and there are always two of them per person on a bed.)

"A floor is to walk on and not to throw things on. It is uncultured."

And still another complaint was about the American habit after finishing a meal of putting the tray of dishes on the floor outside the room.

"This is not done in Russia," I was told the first time I did it. "It makes walking in the halls difficult and, besides, it is uncultured."

It is the supreme reproof. I tried to tell the waitress that it was just as "uncultured" to disturb me in my afternoon rest by knocking at my door two hours after my lunch had been consumed. Whereupon we worked out a quite complicated deal by which, whenever I had a meal in my room, they would get their dishes and I would get my undisturbed rest.

I once had the following exchange with one of the hotel waitresses. Busy as they were, they often found a few minutes to stop for a chat at my table.

"Do you personally live well in the United States?" she asked.

"Moderately well."

"Are there people who live worse?"

"Yes, many."

"Are there people who live better?"

"Yes, many."

"Are there really rich people in the United States?"

"Yes."

"Very rich?"

"Yes."

Proudly: "See? We have no rich people."

"Oh, yes, you have. I met some."

"Ah, but that could have been only the very educated, very cultured ones. It is true, there are rich people among them. But they have to be very cultured."

But one no longer hears the word applied to the use of a handkerchief or a toothbrush, or to wiping one's feet before entering a room. Such acts are now taken as a matter of course, which they were not a generation or two ago. Schools have been most persistent in teaching "cultured" behavior. I heard the word mentioned many times in another connection. A new kind of university has been established, one that does not give degrees, that has no entrance requirements, and does not demand too much homework. It is called a University of Culture, and gives courses in art, literature, music, history of culture. These universities are spreading all over the Soviet Union, many in the various Soviet republics, and are gaining tremendous popularity. They are attended mostly by people who did not have a chance to continue their higher education or who feel that their background could stand some polishing up. I met young and old intellectuals who attended courses in fields which had not been part of their own training. One retired engineer attended lectures on French literature, a librarian a course on the history of painting.

Despite the tremendous emphasis in Russia today on science, the arts are far from being neglected. Russia possesses a tremendous wealth of talented dancers, musicians, actors, performers in every field imaginable. As soon as a child with any artistic ability is discovered—and hardly any remain undiscovered, what with the close state supervision of every stage of life from cradle to grave—he is given every opportunity to develop. He is, however, rarely given an opportunity to strike out for himself in green pastures or to develop his talent along lines that do not conform to party doctrine.

Culture is also dispensed over the radio—along with advertising. In the past, between two parts of a Tchaikovsky or Beethoven symphony, an enthusiastic voice might recommend the best fertilizer for a cornfield or the best grain to feed a horse. There are still plenty of lectures and reports on such matters and there must be many people who listen to them with great interest.

But I also heard uninterrupted excellent music, good storytelling for children, interesting lectures on literature or science. Younger people who had not been exposed to the propaganda barrage of the previous radio era do complain that they get bored with the many agricultural and economic statistics. Those who remember the past are grateful for the present radio programs. Advertisements are never announced in the middle of a program. There are regular periods of fifteen minutes for them. Here is what is advertised:

Names and places and times of lectures.

Names and places and times of theaters, concerts, movies.

Dates of meetings often to be followed by a concert or other entertainment.

Art exhibits.

Special shows in the various parks. One day I heard advertised for one park a circus, for another a water show.

Education institutes—what they teach and their admission rules.

Shoes, clothing, foods, furniture, musical instruments, sports equipment, toys, and whatever is being sold in stores—where it can be bought and what organization manufactures it.

Offers of jobs.

This last, incidentally, takes up most of the time. I was told that, however the jobs are described, they are for the most part calls for unskilled labor, of which there is a shortage. The same person told me that for even highly specialized jobs his organization, an engineering concern, easily gets several applicants but very few for the unskilled jobs. This situation seems to get worse, since most young people continue to study after leaving school. Even if they are not admitted to institutions of higher learning, they continue their studies in evening classes in factories, on farms, or through correspondence courses. By and by they join the army of specialists and only the totally incompetent or those coming from forsaken corners of the Soviet Union are available for unskilled labor. In this connection one also hears talk in Russia, as one does at home, that the introduction of automation and more efficient modern machinery in general may soon completely change the labor situation, which makes people wonder as well as worry. One result may be that the even now quite formidable export of Soviet technical assistants to underdeveloped countries will increase many times.

Once in the course of a discussion of what automation will mean in the Soviet Union, someone mentioned that its introduction of it may bring—besides unemployment—some leisure hours into the Russians' lives. If that happens, another capitalistic problem may become a concern of the Soviets.

TV appeared in Russia only a few years ago and at first not many homes owned a set. It was a great sensation and attraction. People used to travel in the bitterest cold from one end of Moscow to the other to watch it in large groups in the homes of the few fortunates. Now there are many sets. The day after Van Cliburn's first concert on his return trip to Moscow everyone I met told me that he had seen and listened to him on TV. (Few were fortunate enough to get tickets to his concerts, which were sold out for many months before the dates were even announced. About a year and a half before his 1960 concerts lists were oversubscribed. One of the concerts was on a subscription series of the Moscow Philharmonic. I saw an old lady of eighty almost dancing with joy when she was told that her subscription series included a Van Cliburn concert.) The Russians are as much interested in hearing Van Cliburn play as in hearing it confirmed that it was they who discovered him and brought him "fame and glory."

Nowadays even the smallest dilapidated house in Moscow has several aerials. On some there are so many that they make one wonder how a house of such small dimensions could possibly shelter such a number of TV owners.

I never got around to watching Russian TV, though I had intended to do so. I did, however, carefully follow the daily TV schedules in the press and would ask people about their favorite programs. There is, naturally, a great deal of undisguised propaganda, official pronouncements, oratory, slogans, but there are also good lectures, excellent live performances from theaters and concert halls, and amusing as well as lively educational children's entertainment, folk songs, and movies. No Westerns, no Hitchcock, no soap opera, no murders, no horror films, no commercials, no beautiful girls with no other purpose than being beautiful girls.

Many times during my stay in Moscow I was reminded that reading about something is no substitute for seeing. An instance of this came during my first visit to an art exhibit. I had been reading for years that Moscow museums and art exhibits were always crowded, but I was not prepared for the dense throngs.

It was the first Moscow showing of the work of a Russian-born painter, Svetoslav Roerich, the son of the famous old Russian painter, Nikolai Roerich. The younger Roerich had been living for years in India and had married an Indian whose beautiful face graced many of his canvases. I had been urged to see the exhibit by a young woman, a devoted Communist, who had only disdain for anything but completely realistic art. I could not then and cannot now understand why she liked this exhibit so much, since Roerich's painting is to a great extent religious and mystic, anything but realistic, and his brilliant colors, lines, forms and subjects are a far cry from those that distinguish contemporary Russian painting.

Since the young woman had left Moscow before I could ask her, I had to try to find my own explanation. I thought it was because India as a rule is pictured as a great friend of Russia and it would not do to disparage anything from India. Besides, there was a portrait of Nehru which truly is superb, and my young friend worshiped Nehru. But then it occurred to me that this same young woman scoffed at Picasso, who is certainly a much closer friend of communism than Nehru ever was or is. So I still have no explanation for the great success of these so non-Communist paintings among Communists. Could it be that subconsciously there is even among the most faithful party-liners a craving for brilliance and mystery and sheer beauty, and the images of a friendly Nehru and India permitted them to satisfy this craving.

The next exhibit I went to was an enormous one called Sovetskaya Rossiya (Soviet Russia). This museum shows at regular intervals the work of Russian artists only. The art of other Soviet republics is shown either in separate national or in All-Soviet exhibits. Here again there was a constant stream of people. As far as I was concerned, about 90 per cent of the exhibit could have been color photography. A few of the portraits were quite good, and though they left nothing to the imagination they at least revealed the personality of the sitter. But the great majority of the huge canvases were so monotonous, so void of any hint of originality that, even if they were excellent technically, as some experts said, after you had seen a dozen of them the rest seemed like boring repetitions.

After having walked through miles of smiling dairymaids and heroic soldiers and miners I spoke of my disappointment to a friend who is interested in painting. He said that this exhibit showed infinitely more talent than those of even two or three years ago and that he was completely satisfied with this progress. What seemed to me sheer color photography was a great step forward compared with the past exhibits, he said. I accepted his word, but I found these miles of happy people totally uninspiring.

I was told that at an exhibition of modern Polish paintings there were almost daily fist fights between those who welcomed the new forms of art, and those for whom Socialist Realism was an untouchable dogma. Any attempt to shake the foundation is to many orthodox Communists tantamount to being against Marx and Lenin.

I had more discussions in Moscow on modern art than on the U-2 incident or on capitalism versus communism. They were, however, more numerous than lengthy, for most Russians have such strong opinions that the subject is quickly if violently disposed of. And I, who do not consider myself an art connoisseur and certainly no authority on modern art, found myself constantly pleading with them not to condemn it so violently without at least making an effort to find out what it was all about.

Some Yugoslavs who were present at one such discussion expressed great pride that they, contrary to the Russians, paint and exhibit modern paintings, listen to modern music, read all the foreign books, newspapers and magazines they want to, and still consider themselves good Communists. They derided the Russians' old-fashioned taste in art, their total isolation from the outside world, and the provincial narrowness resulting from this. The Russians vigorously fought back and I was glad that the Yugolsavs did the battling for me.

CHAPTER SEVENTEEN

The Return of Religion

For some years before my visit to Russia I had been hearing and reading that many young people, not only in the smaller towns and villages, but even in the cities, were now attending religious services, getting married in church, and baptizing their children there. At the time I left Russia in 1939 such a thing was almost unheard of. What had happened to cause the change? I asked many whys on this. Here are some answers to my "Why did you get married in church?" "Everybody does it. . . . To please my mother. . . . To please my bride. . . . A girl doesn't feel married unless she is married in church. . . . My mother was married in church, so was my grandmother. . . . It is more elegant than just signing a paper in an office."

Apropos of the last answer, the Soviet authorities have lately tried to glamorize the marriage ceremony. The procedure used to be as pedestrian as getting food coupons or declaring a change of address. It is now embellished by a few congratulatory words by the clerk, in some cases even by music. The walls of the marriage offices are painted in bright colors and display pictures of smiling, well-dressed couples instead of—as in the past—illustrations of the dangers of venereal disease and alcohol.

I met young women without any trace of religious belief who married and had their children christened in church without, they said, giving it a second thought. Everybody they knew did it, it was the thing to do. Some years ago this explanation would have been unthinkable, for the propaganda against religion was too shrill, too strong for any but the most deeply religious to resist. Judging by articles I read in the Communist youth press severely attacking such bourgeois conventions, they must be widely observed in Communist circles also.

Though many go through church rituals only because it has again become custom, religion has definitely come back to life in Russia. One explanation I heard was that during the war people facing death had a natural longing for more consolation than the customary official mouthings could give them. Even high Soviet officers had been seen in church before leaving for the front, I was told. Crosses were worn by a large number of Red Army soldiers. Patriotism and religion were the two great forces in supplying the spirit and strength necessary for victory. The first was openly stressed, the second silently but benevolently conceded.

Another explanation was that pressure for a more liberal attitude toward religion was applied by the Allies. The moment the government opened the dike even slightly, the long-suppressed rush was on and it was not an easy task to plug the dike again.

Some people think that the present government tolerance results from the belief that, since religion helped the war effort by encouraging patriotism, it might not be wise to persecute it now; it can perform the same function in the present dynamic reconstruction effort. The church had adjusted itself to the situation, is highly patriotic and nationalistic, and lives in official peace with the government.

There is some feeling that the church is getting too strong, that it has too much influence with the young, and that the government is looking for ways to curtail its appeal without using drastic means, which might boomerang.

It is now applying the methods used elsewhere in the world to attract and hold youths: sports events, communal outings, social get-togethers, and in these activities it shows a great deal of imagination as well as success.

The Soviet authorities feel that the only way to counteract the church's influence is to revitalize their own youth activities. For the young people the shock of the posthumous revelations about Stalin went much deeper than with the older generation, who already knew or suspected much of what Khrushchev revealed. But eventually the effects of the shock, which had expressed itself in cynicism and in a loss of confidence in the party, began to wear off. The party youth organizations had been lying low for many years. They had curtailed their activities during the big purges, since so many of their own ranks fell victims to it on their own account or through their parents.

During the war they were merged into the country's general effort. It was several years after Stalin's death before they sufficiently regained their strength to lead a wavering and lost youth. Now they are moving energetically to counter the dangerous grip that the church had meanwhile gained on some of the young. And again I heard grumbling from some, rejoicing from others, that once more they are beginning to exercise a great influence over children and adolescents.

Their activities, like those of the church, have changed. Endless propaganda speeches, long readings from *Pravda* and dull sermonizing do not keep youth in line these days. What years ago was meant to be auxiliary in youth organizations—the sports, entertainment, dances, and so on—has now become the most important part, and the speeches and propaganda the auxiliary. Both the Communist youth organizations and the church have adjusted to the spirit of the times.

In our hotel I frequently saw bearded Russian priests in long black robes and tall headdresses, with crosses on their chests. They aroused interest only among foreigners and were given an occasional devout glance by a Russian. It was obvious that Russians have again become accustomed to seeing priests in public, at official functions, and wherever other citizens gather. The press, with the exception of *Komsomolskaya Pravda*, which addresses itself to youth, attacked them only rarely, and then without the old venom, and the general public seems completely relaxed about them.

When I mentioned to a friend this matter of the priests wandering in and out of the hotel he, a devout Communist, said that the authorities were really concerned about the renewed strength and influence of the church and that sooner or later there would inevitably be another organized antireligious campaign, probably of a more subtle kind than those of the past.

I heard it said by some foreigners that as in the old days the church served the czar it now serves the Soviet regime. This is true only to a very limited degree. In the Czarist days the church was the right arm of the government. It was powerful in the cities; and in the villages the priest and the local government official were the law of the land. This is certainly not the case today, even though Soviet religious leaders preach patriotism at home and are good Soviet propagandists when they travel abroad. The church has definitely more freedom now than it ever had under the Soviets. But the influence it exerts today is a far cry from the tremendous power it wielded under the czar. There is no doubt that at present it is being used by the Soviet regime for its own purposes. But there is also no doubt that the moment the government thinks it will gain by making a change the change will be made.

On the very eve of my departure an elderly Russian said: "You can tell them in America that in the not too distant future religion will spread so widely in Russia that the government will be helpless to do anything about it." His daughter indignantly disagreed: "This silly tolerance will soon stop, churches and priests will be forbidden to preach their nonsense as they were before." These were the last words on religion in my notes.

CHAPTER EIGHTEEN

The Jews

April 4, a date often mentioned, the day the doctors of the infamous Jewish Doctors' Plot were freed, fell in that year, the year 1953, a few days before Easter. An old shoemaker, a man of eighty, told me that on that day he felt a deep shame washed off the Russian people, a shame which otherwise would have remained forever on his conscience as it would have remained on those of many others. He had heard the news over the radio, and went to church to thank God. He could now celebrate the joyous feast of Easter with a pure heart. His eyes filled with tears when he told me this seven years later, in June, 1960.

I found a great change in the attitudes of Russian Jews since 1939. They have again become conscious of being Jews, as they were under the czars and were not during the first decades after the Bolshevik revolution. But now they are without the consolation they found, even under the czars, in their synagogues and books and press and in a lively close social and communal life. There is no Jewish life as such in Russia today; there is only knowing that one is a Jew. In the early Soviet years no one thought about who was a Jew and who was not; now the identification is always made.

The great charge against Jews originated by Stalin was cosmopolitanism, having ties with the outside world. But it was this that in the first years after the revolution made the Jews among the most devoted internationalists and trusted with the highest posts in the government. Those years are long since gone. Russian nationalism and not internationalism is popular now, and the Jews are definitely the "outs" at present.

Jewish parents of the type who in the past would not have thought of making a distinction invariably mentioned it now if a son or a daughter had married a non-Jew. There were still many intermarriages, but I was told that in general there were fewer now than before not because, as one friend explained, the educated younger generation objected to intermarriage but because in the past some girls had definitely preferred to marry Jews, who were supposed to make better husbands.

In every single case of which I knew where there was a mixed marriage, regardless of which parent was Jewish, the children were registered as non-Jewish. I was told of a case in which a non-Jewish father left his wife and applied for divorce before the child was born, and the Jewish mother registered the child as non-Jewish. People, whether Jews or not, talked about this with a feeling of shame and sadness. They felt that it was dishonest, but they were trying to protect their children from anti-Semitism, the evil roots of which seem to have grown deep.

One Jewish grandfather was extremely bitter when this question came up. He had in his youth fought for the revolution and lost his right arm in the fight. He had been drawn to the revolution because of the Czarist pogroms which he had witnessed as a child, and for many years he remained a deeply devoted Bolshevik. His doubts were first aroused during the purges and were given their final shot by anti-Semitism. For years he hadn't believed that the government really condoned it. Now he did. Several intermarriages in the family, which in the past would have been a completely normal part of Soviet life, had now brought what he called "this dishonesty" into their lives.

"Why put down nationality in questionnaires anyway?" he stormed. "Didn't we fight once upon a time to put an end to these squabbles and quarrels among people? If at least there were a good reason to put down Jew in your passport! But the only reason is to make sure that you don't get a good position or advancement or a chance to travel. Is this what I once fought for and was crippled for?"

This outburst did not contribute to the rosy picture of Soviet brotherly love which some of the younger people tried to present to me.

In some cases the remark that "he (or she) married a Jewess (or Jew)" was not made invidiously. It was simply stated as a fact, like "it is raining today." What struck me was that it was mentioned at all. It never was in the past, at least not by the kind of people from whom I heard it now. Anti-Semitism has not put an end to inter-marriage. It has simply, as it did under czarism, set Jews apart. There are no pogroms, but an ugly and disturbing phenomenon it is nevertheless.

Khrushchev has denied that there is any anti-Semitism in Russia, and as proof he said that Jews have helped to build rockets. This remark originated one of the stories going around Moscow. After Khrushchev's denial of anti-Semitism a young Jewish engineer re-applied for a job that had been refused him before for the obvious reason that he was a Jew. He was again rejected and the reason for it was again obvious. He protested. Hadn't Khrushchev himself said, he insisted, that Jews were helping to build rockets? "That's true," was the answer, "but we are not building rockets."

To my questions about the revival of anti-Semitism, my friends frequently pointed out that, as I knew, the Soviet government during its early decades had fought to expunge any lingering traces of anti-Semitism. However, during the war the government, in its eagerness to arouse Russian patriotic sentiment, removed the curbs it had put on anti-Semitism earlier and, some said, even helped to resuscitate it. This legalized anti-Semitism was given a strong shot in the arm by Hitler's anti-Jewish propaganda, which the Soviet government did nothing to combat either during the war or after it regained the German-occupied territories infested by it. And the reason nothing was done, many said, was Stalin's own strong as well as Khrushchev's less strong but undeniable prejudice.

Another reason, I heard, was that when the Germans were approaching Moscow the majority of Jews fled in panic, many on their own and without any government assistance. The people who remained and were building trenches and fortifications to defend Moscow accused the Jews of having refused to help save the city. Willingly or unwillingly, they ignored what would have happened to any Jew caught by the Nazis.

When during the war I heard rumors of anti-Semitism in the Red Army and in Russia in general I was deeply shocked and at first was inclined to reject them. But when the rumors grew thicker, when in time they definitely ceased to be rumors and became undeniable fact, I began to search deeply in my memory. Had there been signs of it much earlier and I had refused to see them as I had refused to see many other dark spots which would have blackened a picture I did not want to have blackened? Looking back with a completely open mind, I knew the answer was yes. There had been less of it, to be sure, and less chance for it to show itself, since anti-Semitism was then officially condemned. But when, with the blessing of the Kremlin and the help of the war and of Hitler, it did come into the open, it spread quickly.

That the problem will remain for some time is clear when one hears small children ask one another: Are you a Jew? Though it is obviously a topic of conversation picked up at home and they probably have no notion what they are talking about, the idea that there is a definite and important difference between Jew and non-Jew will probably soon become firmly embedded.

During one of the discussions on anti-Semitism a young friend said that Jews were discriminated against only in the foreign service and maybe in one or two other departments. He rejected the opinion of several others present that he, as a Jew, a doctor, would never be sent with a delegation to the West, and certainly not to the United States. He enumerated several scientific and cultural groups that had gone to the United States, each including Jews. He advised me during my visit to the Industrial and Agricultural Exhibitions to look through the lists of names of people famous in the fields of agriculture, plane construction, science, architecture, etc.

I did so and found a number of Jewish names everywhere. During my visit I spent some time at the City Building exhibit in search of material on city planning for my son Victor, who is a city planner in Alaska. One of the directors of the exhibit, after having given half an hour of his extremely busy schedule to an "American tourist who wants Soviet material for an American city planner," as he with delight and pride told everybody present, turned me over to his first deputy, a Jew. This man showed me the exhibit of the new microrayons of which they are so proud, the head of which also was a Jew.

When I reported on my visit to the same group of people the young doctor was triumphant but the others kept insisting that, though Jews were certainly widely employed in jobs of third or fourth importance, one would not find them in the two top categories. Exceptions are the outstandingly talented among them or those who are sent abroad or otherwise played up in order to prove the absence of anti-Semitism in the Soviet Union. One young Jew to whom I talked fiercely defended every word and action of the Soviet government in the foreign field, but when the conversation shifted to Soviet-American student exchanges he abruptly came out with:

"You don't imagine, I hope, that those whom we send to you as exchange students are ever chosen for anything else but their thorough 100 per cent blind devotion to the party? They are sifted through one party organ after another without the slightest concern for their scholastic or human qualities."

I was perplexed at this outburst, but observing his immediate confusion I knew that I would get no clarification from him. I went instead to an unorthodox Communist friend who had often cleared up puzzling points in the past. He was always thoroughly open with me besides being very wise. I told him what I knew about this young man and asked him how could this total devotion to the regime live peacefully in one breast with this thoroughly unorthodox, even anti-Communist sentiment. He answered:

"Don't take his blind devotion too literally. First, he talks in this orthodox way out of a habit which has become his second nature. Second, talking to an outsider, which you are to him, it is hard for a Soviet citizen to talk in any other way. The cold war has made us even more sensitive than we ever were before. As to his outburst —he was no doubt sincere in that. He probably was not able to control his anger and disappointment because, though he is completely loyal and patriotic besides being an excellent scholar, he has little chance of being sent on any exchange program to your country since he is not a party member."

Then he asked:

"Is the young man a Jew?" When I said he was he made an eloquent gesture which said clearly, "Well, what do you expect? He knows that he has no chance to be sent anywhere."

I once mentioned to friends that in one of the Intourist hotels a floorlady told me that she was Jewish, and with tears in her eyes said her entire family in the Ukraine had been wiped out by the Nazis. My friends warned me not to get into conversation with her, insisting that either she had been planted at the hotel in order to find out how foreigners felt about the Jewish problem in Russia or had hidden from the management the fact that she was Jewish. Under no other circumstances, they said, would she have been put in a job where she would be in close contact with foreigners. I was the only one in the room who laughed off this idea as a fairy tale. Who of us was right?

Since I knew a number of Moscow doctors, the Doctors' Plot of 1953 often came up in conversation. They told me that abroad it was incorrectly called the Jewish Doctors' Plot, for there were many non-Jewish doctors involved in it. They admitted, however, that since the majority of the names officially mentioned in the press were Jewish, Stalin's intention had obviously been to put the emphasis on Jews. Every time I asked what the underlying reason for inventing the plot was in the first place—for I personally did not meet a single person who believed in it—I was given the same answer: Stalin had undeniably lost his mind during the last period of his life. The doctors had been unable to give him any relief from the many physical and mental ills that plagued him, and this was his way of getting back at them. The anti-Semitic twist was a by-product of the sick mind of a chronic anti-Semite.

While I was in Moscow a famous doctor, Miron Vovse, died. He was among the best known and most respected of the doctors involved in the plot. While he was in prison a cartoon had appeared in *Krokodil:* A man dressed in a doctor's white coat, a large sharp knife in one hand, in the other a benign and smiling mask—the face of Vovse—half raised to reveal his supposedly real face, vicious, ugly, ferocious, a typical Nazi caricature of a Jew. The cartoon was titled "The Murderer."

Now he was dead, his life considerably shortened by his ordeal, and over a hundred thousand people turned out for his funeral, and mountains of flowers were their silent tribute. I visited a friend's grave several days after Vovse's funeral, and the mountains of flowers were still there. He was well beloved as a physician and as a human being. At the funeral services it was felt that Minister of Health Kovrygina as well as the other notables tried in their speeches to atone for the fact that one of the great Soviet medical lights, a man of outstanding personal qualities, had been so viciously maligned. At the time it happened very few of them had had the courage to lift a finger for him. (Vovse's funeral was a great and spectacular event in Moscow but in vain did I look in *Pravda* for a report on it. The ways of the Soviet press, or rather its silences, are mysterious indeed.)

What is significant about Vovse's story is that by 1953 some few people did dare to speak up for him. During the purges it would have been unthinkable for anyone to stand up for anyone else. And I was told of several instances in recent years when heads of institutions categorically refused to discharge Jewish employees simply for the reason that they were Jews.

This does not change the fact, which no one denies, that there is more discrimination against Jews than against any other Soviet national minority. All, except the Jews, are encouraged by the authorities to cultivate their national arts. All, except the Jews, have schools, a national literature, and a press in their own language. Every nationality, except the Jews, has its own theater, though the Jewish Art Theater, long closed, used to be one of the best in Moscow. Its greatest actor, Michoels, who was in the United States in 1943 as a member of a Soviet cultural group, was killed in a car accident in 1948. According to persistent rumors, he was a victim not of an accident but of a plot. Stalin wanted the popular and respected actor out of the way without too big a scandal.

Under the czars only a very small percentage of Jews could enter a university. There is an unofficial percentage for Jewish students in the Soviet Union too. But in earlier times young Jews who were unable to enter Russia's higher institutions of learning, studied at universities in Switzerland, Germany, Austria, France and England, and returned to Russia to practice their skills. Those whose families were unable to support them received the help of philanthropic organizations in their communities or of foundations whose aim it was to sponsor education. To Soviet young people this was a hard-to-believe tale. To go as a free man or woman to a foreign university!

Even though most of the Russian Jews I met were infinitely more conscious of being Jewish than they had been in the years I remembered, few of them were interested in the Jewish problem on a world scale. They knew nothing about what was happening to Jews in the outside world. Such elementary information as the Soviet vote for the establishment of the state of Israel, its later complete reversal of attitude, the support given to Egypt in its every anti-Israel move, indeed anything that concerns Jewry outside of Russia, was known only to a few who listened to Western broadcasts.

Though the other national minorities fare better than the Jews, that once popular slogan "The brotherhood of all Soviet peoples" no longer fools them. They know very well that being allowed to perform their dances in Moscow's Bolshoi Theater or even abroad does not mean freedom and self-determination for them or an equal status with the Big Brother. And it certainly cannot fool the Russians, who show little interest, respect, or affection either for the national minorities in their own country or for their "brothers" anywhere in the world. I would go further and say that even during my short visit I more than once heard Russians express undisguised contempt for members of the Soviet national minorities.

There are bookstores specializing in the literatures of "brother nations," there are national art exhibits, theater performances. But in Soviet thinking nationalism in reality means Russian nationalism. It would be hard for any Armenian or Tadzhik or Latvian or any other non-Russian member of one of the supposedly independent Soviet republics to get anywhere in one of the prestige fields like engineering or management, even in his home republic and even though the job was completely nonpolitical unless he knew the Russian language. Whenever I broached this subject I found little response. No one was interested.

Neither were the Russians concerned about the people in the satellite countries in which the Soviet government poses as a protector—in contrast to the Western capitalist exploiters. They are interested in their produce, yes. But the Russians I spoke with did not seem to care about or be aware of what lay behind the Soviets' spreading influence in the world at the expense of the West. The spreading was all that mattered. The spreading was good for the Russians. The victims of the spreading were not important.

CHAPTER NINETEEN

The Tourist in Russia

Very soon after my arrival in Moscow I was struck by the fact that, contrary to all my expectations, Russians, with few exceptions, talked little about the U-2 incident, which had occurred only a couple of weeks earlier, and about the worsening of Soviet-United States relations. Moreover, when they did mention it, it was only to say casually and more often than not, in regret rather than in anger, that the U-2 should not have flown over Soviet territory. A sincere regret was expressed that our relations, which had been moving toward genuine friendship, were getting worse again.

The first time I was involved in a less friendly exchange on the subject and was asked reproachfully, "Why did you send the U-2 to spy over Soviet territory?" In an attempt to cut the subject short I answered flippantly, "But I didn't send it." This reply naturally did not satisfy my questioner and he kept on angrily baiting me. He finally provoked me beyond my patience, and I said what I had said on other occasions when provoked beyond my self-control: that if we had an American party in the Soviet Union and in a hundred other countries of the world as the Soviet regime has its Communist parties everywhere, we might not need any U-2's. We would then get our information the way the Soviet government was getting it with the help of Communists and their stooges all over the world.

Everyone in the room vigorously disputed the fact that foreign Communists were disloyal to their own countries and served only the interests of Russia. To what extent they really believed their protests I am not to this day able to judge. Maybe they honestly thought that this was only another capitalist canard. That foreign Communists put their loyalty to the Soviet Union above loyalty to their own countries and therefore considered spying for the Soviet Union a natural consequence of their allegiance was something the Russians have never been told.

All that foreign Communists were doing, it was earnestly explained to me on several occasions, was trying to bring the benefits of communism to the exploited peasants and workers of their own countries. The picture they painted of the United States and of the selfless work of the American Communist party on behalf of those poor exploited people could have been included in *Alice in Wonderland*. Incredible though it sounds, and though a Communist friend once warned me that I must take much that I heard with a grain of salt, they truly seemed to have not the slightest idea of the workings of Communist parties abroad and of their allegiance to and dependence on the Soviet regime, or that Soviet spies had ever been caught anywhere.

At times my exchanges with Russians about the U-2 were frustrating. The Soviet press would quote American sources with which I agreed but which took issue with our government's position. But when I pointed out the disagreement, hoping I had found an additional argument for our freedom of thought and opinion, the reaction was inevitably not the one I had anticipated. As in every other case when I used our right to disagree with official attitudes as a proof of our freedom, it only seemed to convince the Russians that what they were told about the United States was true: that is, that the "American masses," of which I obviously was one, disagreed with the "ruling circles," of which I obviously was not one, just as the Soviet government had always told them.

On higher levels there must have been many strongly felt exchanges between Americans and Russians on the subject of the U-2. But, as I have said, I could detect few signs in my chance contacts with ordinary people that the strong feeling had seeped down to the level of the man in the street. This, of course, does not mean that it may not have existed among other elements of the population. I was told, for instance, that no one working at a sensitive job would ever strike up a casual conversation with a foreigner anyway. Even those friends who had sensitive jobs, talkative as they were on many other subjects, never mentioned the work they were doing and avoided any conversation on such subjects as the U-2 and spying.

As I said earlier, I was in the beginning reluctant to walk around Moscow with a camera. But after my first Sunday I changed my mind. I saw hardly a Russian family that day without at least one camera. After that I never left the hotel without mine. Many times a Russian fellow photographer would come over and look with interest at my German model with the trademark Balda. This in Russian means a dope, a nincompoop, and was always a good opening for a joking remark followed by a friendly discussion of the best angle and light for a picture. And this in turn was inevitably followed by a friendly discussion of life in our respective countries and between our peoples, ending always with the expression of the hope that the U-2 incident was not going to change anything in this relationship.

This total lack of unfriendliness at that time was a constant source of amazement to me. The press was full of venom toward the United States—that is, the Pentagon, the President, the State Department, and Wall Street. But since the attacks were not directed at the American people and certainly not at that time at individual American tourists, I suppose the average Russian felt it was safe to be friendly.

However, it doesn't take much, even in a democracy, to swing public opinion. I have seen it happen more than once in my life. How much less effort does it take in a dictatorship. While I was in Moscow Khrushchev, in at least two speeches, said that nothing should affect friendly relations between peoples even if there was a quarrel between governments, and he specifically mentioned tourism. Russians quoted this whenever the question whether it was safe for them to associate with foreigners came up. I was less sure than they were. I felt that one word, even one hint, in a speech or in the press against one single foreigner could completely change the picture again. Moscow foreign residents with whom I talked about it felt the way I did, but the majority of the Russians disagreed.

"Oh, no," they would say, "this time it is for good; there will always be friendship with visiting foreigners." These last sentences are taken word for word from my notes on the trip.

Not all the Russians, however, were convinced that unrestricted "tourism" was desirable. One friend to whom I expressed some mild criticism of something Russian leaped on my comment as an example of why free travel into the Soviet Union from the United States should not be permitted.

"You see, you yourself bring in ideas contrary to ours—this should not be."

But what about Soviet people abroad? I argued. The handful of tourists or the many diplomats, technical assistants, and UN employees from the Soviet Union and the satellite countries—don't they talk exclusively in terms of their own Communist ideas, unless ready to defect? Why can they go around voicing their ideology abroad and why cannot foreigners do that in Russia? The answer was a lecture, illogical and boring, which I heard so many times that I could repeat it verbatim, to the effect that their ideology had only the good of the people at heart, while ours was really concerned with the interests of the small group of exploiters, etc., etc., etc. When I asked why they were so afraid of such wrong ideas, since they could not possibly influence a Soviet mind, I also heard a recital of stock phrases.

I went to see the U-2, which was on exhibit in the Park of Culture. To avoid having to stand in line with the thousands of Russians who waited to see the U-2 from early morning till the park closed,

I had only to tell the militiaman on duty that I was an American tourist. This was the one time I was reluctant to use my prerogative, but it was also the one time I did not feel like standing in a Moscow line, an opportunity I usually welcomed. But to spend hours in this crowd as an American tourist did not appeal to me.

The behavior of some of the American tourists one sees in Moscow seemed to me anything but calculated to do themselves and their country any good or to encourage the friendliness of the Russian people. Many, of course, are the same kind of tourists one meets nowadays in every corner of the world. But there are, besides, the native sons and daughters returning on sentimental, often tragic, journeys, in the hope of finding some of their kin still alive. And then there is a very special group, received and feted by Soviet authorities, whose principal aim is to take back to their Russian-American, Polish-American, Armenian-American, Ukrainian-American and other such groups a report of what they saw in Russia.

Some of them are genuinely interested and look around with open eyes. Other groups are well infiltrated by fellow travelers; these are the ones who receive special treatment from the authorities and who return with glowing reports unmarred by even a hint of dissonance. I met such a Polish-American group in our hotel, and I can say that it hardly represented the attitudes of the majority of Polish Americans.

Only a few days before I left for Russia I met in my New York neighborhood an American of Armenian descent who was violently anti-American and passionately pro-Soviet. He admitted that he had not felt that until the previous summer when he had heard an Armenian-American group report ecstatically on their trip to the Soviet Union. They dwelt on the wonderful life Soviet Armenians lived, on their great opportunities for work and education.

"Imagine, there were church people among them; they wouldn't tell a lie," he assured me, and in his next breath he branded as a lie every word of criticism uttered and written against the Soviet Union in the United States.

When I saw the way the Polish-American group in my Moscow

hotel was treated and of whom it consisted I thought of my Armenian neighbor in New York. On the other hand, tourists whose outlook is colored by what they have heard from people who have been so deeply hurt in their personal lives that everything looks black are not a reliable source either. I met a few of these and they took back to the United States a picture of Russia that also had little relation to reality. In tourism as in so many other things, the golden mean seems to be hard to achieve.

The fact that the Russians don't have many of the things that we consider essential creates for some Americans a biased point of view and interferes with their grasping how the people really feel. Without a refrigerator or decent kitchen stove or washing machine, they say, how can one possibly be contented with one's personal life? On the other hand, I met some who, remembering the stories they had heard of poverty and shortages, became overenthusiastic when they didn't see starved children asleep in the gutters or have ragged beggars pull at their sleeves, as they had expected, and began to rave about Russia as a paradise on earth.

Once, back in the middle thirties I visited a kolkhoz with some American friends. There was a day nursery for the babies—the first one I had seen in a Russian village. I was deeply moved. Too vivid in my mind were the stories (in literature as well as in life) of women dragging themselves from the fields in an effort to deliver their babies under a shelter and of newborn babies devoured by farm animals. And here the women were working in the fields—as they, to the horror of American tourists, do in most other countries in the world—while their babies were in competent hands, safe, fed, happy. My American companions felt quite differently. They did not compare the present with the past. The only thing they saw, and for which they rejected the nursery out of hand, was that there were no screens on the windows as there would be in an American nursery. Nothing else mattered to them.

I was reminded of this several times when I heard American tourists delivering judgments that were a result of taking the wrong point of departure. At the City Building exhibit I saw models of new apartments that to Moscovites seemed the height of luxury, and they certainly were when compared with what they had had in the past. They were small apartments planned for a family of three or four, and equipped with what to Russians was the answer to their prayers—small furniture easy to move and to clean and a compact efficient modern kitchen.

While I was listening to the comments of the crowd I heard a loud strident voice in English: "But where are the refrigerators?" As a rule refrigerators are bought by the tenants and are therefore only rarely displayed in the model kitchens. "How can you live without one?" the voice went on. "I not only have a refrigerator, I have a large freezer. . . . I shop only once in two weeks. . . . How can you stand those tiny rooms?" And so it went on and on. I walked in the direction of those shrill sounds, and there she was, a representative of the most objectionable type of American tourist, an elderly woman extravagantly made up, overdressed and bejeweled, holding court in the midst of an impatient English-speaking tourist group consisting of Canadians, Britishers, Scandinavians. The poor guide, embarrassed and flushed, could not stop the flow of words since she was under orders to be polite to tourists and to cater to them. Besides being thoroughly distasteful, the woman's long tirade was disrupting the tour's tight schedule. Finally, one of the English-women could not control herself and said softly, "I have no refrigerator either," and her husband added, "I'd much rather have free medical care." Then some of the others joined in, and I whispered to the guide that she should not judge Americans by this one tourist. My whisper was not meant to be too discreet and the woman heard me; afterward we had a little exchange which I thoroughly enjoyed.

Few of the floorladies at the hotel understood English and I was often asked to help them out. Once I found a desperate American at the desk trying to explain something which the floorlady obviously was unable to understand. All the man wanted was to take a nap and be called at a certain hour so as not to miss the ballet. After this had been duly explained to the floorlady we got into a conversation. He was a Kansan and a very angry man. He had an interpreter-guide who not only took him on sightseeing trips but also upon his request translated the Soviet press for him. He was incensed at the way the Soviet newspapers talked about the United States.

In the course of our talk the Kansan admitted that he had never read anything about Russia that did not have a strong anti-Soviet point of view, "and I certainly never will," he angrily added. When I suggested that no battle was ever won without knowing whatever there was to know about the enemy, and that it might be useful at least to try to understand what the other side thinks and does and why, he jumped on me: There wasn't anything a decent American would want to learn about Russia, the Russians and their American stooges told nothing but lies anyway; and he didn't "want any American to read that Communist stuff." I may be mistaken, but judging by what he had to say earlier about the *New York Times* and the *Herald Tribune* he may have included them among the stooges.

I was interested to know what had brought him to Moscow, since he had such violent feelings about it. "They included five days in Moscow in that damned European package!" was his disgusted reply. It was his first trip to Europe and without examining it too closely he chose a package tour that covered over a dozen countries in less than a month.

As such conversations usually do, this one made me feel sad and discouraged. If we who have access to information and are able to satisfy our quest for knowledge and understanding make so little use of this privilege, how can we blame the other side for being ignorant about us? If the Kansas gentleman was keeping a diary of his Moscow visit he probably noted in it that he had met one of those wild American Communists, though before parting I most politely wished him a pleasant nap and an enjoyable evening at the ballet.

If this had been an isolated instance it would not have been very serious but unfortunately I met others like him during my Moscow visit. And as a rule people who hold these views consider themselves

100 per cent patriotic Americans, in their loyalty head and shoulders above those who are trying to learn and to understand what at present is the major problem of the United States.

At the other end of the spectrum are the American tourists who with the enthusiasm and faith devoted by some people exclusively to the Bible repeat everything told them by their guides; they seek no other source of information. I spent some hours listening to my dinner companions quote the wisdom of their guides, propaganda that I had read a day or two earlier in *Pravda*. Attempts to set them straight were as futile as my attempts to set straight the Kansan and his like. Who was I to tell them anything about Russia? The guide certainly knew more than I did.

Fortunately, these two categories of tourists are not the only ones who find their way to Russia these days. There are plenty of travelers who have read a great deal, who think for themselves, and who accept and reject as they probably do at home. I met several who had even mastered some Russian before setting out on the trip.

At times I heard tourists complain that they were being shown only the more attractive features of Moscow. I wondered how many of them on a few days' visit to New York see much more than Fifth Avenue, the theater section, the Empire State Building, maybe the Cloisters. Others complained that the part of Gorki Street away from the center of town was much less glamorous than the stretch that is always pointed out with pride. So is New York's Park Avenue when one gets farther uptown. If only one could convince tourists that if comparisons with home are necessary one should compare equivalent things. One gets a more accurate picture that way.

Occasionally an American tourist in Moscow and others whom I met upon my return told me proudly of the propaganda speeches they made and the arguments they had with Russians. I am not sure that praising everything American and criticizing everything Russian is the best way of making friends and influencing people, especially the deeply patriotic Russians. So I tried whenever possible, whether talking with friends or with chance-met strangers, to keep conversations on a conversational level without getting into heated arguments. I definitely avoided making speeches and using big words. Whenever confronted with attacks on the United States I tried to talk of people, to cite specific examples, to bring up parallels that could be easily understood, to point out the traits Americans and Russians had in common, always trying to remain on a level where minds and hearts could easily meet. It was certainly my experience that theoretical arguments about freedom, economics, equality and so on carried less weight than the undeniable fact that I, who obviously was a representative of neither Wall Street nor "the exploiting or ruling classes," could travel freely, that I could read various newspapers and magazines including those that criticized the President, Wall Street and the Pentagon, and that without the slightest hesitation—or fear—I would agree with criticism of our genuine shortcomings. Often a feature of our life that we would consider trifling and accept without thinking about it—for instance, the freedom with which our papers cartoon American political leaders—made an impression. But what impressed them above all was our freedom to move around wherever and whenever our job, inclination and pocketbook permit.

I once hit the jackpot when I mentioned two letters I had written after a presidential election. One was addressed to the loser, who was my candidate, expressing my deep regret. The other was a long letter to the winner, saying why I had not voted for him and expressing my hope that he would include into his program some of his opponent's ideas which I fully spelled out. The fact that I had written the letters (and that many thousands of other Americans had written similar ones) giving my full name and address without fear of reprisal was impressive enough. But that I received answers and even a long one from the winner was a true sensation. I never failed to bring this up when I needed especially heavy artillery.

I met several American travelers who felt as I did and behaved accordingly, and I am convinced that it is their kind who bring the American picture much closer to the Russians than the propagandists and speechmakers. And since there are many like them traveling in Russia these days, I understand quite well that they are a source of great concern to the authorities welcome as they may be for other reasons. Since they are not obvious agitators who defeat their purpose by their agitation, they do leave a few seeds behind, seeds of doubt and questioning.

I repeat, we the travelers should dispense with the cruder kinds of propaganda. The simple fact that we are free to go to Russia is propaganda enough, especially if the "we" happens to be a teacher, a skilled worker, a modest housewife, a young engineer or doctor, an office clerk, or a student traveling on his or her own money or on a grant. I heard from several Russians that they are not impressed by seeing wealthy tourists, whose presence seems only to confirm what the Russians have always been told—that only the upper class in the United States has any advantages, including the possibility of traveling. It is the non-upper-class travelers who make a great impression in Russia.

In this connection I would like to add my voice to the voices of those American travelers, scientists, scholars, journalists, and students who have returned from trips to Russia with pleas for more exchanges, for more patience, for more mutual understanding.

Few tourists of any nationality have a chance to talk to Russians on their own. I once met a guideless Scandinavian group in a theater. They were delightted to talk with someone who had contact with Russians. It was the eve before their departure and this was the first time they had talked to anyone without an interpreter. More than once when I happened to share a table with visiting foreigners they pumped me interestedly for information about the people and the country. I talked with Indians, Iraqis, Italians, Britishers, Greeks, Afghans. Some of them, whether members of delegations or tourists, were Communists but even they did not seem to have any non-official contact with Russians. Once I got into a conversation with an East German group but a dead silence set in as soon as they found out I was from the United States.

Moscow's foreign residents have even less contact with ordinary Russians than do the tourists. There are militiamen guarding the entrances of foreign embassies as well as the houses assigned to foreigners. Whenever I went to the United States embassy I was politely asked in one way or another by the militiamen on guard what my business was. Once I was asked with a charming smile:

"Are you sure you are at the right address, citizeness?"

My American passport invariably ended the questioning and called forth a snappy salute. I don't eveny those who cannot claim foreign citizenship. Since an eye is kept on all houses in which foreigners live, their Russian visitors are not numerous.

CHAPTER TWENTY

The Death of Boris Pasternak

For over three decades I had been a devoted admirer of Pasternak, the author of *Dr. Zhivago*, as a poet and as a man. I wrote about him in *My Lives in Russia:*

Louis and I once attended a literary "trial" where Pasternak was to explain why he wrote about nature, human emotions, and abstract heroism instead of current economic and political problems as other poets did. After several orators, all insignificant literary pygmies, had poured out poison and wrath on the character and work of the greatest living Russian poet, Pasternak was called upon to answer the accusations. His big blue-gray eyes were wide open but he hardly saw anyone. He looked above the crowd, obviously laboring under a thorough incapacity to collect his thoughts and to put them into plain prosaic words. Several times his lips, thick childish lips, opened as if ready to speak. Finally, he was able to say a few stammering words:

"I cannot write to order. I can only write what I want to write about. I can try to write differently but I don't think I will succeed."

His complete honesty was obvious to those of us who admired him. A girl next to us, with a Komsomol pin, whispered excitedly to her friend, a youngster, whose eyes were filled with sadness and pity for Pasternak:

"Look at his eyes! A real poet by the grace of God!"

In her excitement the young Communist forgot herself and

slipped into the old-fashioned Russian definition of a true poet. But even she, despite her great emotion and admiration for Pasternak, did nothing more than whisper to her friend. The rest of the audience booed and protested, and after a few more malignant orations the meeting was closed. Pasternak was declared beyond the pale of Soviet poetry.

We talked to him after the meeting, if talking is the word for putting questions to a person who does not realize that anyone is speaking to him. An intimate friend of Pasternak told us later that the poet was near suicide that night and had to be closely watched. If the RAPP [Association of Proletarian Writers] had not been liquidated soon afterwards and the attacks on him stopped, the sensitive Pasternak might not have had the strength to live. His numerous friends and admirers were unable to fight for him as long as the RAPP had official party backing. Only after the government condemned the RAPP and its methods did they feel free to show their true feelings. The day when, after a long absence, Pasternak appeared again in public to read his poems, the large hall of the Polytechnical Museum was jammed full. For several minutes the applause and cheers prevented him from starting. For four hours he recited his original poems and translations from Georgian poets to an admiring audience which only let him go after all lights were put out in the hall at midnight.

That happened in the year 1932. In 1960 when I arrived in Moscow I heard confirmed the reports in the American press of Pasternak's serious illness.

On Wednesday, June 1, I heard an American newspaperman mention Pasternak's name on the telephone. I asked him how Pasternak was. He looked at me in astonishment: "Didn't you know that he died the day before yesterday?" I did not know. Neither did the people I had seen during those two days.

On the morning of the next day, the day of the funeral, I called two different friends to find out how to get to Peredelkino where Pasternak had lived and where he died. Though we had spent two summers in the late thirties in the Peredelkino Writers' Village, I had completely forgotten how to get there. Both friends asked me why I was going there. Neither of them nor any member of their families had heard of Pasternak's death, and they were all well-educated, well-informed people.

They had missed the few short lines which had appeared only in the two literary newspapers. There had been nothing in either *Pravda* or *Izvestia*. The short radio news flash announcing his death must have been at quite an unpopular hour since, as I found out later, few people had heard it. The announcement in the papers was not in the name of the important All-Soviet Writers' Union which will go down in history as the body that expelled Pasternak after he received the Nobel Prize. It was signed by the less important Literary Fund, which is a kind of a writers' caretaker and welfare organization. This was certainly meant as a slight to Pasternak. But it must be pointed out that it was the Literary Fund that had really saved Pasternak after his ordeal by not expelling him as the Union did. If it had, his life would have become impossible, for the Fund controls writers' housing, royalties, medical care, and anything else on which a writer's life depends in Russia. Since the Fund could not have acted on its own, I was told that obviously the authorities wanted to give Pasternak a good spanking but not to deprive him of his house and livelihood.

I chose the easiest way to get to Peredelkino. I took a cab. When we were approaching the village the driver said that he would have to ask for directions to get to Pasternak's house. He did not have to. Though we arrived about two hours before the announced hour of the funeral, many cars already lined the street. A militiaman on guard approached us, saluted politely, and asked in a reverent voice: "You are going to Boris Leonidovich?" (Pasternak's name and patrimony) as if we were on our way to pay a visit to a living venerated man. He then politely waved us to a free parking spot.

I joined the stream of people with flowers in their hands walking through the fields toward Pasternak's house. The flowers were added to the mountains of them that surrounded the coffin. By the time the funeral started every room in the house was filled with them. With the exception of not more than a couple of elaborate commercial arrangements they were informal bunches of lilacs, tulips, narcissi, violets, lilies-of-the-valley bought in the markets or on street corners, or picked in the woods or gardens.

There was an expression of deep peace on Pasternak's handsome, noble face. One almost had the feeling of being relieved for him, for his final release from insufferable physical pain as well as from the mental anguish inflicted by contemptible pygmies who had haunted him for decades. After paying their respects people stood quiet around the house and as the crowd increased they spilled out over the garden into the fields and the surrounding woods. Exquisite soft music came from the house for hours. Svetoslav Richter, a devoted friend of Pasternak, who a few months later was to delight American audiences, was the pianist. There was no sign of any religious service though I was told—on the eve of my departure, too late to verify it—that the day before the funeral there had been a Russian Orthodox service in the house.

For hours the huge crowd waited, talking, when at all, in soft voices. There were a great many silent greetings, handshakes, and handkissing. There were tears in many eyes. There might have been some curiosity seekers but they certainly were not obvious. The mood was one of genuine emotion. A man dressed and looking like a character out of early Gorki was half lying at the edge of the woods reciting Pasternak's poetry and there was constantly a circle of listeners around him.

It seemed to me that there were many young rebels in the crowd, some even in high school uniforms. It was nothing I could easily define and describe but they definitely looked very different from a crowd of young Komsomols at a party meeting. Some of them looked as I think young poets should look.

I was told that as soon as the news of Pasternak's death had spread among students they pasted hand written announcements in the railroad station from which the trains to Peredelkino run and in several other places, giving the time and place of the funeral. Considering the lack of official information and judging by the size of the crowd, it was obvious that the students had displayed a great deal of activity.

It was a long wait. The funeral had been announced for four o'clock. Four o'clock came, then five, and a ribbon of people still continued to wind along the path through the fields. Shortly after five the crowd grew quite dense. I learned later that a delegation from nearby collective farms and industrial plants had asked the family to postpone the funeral till after five because many of the farmers and workers wanted to pay Pasternak a tribute. After a while this new wave of people subsided, and the funeral cortege began to form. The flowers from the house were handed out to the crowd and passed over the heads of the people up to the very last rows. It was an endless procession of people and flowers.

When we reached the cemetery and the crowd surrounded the grave the flowers were again passed over people's heads to be piled around the mound. I left soon after the speeches began. I was standing too far from the grave to hear them. A few minutes before I left there was a disturbance. In the middle of a speech a man tried to interrupt the ceremony, crying out that he too was a poet. He might have been a plain crank or of unbalanced mind. But most people suspected that it was a deliberate provocation, intended to create a disturbance, and ignored him. He quickly quieted down. I was told later that after the official speeches had ended and the family as well as most of the crowd had left, many young people, mostly students, remained for many hours reciting Pasternak's poetry.

On the way back the driver said: "He was a great man, it is good that he was so honored. If he hadn't been so meanly attacked, he wouldn't be dead yet." Since on our way out to Peredelkino I had gained the impression that the driver had never heard of Pasternak, he was obviously repeating what he had heard people say at the funeral.

A couple of days later I spent some extremely pleasant hours with a group of young people. I listened with great interest to recollections of their childhood during the war, of the postwar school years, of their present lives, of their dreams for the future. I let them talk, even though at times I had a strong urge to contradict them. I wanted to get a true picture of them, which I wouldn't have had we started an argument. So the harmonious hours went on. Then suddenly a wall arose and the warm atmosphere was chilled.

One of the young people had mentioned Pasternak. Three days after his funeral not everybody in the room knew that he had died. One of them said that he was buried in secret and that no one knew where. There was dead silence when I said that if they wanted to know more about the funeral and where Pasternak was buried I could tell them since I was there. Then some reluctant comment came:

"Probably a few old friends of his were there. . . . Not one of our well-known writers, of course. . . . No young people would think of being part of it."

Three days after the funeral the impression it had made on me was still strong. The faces of the many young people I had seen there rose before me. The result was one of those very rare times during my stay in Moscow when I totally lost my temper and attacked fiercely. I told them that someday Russians would be deeply ashamed of what they had done to one of their greatest poets; that even in Czarist Russia no great writer, even one strongly opposed to the regime, which Pasternak certainly was not, had ever been subjected to the cruelties inflicted on Pasternak; that he had had plenty of opportunities to go abroad and stay there but did not; that when the names of those nonentities who had attacked him were long forgotten Russia would be proud of him and honor him; that I had known him personally and never had anything but deepest admiration and respect for him, something I could not say about those who had vilified him. I told them that I was not interested in personalities at the funeral since I went solely to pay my respects to a great man and to the greatest poet Russia had had for many generations, but that there were many famous artists, writers and musicians there and that I saw hundreds upon hundreds of young people. I think that my uncontrolled outburst left a mark.

Of course, Pasternak's name came up in many other conversations. For instance, I was told, that it was an open secret that some copies of *Dr. Zhivago* had been smuggled in from abroad. And it certainly was no secret that some typists had made good money on the clandestine job of typing the long book in at least four copies and charging one ruble per page. Though I did not come across any Russians who had read the book, everyone I talked with about it had a definite opinion on it. As a rule, depending on their general point of view, people either liked or disliked Pasternak; they either quoted every derogative official pronouncement on him or found reasons to defend him; they either said that *Dr. Zhivago* was a bad book or that it most likely was a very good one.

Some said that there probably would have been less excitement about Pasternak abroad if the book had been published in Russia before it received the Nobel Prize. Others were convinced that the novel would never have received the Nobel Prize if it had been published in Russia. And still others were certain that it would have been impossible to publish the novel in Russia, since it obviously disagreed with the present official interpretation of the events it describes. There was much disagreement about whether Pasternak was prepared to make any changes. One school of thought insisted that he had categorically refused to change even a single word, another that he was ready to make any changes required in order to have the novel published in Russia. Maybe someday we will know the whole truth.

I heard recently that a group of Soviet writers is working on Pasternak's literary heritage. Since nothing in the Soviet Union can be done without a nod from above, the authorities that be have either changed their opinion about Pasternak—or maybe the whole uproar had nothing whatever to do with Pasternak as a writer.

After the arrest of Pasternak's friend, Madame Ivinskaya, and her daughter, American papers speculated widely about the role she had played in his life. I heard little talk about it in Moscow. Since there are no gossip columnists in Russia, only Pasternak's friends knew and talked about this relationship. I heard of it because I knew some writers. Otherwise very few people among the many I met knew about it, and even they showed little interest. The discussions were always about Pasternak as a writer. His love life was not a topic of conversation.

CHAPTER TWENTY-ONE

The Meaning of Freedom

When upon my return I was asked about conversations I had in Russia I used the words "fascinating," "interesting," "exciting." They certainly were that. But not in the sense we mean it when we say conversation was interesting or exciting. The fascination lay partly in constantly opening doors on details of living and thinking which could not possibly be comprehended in America. And partly it was in the realization of how shallow, repetitious, unoriginal is Soviet thinking, if you can call it thinking.

My ten fingers would probably suffice to count the conversations in which people expressed stimulating thoughts of their own, where they grappled within themselves and with others in search of answers and conclusions. The overwhelming majority of my innumerable talks consisted of the same approach, the same reactions, the same pat answers given in exactly the same words. I could not help thinking of Pavlov's dogs. It was fascinating, as I say, and to me, at least, thoroughly terrifying. The slightest criticism, especially, evoked the same automatic, unthinking reaction. Just as the Soviet government constantly attacks the West and is up in arms at the slightest criticism however justified, so are ordinary Russians. They feel completely free to criticize anybody and anything in the Western world, especially in the United States, but are highly intolerant of the slightest criticism directed toward them. Even among the better educated I often met the same attitude. I would sum up in this way the essence of some of the responses I had from people who were conscious of their lack of intellectual freedom:

"How can we possibly indulge now in the luxury of leisurely discussions, how can we give up valuable space in our newspapers or time on the radio, when we still have so much to do to produce the simple things which you have considered indispensable parts of your life for generations now? And even if our people have learned to read and to write, it takes more than one or two generations to polish minds. Give us a little more time, let our minds be polished, our houses built, our needs for a comfortable life satisfied, our military strength assure us of safety, and we too will indulge in free unhurried scrutinies and quests and mental explorations on a higher level. The time has not come yet but it will come."

If the talk was of internal affairs, there would be at times some differences of opinion or even an expression of mild criticism; but conversations on international affairs were thoroughly maddening. All was either utterly black or lily-white. Utterly black, of course, was the United States; lily-white, the Soviet Union. My attempts to present a dispassionate picture, admitting our faults and mistakes, failed dismally. "You see, you say it yourself!" was the inevitable triumphant reaction.

At times the Russians were outright illogical; complaining about things which they would in the same breath heatedly defend if I agreed with them. But then let any American remember how on a trip abroad or talking with a foreigner in the United States he will stoutly rise to the defense of anything the foreigner criticizes though he himself may have blasted away at it a moment earlier.

Restricted though this sensitiveness made many conversations, it was infinitely easier now to involve Russians in prolonged discussion than it had been in the late thirties when people were afraid of their own shadows. Then any criticism of the obvious defects of Stalin's rule was private and whispered, and confined to close friends. Now people feel much freer to say openly what they think. They are once more the great talkers they used to be. During the Years of Silence —the purges—the Russians ceased to be themselves. They are themselves again. Young and old, at the slightest provocation, get into endless arguments. They are pat, predictable, rarely profound or introspective, but at least people talk again. And they talk without lowering their voices, unless the conversation shifts to too dangerous subjects. To me it was a source of great enjoyment to watch and hear people again indulge in their favorite pastime.

One evening when the room rang with loud dissenting voices an older friend told me that it was music to his ears, though they were talking about nothing more controversial than the decorations of a new subway station.

"There were so many years when no one dissented," he said, "and when in every room of this very apartment all talking was done in whispers."

Even among the Intourist workers, whose job is dealing with foreigners and therefore demands more reserve, there was less parroting of official slogans than formerly. In chats during their off-work hours they expressed opinions of their own on books, plays, architecture, or art, frequently disagreeing among themselves and at times even with a *Pravda* review. Minimal as their independent thinking on a few limited subjects would seem to a Westerner not familiar with Soviet ways, it seemed of great significance to me.

Several times when I sincerely praised something I heard the complaint that has also been made officially: while people are in the Soviet Union they praise everything, but when they are back home—they criticize. I honestly tried to explain but this was not an easy task. The Russians did not seem to realize that, first, they make it difficult to continue a friendly conversation after one has expressed even the slightest criticism. One therefore ceases to criticize anything in their presence, which doubtless creates the impression that one is thoroughly pleased with everything. Second, that one sincerely admires the many achievements. Third, that we consider honest reporting requires one to present both sides of the picture— the good as well as the bad.

I wonder whether I ever convinced anybody. For Russians, who are trained to see only the rosy side as far as their own country is concerned, criticism, even if accompanied by praise, implies enmity. Nothing fundamentally negative about the Soviet system ever appears in the press, and the Russians are conditioned to consider the slightest criticism of their system a betrayal. This is a deep source of fundamental misunderstanding. When in the course of these exchanges I would ask why it was all right for them to criticize the Western world so fiercely, pointing out that Soviet journalists and travelers never report anything good about the West, I received several times the startling but sincerely meant reply:

"What is there to criticize about our system? But the capitalist system is thoroughly wrong."

There were other responses, of course. Not everybody was sure that the Soviet system could ever bring them freedom. On the other hand, I did not get the impression that Russians necessarily associate the West with freedom. Their minds have been too filled with the defects of the West, with all the derogatory information they get on the capitalist system and private trade. It is hard to associate the evils they hear about our world with the lofty ideal of freedom.

What today's Russians know of private enterprise in Russia is that it is sly, illegal, fraudulent, more often than not connected with stealing and cheating. They have not known private enterprise based on anything else. The short few years in the twenties when private trade was permitted are ancient history, nor was it conducted then with integrity.

The same goes for the word "capitalism." To them it connotes only imperialism, exploitation, colonialism, excessive poverty beside excessive wealth. For example, when I would point out that our workers were allowed to strike, whereas theirs were not, I would be told quite seriously:

"Of course! Your workers need strikes to protect them against exploitation by the capitalists. Otherwise they would starve and freeze. But ours? Ridiculous! Against whom would Soviet workers strike?

Against themselves? Against their own government, which is satisfying all their needs and demands?"

The Russians do not call our world a free democratic world, for that phrase has been taken over to describe their own world. "Social democracy" is a bad word since Social Democrats have for decades more consistently fought communism than many a bona fide, dyed-in-the-wool capitalist for whom trade with Communists doesn't seem such a bad idea. Forty-three years of distorted history and perverted terminology have obscured visions and produced plenty of cobwebs in minds and in words. I never felt this so strongly as when our conversations touched on ideals of freedom, and on the differences between East and West, using the same words which to me and to the Russians had totally opposite meanings.

Freedom and its meaning was the subject of one of the best talks I had during my visit. It was with an old friend whom I had seen several times, but always in a crowd, and he had never said anything revealing or different from what others said. This time he had maneuvered it so that we were undisturbed for a couple of hours and he unexpectedly opened up. When he asked whether I could visualize living in Russia again, I most emphatically said no. Why so emphatic? he asked. I could not breathe without freedom, I said. What is freedom? came his question. This man is a scholar, a philologist. He has traveled abroad, he reads French and English, and has access to American, English and French newspapers, magazines and books. His questions were not the usual ones, easy to answer. He asked whether I considered the United States a truly free country.

"Why," he asked, "can anyone, even a crank, say whatever he wants to say in London's Hyde Park, and what are your authorities afraid of in New York's Union Square?"

Other questions were:

"Why are you so afraid of your American Communists? The Italian and French governments have so many more of them, and they are much less jittery about them. Why is the American so suspicious of anyone who expresses ideas contrary to his own? And what is the average American's attitude anyway? Is it one way according to the Declaration of Independence or the Gettysburg Address and another according to what McCarthy or Edgar Hoover or Dulles decided at a given moment?"

And: "Does freedom evolve or is it being declared? Is it declared in general terms or in detail? Who in the United States defines the detailed terms today?"

He agreed with me that he was not free, that Russia was not free, that no Communist country was free. He insisted that he was not attacking me or the United States. He was trying to define for himself, he said, whether the freedom we have in the United States was real freedom and whether we lived up to the words we pronounced in the name of freedom. He wanted to create in his mind a picture of real human freedom for which he could strive and he was not sure he saw the image of this freedom at present in the United States. It had been easier for me with people whose arguments against the United States were simple to answer and to destroy than with a wise-thinking man who was searching for the same ideal I was and who saw fault where I saw fault.

At the end of our conversation, however, he told me that, because I did not contradict him in what he knew was true, and because I tried to be honest with him, I had convinced him that Americans are free to think and even to act when freedom is being attacked. That was good enough for him, he said, even though not all Americans seemed always to use this right to act. And, he added, this would help him keep his faith that someday freedom of the human spirit would prevail. It was a hard, interesting, and satisfactory talk, as well as the only one of the kind I had in Moscow.

Most Russians, it was apparent, believe sincerely that only under communism can there be total satisfaction of all human needs, equal opportunities for all, no exploitation of man by man. The fact that they are far from their goal does not interfere with their belief.

"The road toward our lofty ideals is a long and arduous one," I was told. "We have gone a long way on it and we keep going."

When I expressed doubt, pointing out the obvious digressions from their ideals that seemed to lead in the opposite direction, they usually counterattacked.

"How about your own lofty ideals? You are supposed to have reached your goals. How do they fit with segregation, slums, underprivileged children?" Invariably they would quote news stories from our own press. More than once, defending our society and our way of life, I had to compromise with my own conscience. The picture of four-legged pets snugly clothed in fur coats and rubbers in a city where inadequately clothed and fed children live in unheated, rat-infested slums at times interfered with my words about freedom, equality, opportunities for all.

The issue of segregation gave me the most trouble. I found it impossible to make anyone understand that what happened in a school in the South was definitely not ordered by Washington. The woman I was talking with, like the others, would accept nothing except what she had been told by her own government through the press and radio. And what she read and heard was that the American government treated Negroes in a bestial way.

I spoke with several Americans who had contact with Russians, and they were unanimous on this: the racial problem is a tremendous blot on our national reputation. In all sincerity some Russians asked me to explain to them how our treatment of the Negro could go hand in hand with the widely quoted ideals of American democracy. Others, less kind, would throw at me cruel but undeniable facts reprinted in *Pravda* or *Izvestia* from the American press. Of course, there is a great deal that one can and does say in answer: That there is progress, that the government is not responsible for discrimination, that many of us are dissatisfied with the slowness of the progress, that we are certainly trying to do something about it. But these are insufficient answers and they sound flat when one is defending democracy in a city filled with dark-skinned students and visitors who can eat anywhere they want and sleep in any hotel.

I wondered at times whether it might not be a good idea to send some of our most rabid segregationists to Russia. They pretend to be patriotic Americans. Maybe if they saw for themselves the great harm they are doing to their country their patriotism might win out over their racism.

There is no doubt in my mind that Communists have clutched at our discrimination issue not because they have any special warmth for or interest in Negroes—they have shown plenty of inhumanity and brutality toward their own national minorities—but because it suits their purpose of attacking the United States wherever possible, and this is such a useful and easy issue to exploit. If deprived of it they will readily and efficiently find another issue. It so happens, however, that the segregation issue has a universal appeal at this special moment in human history. What better way of making friends in the young emerging Africa? And with the help of Communist parties all over the world the Soviet government can and is doing us endless harm in exploiting it with great efficiency and excellent results.

The Russians know even the tiniest detail about Little Rock, for instance (as they no doubt learned later about the University of Georgia, the sit-ins, the refusals to serve food to African UN delegates, etc.), but because of their lack of communication with the West they are totally ignorant of any world problem, however vital, that the Soviet government does not deem it necessary to inform them about.

CHAPTER TWENTY-TWO

Russians and the Outside World

Even conversations about the United States could be friendly and congenial as long as we stayed on the subject of everyday life or touched only lightly on politics. I rarely touched on the fundamentals of politics with old friends whom it might disturb; I did not want to have upsetting discussions with them. Not that I was eager for hot arguments with anyone, but as I have related more than once fur flew the moment we touched on the structure of our countries, the responsibility for the failure of the summit conference, the United States bases, spying (nothing was ever denied with more vehemence than the existence of Soviet spies abroad), or free elections.

At the risk of being overrepetitive I must say again that especially in conversations about our different systems of government there was not much sign of a bridge of understanding. Quickly gone then was the atmosphere of a friendly give-and-take which I tried to maintain whenever possible. Long-forgotten pages of Jack London and early Upton Sinclair rang in the air. I was once asked, for instance:

"Why do the American police beat striking workers to death?"

I laughed. I honestly thought it was asked as a joke. It was not. The United States these people were talking about had no resemblance at all to the one we live in today. This does not mean, of course, that they are not extremely well informed about our problems. They know about the number of unemployed, they know about the plight of the migrant workers, about the slums in the big cities, the overcrowded schools, crime, juvenile delinquency, the high cost of sickness, and of course Little Rock, as well as any other aspect of our segregation troubles. When I would say that many Americans are quite conscious of our own shortcomings and that we are trying to remedy them and often succeed, I made little impression. Their own press, they believed, was a more reliable source of information than an American visitor. Nor had they any idea of what the active participation and influence of private citizens can bring about. Neither can they understand that the American government is not powerful enough to eliminate overnight whatever evil it wants to eliminate.

"Why is there nobody in the United States besides the Communist party to take the side of the workers and peasants?" I was asked more than once. It was dreadful, they thought, that since the party was persecuted and its members were rotting in prisons the unfortunate American workers and peasants were left without any protection whatever. I wonder whether my attempts to give a more realistic picture of the membership of the American Communist party, of how few "workers and peasants" belong to it, and of the status of the American workers and peasants, met with any great success. The Russians' image of the United States is so utterly unrealistic and at times so funny that a good laugh should have been the only answer but that would have been taken as a sign of my heartlessness toward the fate of those poor downtrodden Americans.

Once a very young salesgirl at a GUM counter asked me in a voice full of compassion about the suffering of the American working class. I tried my best to prove to her that her compassion was slightly misplaced. I spoke of our unemployment, of which the Russians are told a great deal, and about unemployment compensation, of which they hear nothing. I delivered a real lecture trying to explain the problems of overproduction, seasonal unemployment, automation, etc. There were a number of people waiting for the attention of the salesgirl, but no one objected to our protracted conversation and some eagerly participated in it. I doubt, however, that what I said had any effect. I may have put one or two new thoughts into the young salesgirl's head, but the pity she carried in her heart for the tragic fate of the downtrodden American workers was probably too deep-seated to be shaken.

One evening with several young people around we talked about the purges, the postwar terror, the Hitler pact, the Doctors' Plot, and much more. There was the usual reaction to whatever was considered negative: Stalin's errors and the mysterious "inevitable historical process." Then, when I was asked questions about the United States I spoke at length of the tremendous changes, social and economic and cultural, which I had witnessed in the United States since I first went there in 1916. I told them of the disappearance of sweatshops and child labor, of the introduction of social security, of minimum wages, of legislation against racial discrimination, and so on. The reaction was a totally unexpected one.

"Oh, yes," said one of the young men, "that was only natural. The Bolshevik revolution had forced the whole world to adopt its humane concern for people, especially for workers and peasants. The American people would otherwise have revolted against their government. Your ruling classes were forced to do it by us."

Several heads nodded approvingly, and again I was shocked over their total lack of understanding of the outside world. Suppose I had told them that among the American labor leaders who had been most prominent in the fight for better working conditions they would find the most outspoken opponents of the Soviet Union? Once more I would have been accused of lying; that would have been all.

During the same evening I brought up, as I often did, our freedom to disagree, to discuss, to express our differences openly. I could have recited the answers I received: we don't need different parties, opposition, discussions, all that you in the capitalist world need. Our Soviet regime has eliminated the necessity for individuals to do anything for the people; the government takes care of them.

One of the young men, whom I had known as a baby and who was usually most affectionate and friendly, expressed pity for me for being so obviously wrong and naïve. His wife, worried lest I might be insulted (which I certainly was not), brought out a tray with refreshments and a topic more familiar to the young people than to me: American jazz, and the evening ended with the usual warm fellowship.

I tried constantly to get to the bottom of this illogical contempt for everything American and rejection of things to which the Russians themselves so obviously aspire. Their answer invariably was that only the wealthy are able to enjoy these things in the United States, but that when they become available in the Soviet Union everyone will enjoy them, the Kremlin and those on the farms, and therein lay all the difference.

At times I succeeded in exercising the necessary patience and self-control to listen to the fantastic views of Russians on the Western world. Occasionally I even succeeded in expressing a thought or two without being too fiercely attacked. But the only truly quiet conversations on foreign affairs I had was with faithful older party members. Their unshaken faith in the final triumph of communism is so deep-seated that any contrary suggestion can mean only a total lack of understanding on the part of the dissenter. Why waste time arguing when life itself keeps arguing for them and proves communism right?

Several times during conversations about the United States people quoted violently anti-American articles from the Soviet press, reprinted from French, Swedish, Indian, British, and other papers. But never did anyone mention that the authors of these articles were either active Communists or Communist sympathizers who would under no circumstances express a pro-American point of view. Such articles are widely distributed as representative of the general world opinion on the United States.

The Stalin-Hitler pact came up in many conversations on foreign affairs. To most people it was news to hear of the strong reaction of the Western world to the pact, of the many Communists all over the world who left the party because of it. Nor did they have any idea of the struggle in the United States between isolationists and interventionists, of Roosevelt's attitude, of England's. In short, the great majority of Russians knew nothing about the problems of the Western world, whether past or present.

There are a few stock phrases that must be in all textbooks since all kinds of people used them constantly. Here is one of them: The West has no other aim but first to weaken and finally to destroy the Soviet Union, though capitalism itself is sentenced by history to an imminent death; communism is taking over as the wave of the future.

The Russians appreciate foreign goods, they envy the number of gas stations and the accessibility of auto-repair shops, the amount of living space and wealth of consumers' goods, admire foreign cars and the elegance of foreign tourists. Above all they envy our freedom of travel. But none of this interferes with their fundamental belief that our system—and therefore all its achievements—is based on exploitation, while the Soviet Union, as soon as it catches up with the United States, will possess everything the Americans enjoy today but no one will be exploited.

This word "exploitation" was used constanty, but I heard much less mention of the word "inequality," though in the past the two words were often linked. I presume that it is hard for even the most enthusiastic Soviet patriot not to realize that Soviet society is far from having achieved equality. Those with whom I could talk without reservation admitted, some with genuine sadness, that there was much less equality in Soviet society today than there had been in the earlier Soviet years.

Once in the course of a discussion on Soviet citizens' hopes of traveling abroad, I said that there might be a risk in exposing Russians to the freedom and general way of life in the Western world. I was rudely cut short by one of the men:

"This is humbug! Our standard of living is going to be as high as yours very soon now and there will be nothing for us to be impressed by. No one is afraid of our being exposed to your capitalist ideas and to your distorted notions of freedom."

According to him, the one and only problem was foreign exchange which, he insisted, was going to be settled as soon as the currency reform took place.

As I have said before, there is a definite block in people's minds where foreign affairs are concerned. We would have a friendly give-and-take on a thousand and one topics but the moment the Soviet Union versus the outside world came up minds closed and genuine discussion became impossible. Even those violently opposed to almost everything Stalin did in domestic affairs accepted without question his annexation of other countries or his breaking of treaties and promises. And they would definitely deny that he was in any way responsible for the cold war.

One old Communist friend who was critical of many of the Kremlin's domestic policies, under both Stalin and Khrushchev, spoke for many others when he stanchly defended all Khrushchev's activities in the foreign field. In the case of Stalin he disapproved only of the pact with Hitler in 1939. He had felt very strongly about it at that time but, he added, he later understood the necessity for it. The Soviet government had no choice, he said.

"If we had not signed the pact, Hitler would have thrown his entire might against us and do you think that even one Western power would have raised a finger to save us?"

Once in the course of an argument I mentioned that I remembered how Lenin's decision to give Finland and the three Baltic states—Latvia, Lithuania and Estonia—their independence after the 1917 revolution was hailed as proof that the Soviet regime believed in national self-determination and freedom for other peoples. Hadn't all the outright annexations under one guise or another after the last war been retreats from Lenin's vision of what Soviet Russia should have been? I asked.

Oh, no, was the consensus of the replies. Lenin acted at that time solely out of military and political expediency, because the Soviet regime was weak, never out of any conviction that this should remain Soviet policy in the future. As soon as it was possible to correct it Stalin did so. Besides, I was told, Finland was still independent, and as to the Baltic States, they were so small and weak economically that they were much better off as part of a big strong country like the U.S.S.R. I asked whether the peoples of these countries had been asked how they felt about it, and how this fitted in with Soviet advocacy of independence and freedom for even the tiniest and weakest African or Asian country, which might also be better off under the tutelage of a strong Great Britain or France. The answers were a literal repetition or rehash of *Pravda* editorials on wicked Western colonialism and imperialism, and the brotherly, selfless Soviet concern for the meek and weak of this earth.

During that same evening, after listening to an account of what Russia went through during the past two decades, I gave a chronology of that period the way I saw events: the pact, the war, the war conferences, the taking over of the satellite countries, the blockade of Berlin, Korea, and the total change in United States' attitude as a result of these events. Fierce denials of any Soviet wrongdoing were showered on me. My interpretation, mildly as I tried to word it, was contrary to every account and interpretation they had ever heard. The chasm between our attitudes was hopelessly wide. When I reached the hotel that night I was sad as well as worried.

Once I asked a friend whether it was right to have forced Czechoslovakia into communism when so few of her people had wanted it? This man had known Czechoslovakia well and had no illusions about the insignificance of the Communist party there. His answer to my question was the answer of an orthodox Communist: the Bolshevik revolution of 1917 was made by a few for the sake of the many. There were few Communists in Czechoslovakia in 1948, that was true. But neither were there many Bolsheviks in Russia in 1917, he said; the masses were won over later, and they were in Czechoslovakia too. Now the people there were satisfied and of course would not want to return to capitalism. He fiercely denied that the coup was instigated by the Russians. It was solely the work of Czech Communists, he was convinced of that. Will I ever know whether people were trying to fool me when they said these things or did they sincerely believe them?

Several people told me that the satellites were happy to be under the protection of Big Brother Russia and did not mind in the least giving up some of their independence for this protection and assistance, since their independence was being threatened by imperialists. Some Russians, however, told me that they resented the help sent to the satellites during the first years after the war when Russia herself needed every morsel of food and every piece of machinery. When I suggested that possibly the satellites had sent some food and machinery to Russia during those years instead of the other way around, it was indignantly denied and I was, as on many other occasions, accused of a total ignorance of world affairs.

I gained the impression that many Russians really believed that the satellites' ties with Russia were entirely voluntary, the result of popular demand. Incidentally, I was not supposed to use the term "satellites" in Russia. "Socialist countries" is the only proper expression to use. They were completely free and independent and no one's satellite, I was told in Russia as well as in New York, where a European Communist corrected me when I used the word "satellite" in his presence.

In all these conversations it seemed that no countries except the United States and the Soviet Union mattered at all. There was obvious indifference when France or England or Sweden or Canada or Egypt or India or Cuba or any other country was mentioned. And in some cases there was a tone of disdain when the names of the new African or smaller Asian countries came up. The press, of course, gave plenty of space to anything that happened in even the smallest country on earth if it in any way added to the prestige of the Soviet Union or hurt the prestige of the United States. However, I found little reflection of that interest in the population. For them it seemed there were only two countries worth talking about. The others were merely pawns in the game between the Big Two. Very few of the older people and none of the younger ones were in the least concerned about complicated problems of the new Asian and African countries, or realized to what extent the West was interested and was helping in the underdeveloped countries' struggle against poverty and disease. That anyone besides the Soviet Union would understand the needs of these countries and would offer assistance had never occurred to them. It also sounded unbelievable to them that there might be underdeveloped countries, especially among those who only recently became independent, who would look for non-Communist ways and means to achieve progress and end poverty.

Several times I was asked: "Why are Americans always opposed to Soviet policies?" It was at times hard for me to judge whether my questioners, so many of them chance acquaintances, were always genuinely in search of an answer or used such questions merely as an opening for anti-American propaganda.

I remember especially well a conversation in a family where I spent a couple of hours purely accidentally. I had come to visit neighbors but they were out. The mother of the family asked me to wait in their room. I had not met these people before and never saw them afterward, but somehow this remained in my memory as one of the pleasantest exchanges I had with Russians. After they had in a not too unfriendly tone enumerated their grievances against the United States and the Western world, they gave me the floor.

Also in as friendly a way as possible I enumerated in concrete terms my criticism of Soviet policies and asked them whether they had always agreed with all of them.

"Did you agree," I asked them, "with the purges, with the pact, with the Doctors' Plot, for instance, with all the degradations you suffered under Stalin?"

"Of course not" was the emphatic answer, "but all that is gone and can never happen again."

That they really believed this could not be doubted, and my suggestion that such things might happen again was definitely rejected. I have not always succeeded but this was one of the few cases where I think I did in some degree penetrate the concrete wall of the habitual word associations and put at least some of the words in their proper context. Among the most rigid word associations which these people too kept repeating are: Wall Street-Pentagon-Rockefeller (or Ford-Morgan-Harriman, the name doesn't matter); Democrats-Republicans-exploitation of workers, peasants, Negroes; capitalism-fascism-Franco-Chiang Kai-shek-American bases abroad.

Toward the end of our conversation I asked them as I had asked so many others:

"Why can we, in the United States, praise the good and criticize the defects in talking and writing about our own country or about England, Argentina, India, Ghana, or any other spot on earth you name? Why should we forever treat the Soviet Union as a sacred cow, as a paradise on earth, where nothing wrong is ever said or done? Why can you go on vilifying us while we are considered criminals, reactionaries or Fascists if we criticize even the same things you consider wrong and which Khrushchev himself admits are wrong?"

I received an answer only to my last question:

"But Khrushchev has said all there is to be said about the past errors. What is there to talk about? Why waste time and chew forever on a past that is gone?"

To my question: "Do you agree with everything that has happened since Stalin's death?" the answer was: "Of course! If occasionally a mistake is made, Khrushchev admits it and corrects it. There is nothing for us to worry about now."

Our conversation was friendly, we patiently listened to one another, which did not always happen in Moscow, we did not once fly at each other, each honestly tried to understand the other's thoughts and feelings.

Though we had met only two hours earlier, our visit ended in friendship and even an embrace from the younger, 15-year-old, daughter. Despite our deep fundamental differences, a human contact was established between our two worlds which someday may prove to have been more useful than if we had parted enemies over the question of who wrecked the Paris summit conference.

I never felt that our deep disagreements affected the friendly attitude of Russians toward me personally. They would, however, never make a secret of their glee over American setbacks. I was in Moscow during the anti-United States demonstrations in Japan, which resulted in the cancellation of President Eisenhower's trip. I asked several people whether these particular demonstrations or, for instance, the rejection of certain American policies in Japan and in other non-Communist countries might not be rather a confirmation that there was more freedom of expression in the non-Communist world than proof of "despicable Wall Street-Pentagon exploitation"? But, no, that is not the way Russian minds work. To them every anti-American demonstration in the world, wherever it takes place, proves only the fact that capitalism was and is fundamentally wrong and that people everywhere fight against it.

The most doubt I ever encountered concerning Soviet foreign policy concerned Hungary. Quite a number of people suspected that the Soviet action might have been wrong, that the revolt was a truly national uprising against a foreign rule, that Fascists and foreign capitalists were not behind it, that youths and workers led it. The doubters sensed that what was reported to them was not the true story. But they had no way of knowing the truth since the Voice of America as well as other broadcasts from abroad were completely jammed at that time. But even the doubters were not too concerned about the Hungarians. If keeping Hungary under total Soviet control was good for Russia, that was all that really mattered.

In discussions on Hungary the word "freedom" would inevitably come up. I would then ask what people meant when they used or heard the word. The answers were of great variety. For some it meant the right to choose or change one's profession or job, or to go on a vacation wherever one chose, or not to be afraid to associate with whomever one wanted to. Or, as one woman put it:

"Freedom means being able to choose who it could be when you hear a knock at your door in the middle of the night. In the past it could have been only the secret police, now I can choose between an out-of-town relative or a friend dropping in, or a drunken neighbor mistaking his door."

One man said freedom meant not being afraid of one's own

shadow, to another it meant straightening his back. A few used the opportunity to give me another lecture on freedom from exploitation, from slavery, from injustice, from discrimination, and all the way down the line. Whether the discussion on Hungary shifted to freedom or to anything else, it was a topic that several I talked with seemed glad to drop. Hungary seems to have aroused doubts in them which they would rather suppress.

If it was obvious that Hungary had aroused some doubts in the minds of the Russians, it was also obvious that they spoke of China with great reluctance. During my stay in Russia hardly anything appeared in the papers on China and still less mention of it by the people I talked to. Whenever, in order to get a reaction, I raised the question of China or Soviet-Sino relations with people who, I was certain, must have been thinking about it, their response was noncommittal and vague:

"I love Chinese art. . . . Isn't the Chinese theater interesting? . . . I wish I could go there on a trip."

Once in a discussion about India and Asia in general someone said:

"It's true the revolution in China has brought a great upheaval and has demanded great sacrifices. But weren't the sacrifices worthwhile in order to eliminate disease and hunger and child mortality, and establish freedom from exploitation? Wouldn't the people of India be much better off under a Communist regime as the Chinese are now?"

This was echoed once or twice by the comment that communism has saved China from starvation and total ruin. But there was never a word about possible Soviet-Chinese conflicts.

Those who had personal experience with Chinese who were working or studying in Russia spoke with contempt of their overzealousness. A young Russian engineer told me of his Chinese colleague on a Siberian job. Every morning the Chinese was at work when the Russians were still fast asleep. He usually left before breakfast at dawn. After the evening meal the Russians spent their time at the movies, dancing, playing cards, and so on. The Chinese, after eating much less than his colleagues, would immediately go back to the plant and returned to his room only for a few hours' sleep. Not once during the three months they had spent together did he join the Russians in their leisure. They were far from admiring his diligence; indeed, they made fun of him, thought him queer, and had nothing to do with him. My young engineer friend and most of his Russian colleagues were members of the party. But they belonged to the young Soviet generation which had learned to play although deeply devoted to its work.

It seems to me that the Russians neither feel any intimate bond with the Chinese because they are Communists nor fear a conflict in the future, ideological or any other. They are not in the habit of concerning themselves with things they never read about in the press or hear over the radio. Whatever difficulties Khrushchev may have with the Chinese do not yet worry the Soviet man in the street.

I heard several anecdotes in Moscow about China. I liked best the shortest of them: There are three kinds of movies in Russia—good, bad, and Chinese.

CHAPTER TWENTY-THREE

Departure

In the past I had known Russians to whom the Soviet regime had meant hell and others to whom it represented heaven. A few of the first, but by no means all of them, still felt the same way. The old enthusiasts were even more enthusiastic. And the general atmosphere was certainly one of loyalty to the regime.

It saddened me, however, to find even among the most devout Communists much less of the excitement and enthusiasm that had characterized the twenties and thirties. Having tasted the material satisfactions of an improved economy, having savored the promise of still better things to come, and having gained a certain confidence that the people who are running the country at present are not going to revert to Stalinism, the Russians are beginning to settle down inwardly. And of course they realize that there is little they can do to change things, anyway. As a result of all this, people are generally in a much quieter mood than during the turbulent twenties and early thirties.

But isn't there the same absence of heat and passion elsewhere in the world too, compared with the excitement of two or three decades ago? I do not know Asia and Africa but I do know the United States and Europe, and the only passionate reaction I have encountered during these past years in the United States or in

Western Europe was in Vienna in 1956. During the weeks when the torrent of Hungarian refugees poured into Austria I saw for myself how the imagination of European youth was fired as it had been in the thirties by the Spanish Civil War.

It was hard for me to believe, during my weeks in Russia, that an event occurring outside the Soviet Union had so aroused the emotions of the Russian people, aroused them as hardly anything else ever had. At that time a tidal wave of deep sympathy for their Spanish brothers and an idealistic desire to help swept the country. The feeling was at first government inspired; it could not have been otherwise in the Soviet Union. Nevertheless, it was completely genuine, and among our Russian friends the Spanish war was—next to the purges—the main topic of conversation. But not once during my visit, when I brought up the subject and recalled the deep emotional participation of the Russians, did I find even a hint of a response. The older generation was too preoccupied with what had happened after that. For the young people it was not even a page out of history but boiled down merely to: "the Germans were trying out weapons for their future aggression against the Soviet Union." Not one person was able to tell me anything about any of the many Spaniards, mostly children, who came to Russia at that time and were received with an emotion bordering on adulation. Some of the people I asked about it had then enthusiastically attended every meeting about Spain, had invited Spanish children to their homes, had sacrificed some of their meager belongings to drives for Spain. Now it was a page of history torn out and lost.

Among the people with whom I discussed the Spanish war were several who, by the sheer logic of their backgrounds, should have been irreconcilable enemies of the Soviet regime. They were not. Their lips seemed to be sealed against even a single word of indignation or protest. Indeed, I met some who were reconciled to their fate to an almost enthusiastic degree. In not one of those people did I detect a sign of anything even remotely resembling genuine opposition.

A not very orthodox Moscovite who had much fault to find with

Soviet domestic policies said that should there be a free referendum today at least 90 per cent of the people would give a definite yes to Khrushchev and the Soviet regime. As was my custom, I asked several more people the same question and the answer was always the same, with a slight variation in the estimated percentage. Some added that, of course, in the past, especially in the thirties, the answer would have been a different one. And a few said that they would vote for Khrushchev, though they don't by a long shot agree with everything he does, because someone else would be so much worse.

These latter were people who had preserved their capacity to think for themselves to a certain extent and were searching for ways to improve what they thought was wrong. There are probably not many such people around, and even these few were by no means anti-Soviet or pro-Western or ready for any kind of anti-Soviet activity. They were above all Russian patriots. They would like to see the Soviet regime democratized, they would like to improve and to modify it—but certainly not to overthrow it. By no means did they seem to me likely material for counterrevolutionary subversive activities.

Deep as is their patriotism, however, it seems to me that the loyalty of the Russian population to the Soviet regime springs to a great extent from the betterment in their living conditions. I could not help reflecting that if people are to strive exclusively, and at any cost, to satisfy their material well-being, then the way the Soviet government rules its subjects may be the right way. But if other things are important—human dignity, spiritual and personal freedom, the right independently to search for answers and to reach conclusions—it certainly is, to say the least, totally wrong.

And unless before too long there is more genuine contact with the outside world than conducted tours for foreigners, more contact with peoples and literatures (past and present) which mirror these demands, the seeds of a craving for more spiritual values which still flutter around in search of a fertile soul will perish. The resulting future Communist society is, to me at least, a thoroughly terrifying one. Often in our discussions of Soviet goals, material or spiritual, the question arose of whether the end justifies the means? All Communists and most non-Communists answered in the affirmative, and some of them were quite scornful of my loud *no*. Whenever upon my return I spoke of this, I never once heard an affirmative from my American friends.

Again, when I talked with Russians about the price to be paid for their achievements, we were as far apart as people could possibly be. To me, the question whether the tremendous sacrifices that the Russian people made for the sake of a better material life were unavoidable is not hard to answer. The answer is a flat no, of course. The Russians feel differently about it. Their arguments run on these lines:

They are sure that they would have been crushed long ago had they not been ready to make sacrifices. During the first years after the revolution there was the real danger of the weak regime being overthrown by opposition inside with the help of the outside world During the Five-Year Plans every bit of energy and nerve, however inhuman the cost, had to be utilized to build the country's strength. The whole world was out to crush the Soviet Union, and it had to be able to stand on its own strong economic, military and industrial feet.

All this may have had some basis in the twenties and thirties. But I could never accept the arguments brought to defend the postwar Soviet acts. There certainly was no danger then of the Soviet government being overthrown from outside. The friendly relationship with the West built up during the war, as well as the general desire for peace, was so great that a modus vivendi could certainly have been reached had the Soviet leaders either wanted to understand or had they correctly understood the outside world. For me, there can be no justification of the postwar Soviet terror, as there was none for the prewar one, and as there is none for the vicious anti-Westernism that is poisoning the minds of the Russians and is certainly anything but conducive to an easy solution of the world problems. (I am not entering here into a discussion of the

West's behavior, which at times could also have stood a great deal of improvement.)

If the fog created by the bombastic propaganda hammered into the Russians' heads could be cleared away and those heads could once again, as they did even under the tyranny of the czars, ponder the ideas and the ideals of a civilized world, they might agree that there must have been more human ways to become full-fledged members of a twentieth-century world community than by the barbaric methods of an Ivan the Terrible or a Hitler or a Stalin. I did not find too many signs that minds were clearing.

Some of the older Russians I talked with remembered that in the early years of the Soviet regime it was assumed that the rigid controls set up by the young revolutionary government would be relaxed as soon as external and internal peace was established. Nowhere in those early years was there a hint, at least that I could discern, that the suppression would remain a permanent feature and would grow worse as the years went by; that gradually the government would have power over every waking hour of its citizens, over the places they lived and worked, over the thoughts in their heads, the books they read, the friends they chose. But it did happen. Now there has been some relaxation of the control—not much, but enough for people to feel that the air they breathe is somewhat fresher, and to be duly appreciative. In this I cannot join them. That the window in a prison has been slightly opened may be a source of joy to those who are inside. But I like my windows not to be in a prison to begin with.

Some Russians sounded so delighted with things as they are and so hopeful for the future that at times I wondered: Maybe I am the one who is mistaken and not those who rejoice over the return of the Siberian exiles and over the rehabilitation of the reputation of the host of those who were killed by a merciful shot or perished in agony in a labor camp. Maybe those are right who see the dawn of a new happier life because a man is not afraid any more to say hello to an old friend; because a kitchen pot is more attractive, and new houses and transportation more plentiful. I never wondered for very long. I am unable to accept the right of a government to sacrifice millions of people, even for the sake of a brighter future, without asking them whether they are willing to sacrifice themselves and their families.

I certainly deeply enjoyed my trip. I was happy beyond words to see old friends whom I had feared I would never see again. I was overjoyed to hear laughter and to see the sparkling eyes of the young. But as far as I am concerned no improvements can under any circumstances justify the human sacrifices they cost; the immensity of which it is hard for the outside world to imagine.

There was another thing about my visit that saddened me. Despite my friends' lack of fear to receive me in their homes, whenever it came to the question whether we should correspond the response inevitably was: let's wait till you come again. To me this is rather frightening.

Here I spent a month seeing people, some old friends, some new ones to whom I grew attached, people who are unconditionally loyal to the regime, and I can't write them a letter. Not even a few words to tell them about my return trip, how I found my family and grandchildren about whom we had talked so much. I can't tell them what a joy it was for me to have seen them. I can't thank them for their warm and generous hospitality. I can't do any of the things so normal in our world, so thoroughly unpolitical, so purely human and personal.

It is true that some among the younger people said that it was all right to correspond, that it was not the way it had been in the Stalin days, that there was nothing to fear now. Some friends in the United States also told me that it was safe to correspond with Russians now, that many Americans do it these days. Maybe. But I remember too well how in the past lives were ruined because somewhere in the outside world there was a relative or a friend. And at times I had heard in Moscow the same doubt: "Who knows whether someday it will not again be a crime to know someone in the West?" And so—no letters will be written to any Moscow friends, and this is a source of great sadness for me.

In the end I was at times infinitely bored and exasperated at hearing the same things over and over again as if most Russians had built-in phonograph records. Often I wished I could have called them liars. Unfortunately I could not always have done so with a clear conscience.

Hard as some of our exchanges were for me, I managed to remain calm most of the time. On some occasions I even succeeded in presenting fully my own side of the picture. Only once did a conversation end in disaster and I never saw this couple again though I had known them quite well in the past. Their attack on me was so fierce and at the same time so idiotically senseless that it would have been of no use for us to meet again.

Disagreements did not necessarily end a good relationship. Accidentally, through an official of a satellite embassy, an old friend of ours had learned that some members of the Fischer family had criticized the Soviet Union. After we exchanged reports on our families (he had lost his only son in the war) he looked around the neighboring tables in the café and asked in a conspiratorial whisper, his eyes wide open in disbelief:

"Can it be true that the Fischers have said unfavorable things about us?"

Our long friendship was not affected by my answer, but the conspiratorial whisper and his disbelief showed how very unconditioned even the more thinking Russians—he was one of them—are to criticism. I fear the enormous danger implicit in this attitude. By the end of my stay I should have been used to their way of thinking but I was not, and even up to the very last exchange with some Soviet officers at the airdrome lunch counter on the morning of my departure from Moscow I was not.

It was easy for me to say good-by to Russia in 1960. There were no roots to be pulled up this time, no dreams to bid farewell to. And I did not leave tragedy behind as I had in 1939, because as far as I could judge people did not consider their lives tragic. Uncomfortable, hurried, noisy maybe, but hopeful. If they have forgotten or never knew some of the old dreams that had once inspired me and if they are willing to erase from their own memories the agonizing days of Stalin, who am I to judge them and to say they shouldn't?

The last days in Moscow were filled with sentimental farewells, gift shopping, and an intense desire to be on my way. Pleasant and interesting as my stay had been beyond any expectations, I could hardly wait to board the plane going west. Remembering my experience on the day of arrival, I felt that I would not be sure of a safe return until I had reached Belgian soil. As on my arrival, I had the Intourist car and driver all to myself and he too displayed great energy in his efforts to add to my education, but this time I was a less attentive listener. All I wanted was that it should be an hour or two later.

Though it was definitely a breakfast hour, there was no coffee or tea at the airdrome lunch counter, only chocolate, cookies, candy, oranges. Two Soviet officers helped me overcome my disappointment about the lack of coffee by inviting me to sit with them. They shared their cookies with me and I reciprocated with oranges. And so I had my last conversation in Moscow. These officers, charming and intelligent, knew a great deal. They knew about every rocket failure in the United States, every detail of German rearmament, every expression of anti-American feeling anywhere in the world, about French trouble in Algeria, and everything else detrimental to the image of the West. But they had no inkling of any world problems except the East-West problems. They had no idea what I was talking about when in the course of our conversation I mentioned the exploding world population or the lowering of class barriers in the non-Communist world.

Finally this conversation came to an end too, and after a huge amount of slow paper work and all kinds of exasperating delays there came the hour to which I had been so anxiously looking forward. What a joy it was after a month of seeing nothing but Soviet newspapers to find on the plane the Belgian papers of the same day and the London *Times* of the day before. I had known all along, of course, how one-sided and full of falsehoods the Soviet press was but not until I read a Western paper again did I realize the full extent of their bias. A very few hours later in Brussels I experienced the pleasure of holding in my hands the European editions of the New York papers and read the same news I had read in the morning Soviet papers. It was extremely hard to realize that it was the same news.

Epilogue

In Moscow I was deeply shocked by the total lack of understanding of the United States. I was no less shocked by some of the reactions I met with upon my return home. To be correctly informed is certainly no less important in the United States than it is in the Soviet Union. Yet it was clear to me that many Americans' picture of Russia is far from correct, and is based less on the dispassionate, objective information available than on time-worn and superficial slogans and catchwords.

To stress Russia's achievements and advances would only play into the hands of American Communists, I was recently told. The influence of the American Communist party on American minds does not worry me in the least. Their role as unswerving tools of Soviet foreign policy and their tedious cant are so ridiculously obvious and so foreign to the American mind that they destroy themselves.

What troubled me in all the talks after my return was the lack of genuine strong liberal thinking, the kind of thinking that could counteract the fuzziness that permeates the minds of some decent Americans who let themselves be mesmerized by the lofty Soviet talk of peace, friendship, disarmament, racialism, colonialism, exploitation, and so on.

And no less alarming was the fierceness with which some of my listeners rejected the idea that there was anything good to be found in Russia. Such blind branding of all favorable information about Russia as an a priori lie leaves us ignorant and ill-prepared for the future. It deprives us of any intelligent appraisal of what really goes on in the Soviet world and exposes us to unnecessary surprises and unexpected shocks.

I felt at times genuine animosity among my listeners when to sarcastic questions like "Do they teach them anything besides communism and how to build rockets?" or "Do they know how to use a handkerchief?" I would tell them truthfully what I had seen there. Nothing but a negative report was acceptable, however, and in a few cases I could sense a suspicion that I had been thoroughly brainwashed by the Communists. When I met this attitude in Russia, where every favorable word about the West was by many considered a sheer lie and propaganda, and criticism of the Soviet system equal to treason, I found it regrettable but understandable. Meeting it in the free air of the United States was frightening.

If I had one wish to make in the field of Soviet-American relations it would be that the day will come when it will be possible for an American after a trip to Russia to say, for instance, that Moscow children look happy and healthy, that there are more parks in Moscow than in New York, that more books are read and plays seen and good music listened to there than in the United States, without being suspected of disloyalty to the United States. And that the day will come when it will be possible for a Russian to travel to the United States and to say after his return that it was a pleasure to read newspapers of different points of view and to report truthfully on other aspects of our life that impressed him, without being suspected of being a traitor to his country who had sold his soul to Wall Street.

During my stay in Russia I often felt annoyed and depressed by the absence of a clash of minds, by the dearth of original ideas, by the endless repetition of the official line. And then I felt guilty for being annoyed. For a long time the Russians have heard and read only one opinion. How else can they be expected to think or talk?

I felt infinitely more depressed when upon returning home I heard Americans talking in clichés, with few ideas of their own, religiously repeating the words of their favorite columnist or commentator. I don't like the Soviet regime, its ideology, and what it does to the human being, but I will always defend the Russian people for being politically unsophisticated and inarticulate. They could hardly be otherwise. I cannot defend us for being so politically shallow as to discuss seriously an American President's "TV projection" instead of his ideas.

After one of my reports on the trip a woman complained:

"Why aren't we told these things?"

But we are. There is no excuse for any American who can read to be totally ignorant of Russia. There is certainly no dearth of books on Russia, many of them good, some even excellent. There are magazine articles and news reports by experts. Therefore, the appalling ignorance I encountered among people who are supposed to read and to think astonished me.

Once I was asked:

"What's the use of knowing what the Russians are told about us? It's all lies anyway."

Let us accept this and assume that every word the Russians are told about us is untrue. We still have to know what they are being told. To follow the example of the Russians and prohibit the teaching of Soviet attitudes in our schools as they prohibit the teaching of ours is certainly not the right way for us to understand the Soviet Union and prepare for the future. To be told that Marxism and communism are nothing but bad words gives us a soothing feeling and helps us to ignore them. But it is hardly a way of behavior worthy of the United States.

At times when my American listeners objected to whatever positive I had to say about Russia, they would trot out words and phrases usually reserved for Fourth of July speeches. They are beautiful words, but I wondered how often we translate these words into deeds? To be well fed and well clothed and well housed is not enough. It seems to me that now more than ever before we have to be on our guard and watchful that our glittering gadgets do not win over ideas. However communism describes itself, it is a thoroughly materialistic ideology. We have such an abundant arsenal of excellent ideas and ideals that if put into practice they may be infinitely more efficient than nuclear war heads.

If we were ready to give up even a small part of the energy and time that we concentrate now on our comforts, on easy entertainment, on personal gratification, on achieving higher status . . .

If we devote less time to criticizing the Russians, if we could avoid becoming hysterical every time Khrushchev says or does something we don't like, or someone says or writes something favorable to Russia, or the Russians perform some spectacular feat . . .

If we would once more become sure of the road we want and intend to follow, and faithfully and confidently follow it, rejoicing over our advances and successes, and working to eliminate our shortcomings . . .

If we would try by deeds to make the United States the symbol of freedom for the individual that it once was to the peoples of the world . . .

Then we could hope that those who are searching for a way out of their poverty and for a life of freedom and dignity would turn to us instead of to communism.

If I have permitted myself, besides reporting on my trip, to express also some political reflections, it certainly is not because I consider myself a political expert. Far from it. It is only because as a citizen of a democracy I consider it my right to say what I think and feel on an important subject, one to which my background and experience have brought me close.